Real Math™

Stephen S. Willoughby
Carl Bereiter
Peter Hilton
Joseph H. Rubinstein

Lacey D. Cooper
Vice President and Publisher,
Mathematics

Jean J. Pedersen,
Curriculum Consultant for Geometry

Open Court   La Salle, Illinois

The Calculator Activities are based upon work supported by the National Science Foundation under Grant No. MDR–8896131. Any opinions, findings, and conclusions or recommendations expressed in this publication are those of the publisher and do not necessarily reflect the views of the National Science Foundation.

Photography
Charles P. Gerity
Lew Harding

Cover Design
James A. Buddenbaum

Illustration
George Armstrong
Dev Appleyard
JoAnn Daley
Larry Frederick
Dennis Hockerman
Diana Magnuson
Dick Martin
Robert Masheris
Bill Miller
Phill Renaud
Rob Sauber
Yoshi Sekiguchi
Dan Siculan
Jim Teason

OPEN COURT, Thinking Story, and ✺ are registered in the U.S. Patent and Trademark Office.

Copyright © 1991, 1987, 1985, 1981
Open Court Publishing Company

All rights reserved for all countries. No part of this book may be reproduced by any means without the written permission of the publisher.

Printed in the United States of America

ISBN 0-8126-0633-7

How close is your estimate?

Estimate.

1. What things will you estimate?

2. How many did you estimate?

Check your estimate.

3. How many did you count on your first try?

4. How many did you count on your second try?

Discuss the Thinking Story® your teacher will read from *Bargains Galore*.

Find the numbers that are written twice.

1. Start at 8.

    8 12 10 11 9 16 14 18 11 13 15 17 13

2. Start at 47.

    49 51 47 52 56 55 50 53 57 48 50 52 54

3. Start at 96.

    105 97 102 96 101 106 99 103 100 104 99 106 98

4. Start at 379.

    387 381 388 382 386 379 383 385 380 383 382 384

How many cookies? Show the number with your response card. Then write it.

1. One hundred thirty-two

Show.  Then write. ■

2. Twenty-seven

Show.  Then write. ■

3. Two hundred five

Show.  Then write. ■

Count up or down. Fill in the missing numbers.

1. | 7 | 8 | | | | 12 | | |

2. | 17 | 16 | 15 | | | | 11 | |

3. | 86 | 87 | | | | 91 | | |

4. | 431 | 432 | | | | 436 | |

5. | 807 | 808 | | | | | 813 |

6. | 707 | 706 | | | | 702 | |

7. | | | 421 | 422 | | | |

Roll a Number Game

Each child in Jane's class measured the length of the room in shoe units. Jane made a graph of the results. Make a graph for your class.

LESSON 3

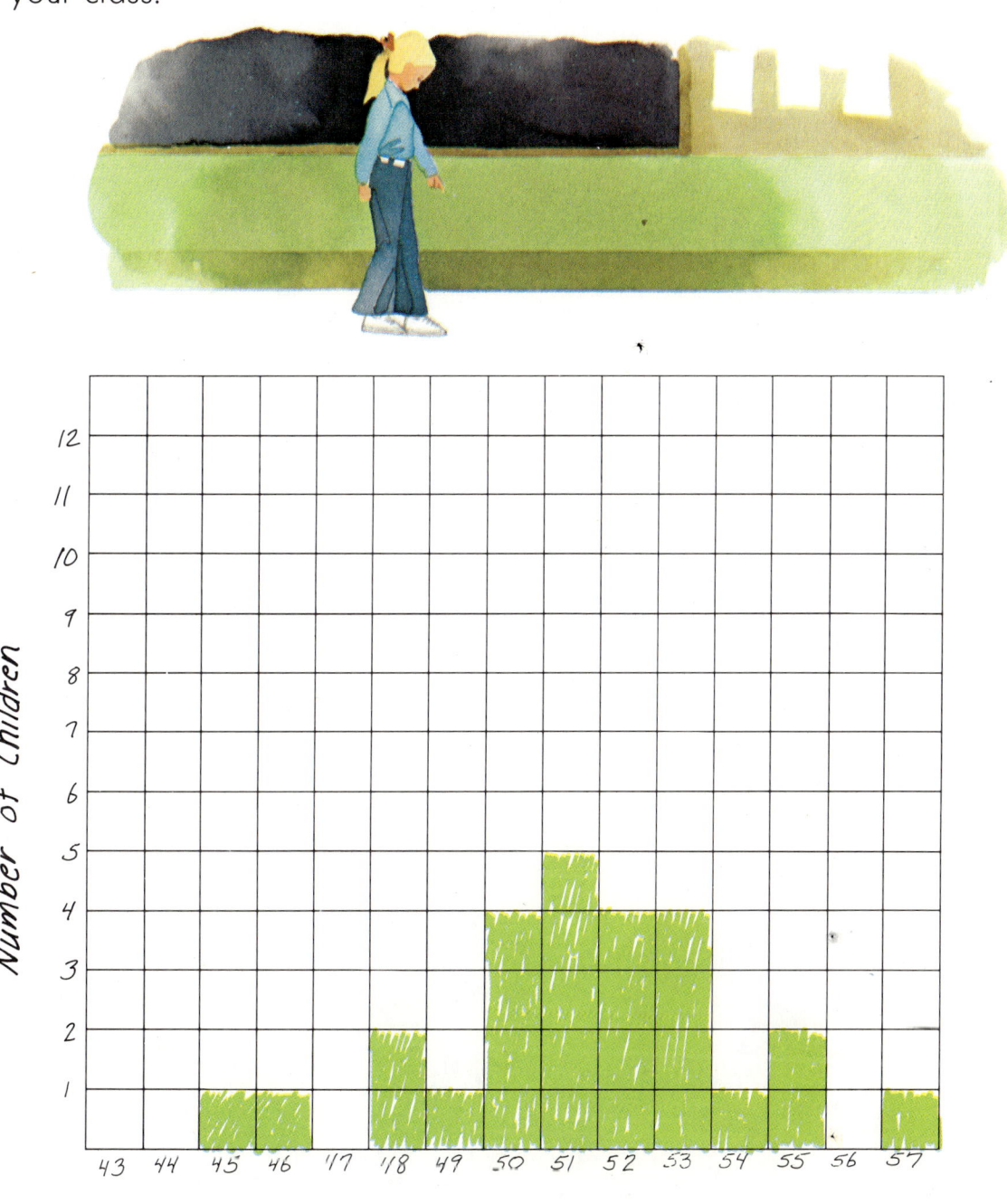

LESSON 4

Count up or down. Fill in the missing numbers.

1. | 997 | 998 | | | | 1002 |

2. | 2076 | 2077 | | | | 2081 |

3. | 6543 | 6542 | | | | 6538 |

4. | 4096 | 4097 | | | | 4101 |

5. | | | 7238 | 7239 | | 7241 |

6. | | | 1010 | 1011 | | |

7. | 9995 | 9996 | | | | |

Counting and Writing Numbers Game

Add.

LESSON 5

1. $3 + 1 = \blacksquare$
2. $8 + 2 = \blacksquare$
3. $2 + 7 = \blacksquare$
4. $9 + 9 = \blacksquare$
5. $2 + 8 = \blacksquare$
6. $1 + 7 = \blacksquare$

7. $8 + 5 = \blacksquare$
8. $7 + 10 = \blacksquare$
9. $4 + 10 = \blacksquare$
10. $10 + 9 = \blacksquare$
11. $8 + 3 = \blacksquare$
12. $7 + 8 = \blacksquare$

13. $\begin{array}{r} 7 \\ +8 \\ \hline \end{array}$

14. $\begin{array}{r} 6 \\ +5 \\ \hline \end{array}$

15. $\begin{array}{r} 8 \\ +1 \\ \hline \end{array}$

16. $\begin{array}{r} 9 \\ +3 \\ \hline \end{array}$

17. $\begin{array}{r} 4 \\ +7 \\ \hline \end{array}$

18. $\begin{array}{r} 10 \\ +3 \\ \hline \end{array}$

Subtract.

1. 8   2. 20   3. 10   4. 17   5. 9   6. 14
  −1   −10   − 2   −10   −3   − 9

7. 7 − 2 = ■   12. 12 − 7 = ■
8. 10 − 3 = ■   13. 15 − 8 = ■
9. 11 − 8 = ■   14. 15 − 7 = ■
10. 13 − 4 = ■   15. 16 − 9 = ■
11. 16 − 7 = ■   16. 12 − 9 = ■

Roll a 15 Game

4 + 8 + 2 = 14
I'll stop.

Use play money or objects to act out the stories.

1. Robert has 3¢. He wants to buy a cup of lemonade for 8¢. How much more money does he need?

   3 + ■ = 8

2. James has 2¢. He wants to buy a comb for 12¢. How much more does he need?

   2 + ■ = 12

3. Amy had 10¢. She bought some cookies. Now she has 4¢. How much did she spend?

   10 − ■ = 4

1. Coco had 15 bananas. He ate some. Now he has 7 bananas. How many did he eat?

   $15 - \blacksquare = 7$

2. Alicia spent 15¢. She has 5¢ left. How much money did she start with?

   $\blacksquare - 15 = 5$

3. Inger gave her friend 3 marbles. Inger now has 7 marbles left. How many did she start with?

   $\blacksquare - 3 = 7$

Do these problems. Watch the signs.

1. $4 + \blacksquare = 9$
2. $\blacksquare + 5 = 9$
3. $8 + \blacksquare = 15$
4. $9 + \blacksquare = 15$
5. $4 + \blacksquare = 11$
6. $\blacksquare + 8 = 11$

7. $14 - \blacksquare = 4$
8. $\blacksquare - 3 = 10$
9. $18 - \blacksquare = 8$
10. $\blacksquare - 7 = 6$
11. $\blacksquare - 4 = 4$
12. $7 - \blacksquare = 3$

Frog Pond Game

Missing Term Puzzle

LESSON 7

Do these problems. Watch the signs.

1. 9 + 4 = ◼
2. 4 + 9 = ◼
3. 13 − 4 = ◼
4. 18 − 7 = ◼
5. 9 + 9 = ◼
6. 16 − 8 = ◼
7. 6 + 6 = ◼
8. 6 + 7 = ◼
9. 4 + 8 = ◼
10. 9 − 4 = ◼

11. 11 − 4 = ◼
12. 18 − 9 = ◼
13. 7 + 7 = ◼
14. 7 + 8 = ◼
15. 13 − 8 = ◼

Roll 20 to 5 Game

My score was 2.

My score is 6. I win.

Do these problems. Watch the signs.

1. $20 - 10 = \blacksquare$
2. $18 - 10 = \blacksquare$
3. $13 - 10 = \blacksquare$
4. $18 - 8 = \blacksquare$
5. $5 + 5 = \blacksquare$
6. $10 - 8 = \blacksquare$
7. $9 + 8 = \blacksquare$
8. $15 - 8 = \blacksquare$
9. $11 - 3 = \blacksquare$
10. $16 - 9 = \blacksquare$
11. $19 - 10 = \blacksquare$
12. $17 - 10 = \blacksquare$
13. $16 - 6 = \blacksquare$
14. $15 - 5 = \blacksquare$
15. $10 - 7 = \blacksquare$
16. $10 - 4 = \blacksquare$
17. $8 + 8 = \blacksquare$
18. $12 - 4 = \blacksquare$
19. $0 + 7 = \blacksquare$
20. $13 - 9 = \blacksquare$

LESSON 8

1. The score is 6 to 3. The Tigers are winning. How many runs behind are the Cubs?

2. The game will last 7 innings. The teams have played 4 innings so far. How many more innings will they play?

3. The Tigers have 11 hits so far. The Cubs have 7. How many hits have there been in the game?

4. The umpire brought 12 balls to the game. Some were lost. There are 9 balls left. How many were lost?

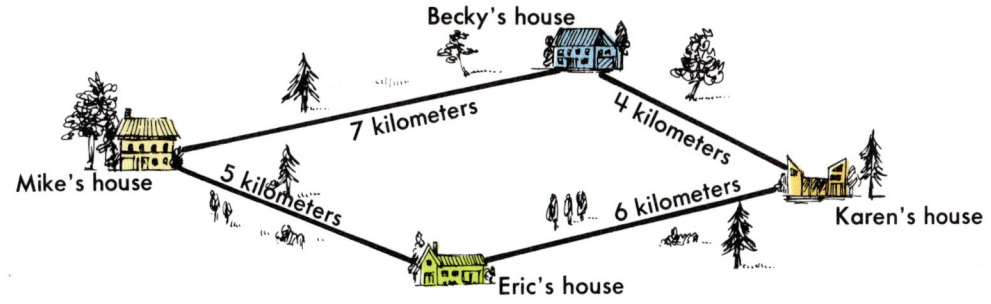

1. How far is it from Eric's house to Karen's house?

2. How much farther is it from Becky's house to Mike's house than from Becky's house to Karen's house?

3. How far is it from Eric's house to Karen's house and then to Becky's house?

4. How far is it from Mike's house to Becky's house to Karen's house?

5. How far is it from Mike's house to Eric's house to Karen's house?

Discuss the Thinking Story®

LESSON 9

Do these problems. Watch the signs.

1. $10 + 5 - 7 = \square$

2. $12 - 5 + 6 = \square$

3. $6 + 9 - 3 + 3 = \square$

4. $4 + 4 + 4 - 6 + 8 = \square$

5. $7 + 4 - 8 + 10 = \square$

6. $15 - 10 + 5 + 4 - 7 = \square$

7. $3 + 3 + 3 + 3 - 10 + 2 + 2 = \square$

8. $6 + 6 - 2 + 9 = \square$

9. $7 + 3 + 8 - 9 - 9 + 4 = \square$

10. $13 - 8 - 3 + 5 + 3 + 9 = \square$

Do these problems. Watch the signs.

1. 7   2. 5   3. 15   4. 9   5. 7
   +8   −4   − 6   +8   +4
   ──   ──   ───   ──   ──

6. 18   7. 15   8. 14   9. 5   10. 9
   − 9   − 6   − 8   +7   +9
   ───   ───   ───   ──   ──

11. 10   12. 14   13. 17   14. 13   15. 16
   +10   − 4   − 7   −10   − 6
   ───   ───   ───   ───   ───

16. 20 − 10 = ■   21. 4 + 9 = ■

17. 17 − 8 = ■   22. 2 + 8 = ■

18. 5 + 9 = ■   23. 3 + 9 = ■

19. 6 + 6 = ■   24. 10 + 6 = ■

20. 8 + 8 = ■   25. 8 + 10 = ■

17

LESSON 10

Check yourself.

1. 7 + 8 = ■
2. 19 − 10 = ■
3. 4 + 4 = ■
4. 3 + 7 = ■
5. 8 − 2 = ■
6. 14 − 8 = ■
7. 17 − 9 = ■
8. 9 + 7 = ■
9. 6 + 6 = ■
10. 11 − 4 = ■

11. 3 − 3 = ■
12. 9 + 9 = ■
13. 15 − 9 = ■
14. 13 − 4 = ■
15. 3 + 9 = ■
16. 8 − 7 = ■
17. 1 + 8 = ■
18. 16 − 7 = ■
19. 6 + 7 = ■
20. 10 + 5 = ■

Number correct ■

3 tens and 12 = 42

Write the standard name for each of these.
You may use materials to help.

1. 2 tens and 8 = 28
2. 5 tens and 12 = 62
3. 6 tens and 15 = ■
4. 4 tens and 0 = ■
5. 7 tens and 16 = ■
6. 0 tens and 14 = ■
7. 8 tens and 3 = ■
8. 8 tens and 13 = ■

9. 4 tens and 10 = ■
10. 3 tens and 0 = ■
11. 3 tens and 7 = ■
12. 3 tens and 17 = ■
13. 6 tens and 17 = ■
14. 11 tens = ■
15. 13 tens = ■
16. 17 tens = ■

LESSON 11

2 hundreds and 14 tens = 340

Write the standard name for each of these.
You may use materials to help.

1. 2 hundreds and 8 tens = 280

2. 5 hundreds and 12 tens = 620

3. 4 hundreds and 0 tens = ■

4. 4 hundreds and 10 tens = ■

5. 4 hundreds and 17 tens = ■

6. 1 hundred and 17 tens = ■

7. 0 hundreds and 17 tens = ■

8. 0 hundreds and 13 tens = ■

Write the standard name for each of these.
You may use materials to help.

1. 7 tens and 5 = ■
2. 7 tens and 15 = ■
3. 7 hundreds and 5 tens = ■
4. 7 hundreds and 15 tens = ■
5. 3 hundreds and 10 tens = ■
6. 3 tens and 10 = ■
7. 0 tens and 16 = ■
8. 0 hundreds and 16 tens = ■
9. 16 tens = ■
10. 18 tens = ■
11. 20 tens = ■
12. 9 hundreds = ■
13. 10 hundreds = ■
14. 11 hundreds = ■

$1000 Bills Game

LESSON 12

25 + 47 = ____?

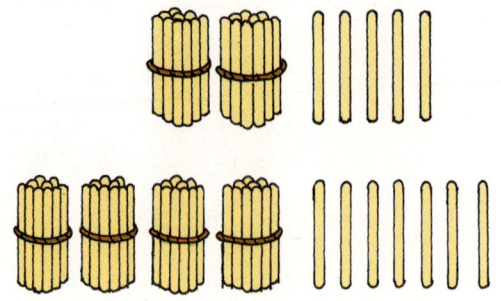

$\quad$ 2 tens and 5 $\qquad$ 2 5
$+$ 4 tens and 7 $\qquad$ + 4 7

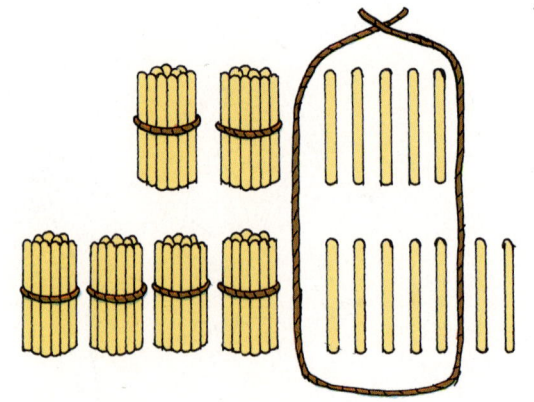

$\qquad\qquad$ 1 ten $\qquad\qquad$ 1
$\quad$ 2 tens and 5 $\qquad$ 2 5
$+$ 4 tens and 7 $\qquad$ + 4 7
$\qquad\qquad\qquad$ 2 $\qquad\qquad$ 2

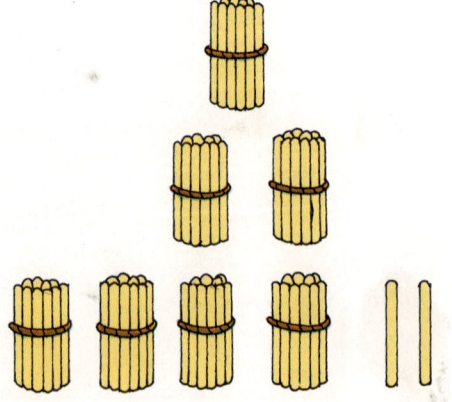

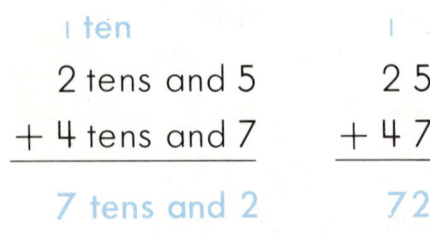

$\qquad\qquad$ 1 ten $\qquad\qquad$ 1
$\quad$ 2 tens and 5 $\qquad$ 2 5
$+$ 4 tens and 7 $\qquad$ + 4 7
$\quad$ 7 tens and 2 $\qquad$ 7 2

Add. Use sticks or other objects to help.

1.   ¹43
  +28
   71

2.   57
  +29

3.   36
  +51

4.   36
  +54

5.   19
  +38

6.   25
  +25

7.   43
  +20

8.   43
  +30

9.   82
  + 9

10.   16
  +37

11.   17
  +37

12.   45
  +45

Roll and Add Game

13.   35
  +45

14.   34
  +45

62 + 73 is 135.

LESSON 13

Rewrite to show ten more ones.

42 = 3 tens and 12

1. 27 = ☐ tens and ☐
2. 80 = ☐ tens and ☐
3. 68 = ☐ tens and ☐
4. 70 = ☐ tens and ☐
5. 21 = ☐ tens and ☐

6. 51 = ☐ tens and ☐
7. 52 = ☐ tens and ☐
8. 62 = ☐ tens and ☐
9. 16 = ☐ tens and ☐
10. 12 = ☐ tens and ☐

Jan has four $10 bills and three $1 bills. She must pay Mr. Gómez $8.

11. How can Jan pay $8?

12. How much will Jan have left?

Rewrite to show ten more tens.

230 = 1 hundred and 13 tens

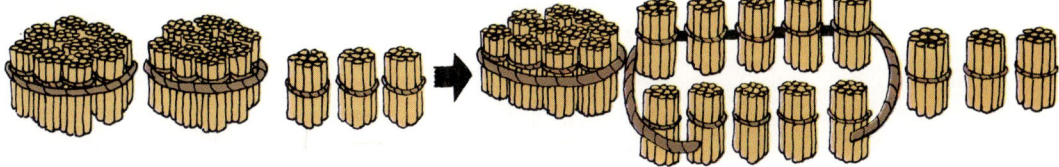

1. 420 = ▩ hundreds and 12 tens
2. 700 = ▩ hundreds and 10 tens
3. 760 = ▩ hundreds and ▩ tens
4. 160 = ▩ hundreds and ▩ tens
5. 240 = ▩ hundreds and ▩ tens
6. 500 = ▩ hundreds and ▩ tens
7. 580 = ▩ hundreds and ▩ tens
8. 980 = ▩ hundreds and ▩ tens

Mrs. Taylor has one $100 bill and two $10 bills. She must pay Mr. Olson $30.

9. How can Mrs. Taylor pay $30?
10. How much money will she have left?

Rewrite to show no hundreds and then more ones.

205 = 20 tens and 5 = 19 tens and 15

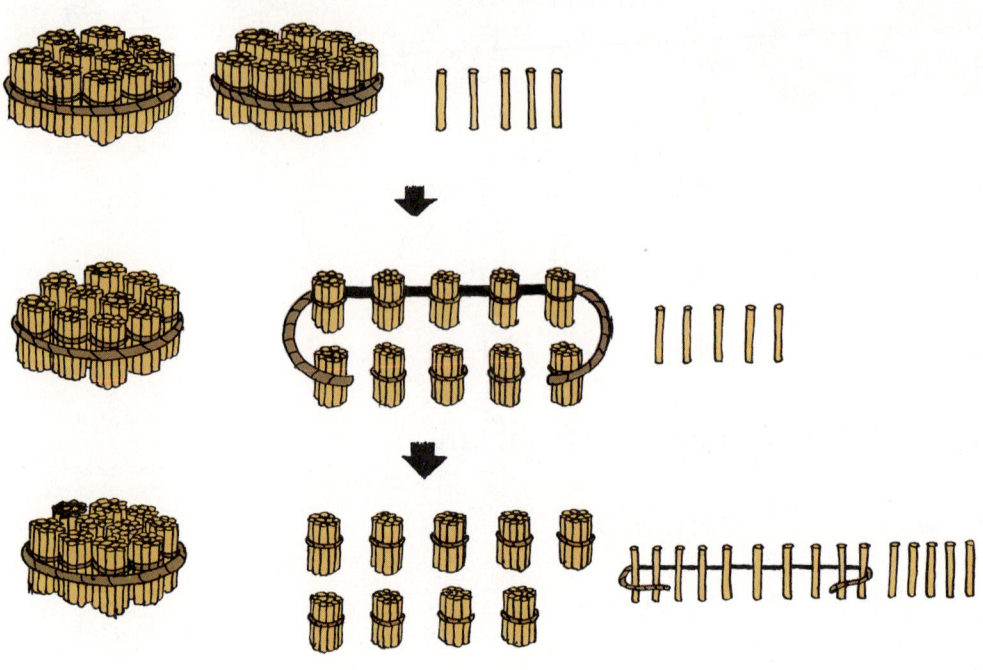

1. 307 = 30 tens and 7 = 29 tens and ■

2. 600 = ■ tens and 0 = ■ tens and 10

3. 604 = ■ tens and ■ = ■ tens and ■

4. 809 = ■ tens and ■ = ■ tens and ■

5. 700 = ■ tens and ■ = ■ tens and ■

6. 707 = ■ tens and ■ = ■ tens and ■

$31 - 14 = \underline{}$

3 tens and 1	3 1
− 1 ten and 4	− 1 4

2 11	2 11
3̸ tens and 1̸	3̸ 1̸
− 1 ten and 4	− 1 4

2 11	2 11
3̸ tens and 1̸	3̸ 1̸
− 1 ten and 4	− 1 4
7	7

2 11	2 11
3̸ tens and 1̸	3̸ 1̸
− 1 ten and 4	− 1 4
1 ten and 7	1 7

Subtract.

1. $\overset{3\;13}{\cancel{4\;3}}$
   $-2\;9$
   ────
   $1\;4$

2. $8\;6$
   $-3\;7$
   ────

3. $8\;7$
   $-3\;7$
   ────

4. $2\;8$
   $-1\;9$
   ────

5. $3\;8$
   $-1\;9$
   ────

6. $5\;0$
   $-2\;5$
   ────

7. $7\;5$
   $-5\;0$
   ────

8. $7\;5$
   $-2\;5$
   ────

9. $6\;1$
   $-4\;7$
   ────

10. $9\;4$
    $-4\;6$
    ────

11. $9\;0$
    $-4\;5$
    ────

12. $8\;0$
    $-4\;5$
    ────

Roll and Subtract Game

I'll subtract 19 from 37.

13. $7\;2$
    $-3\;8$
    ────

14. $6\;1$
    $-2\;4$
    ────

Martin has 75¢.

1. Can he buy popcorn and go on the ride?

2. Can he buy ice cream and go on the ride?

3. If Martin buys popcorn and ice cream, how much will he have left?

4. There are 27 children in Mrs. Pinto's class. 15 are boys. How many girls are in Mrs. Pinto's class?

5. In Mr. Epstein's class, there are 13 boys and 16 girls. How many children are in Mr. Epstein's class?

Kim has 46¢. Nancy has 38¢.

6. How much do they have altogether?

7. How much more do they need to buy the plane?

Mrs. Germano started at home. She drove 32 kilometers east. Then she turned around and drove 17 kilometers west.

1. How far is Mrs. Germano from home?

2. How far has she driven?

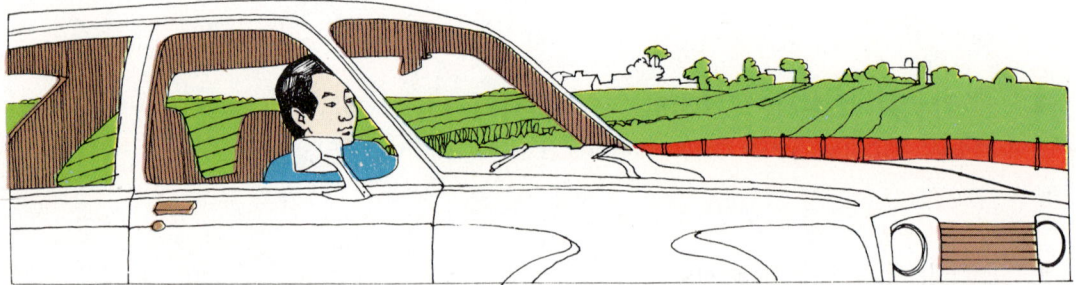

Mr. Cheng started at home. He drove 32 kilometers east. Then he drove 41 kilometers east.

3. How far is Mr. Cheng from home?

4. How far has he driven?

Mr. Cheng drove 73 kilometers. Mr. Smith drove 61 kilometers.

5. Who drove farther?

6. How much farther?

7. How far apart are they?

1. Marie had some records. She gave 12 of them to her brother. She has 19 records left. How many did she start with?

2. Mr. Batra lives 18 kilometers from Bigtown. He drove there and back. How far did he drive?

3. Kevin had 80¢. He spent some money at the bakery. Now he has 28¢. How much did Kevin spend?

4. Zelda's tomato plant is 38 centimeters tall. One week ago it was 25 centimeters tall. How much did it grow last week?

1. How much will the ball and truck cost?

2. How much will the shell and crayons cost?

3. How much will the book and yo-yo cost?

4. Luis has only $1.
   At most, how many of the 6 things can he buy?

5. Which of the 6 things can Luis buy?

Roll a Problem Game

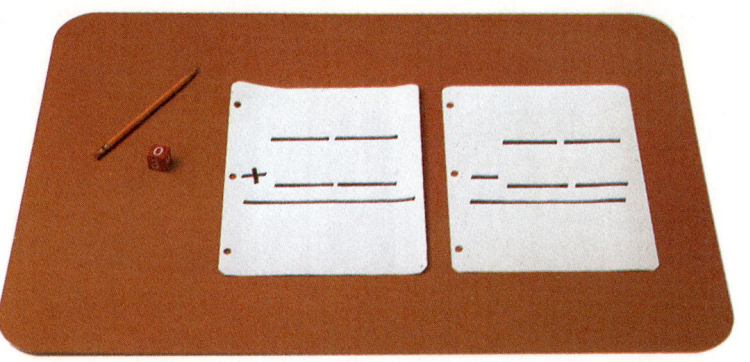

LESSON 17

1. One month ago Moppet weighed 19 kilograms. Now he weighs 26 kilograms. How much weight did Moppet gain last month?

Peter has 30¢. Suppose he earns 65¢.

2. How much money would Peter have?

3. Would Peter have enough money to buy 2 books that cost 45¢ each?

Buffy is 73 centimeters tall.
Flip is 78 centimeters tall.

1. Which dog is taller?

2. By how much?

3. Which town is farther away?

4. How much farther?

Discuss the Thinking Story®

Do these problems. Watch the signs.

LESSON 18

1. 18
   +47
   ———

2. 63
   +27
   ———

3. 63
   −27
   ———

4. 85
   −35
   ———

5. 91
   −64
   ———

6. 43
   −41
   ———

7. 72
   −28
   ———

8.   8
   +74
   ———

9. 39
   −37
   ———

10. 51
   −49
   ———

11. 32
   − 9
   ———

12. 17
   +87
   ———

Number correct ■

LESSON 19

$436 + 287 = \underline{?}$

Use play money or other objects to follow this example.

```
  4 3 6     Start at the right.
+ 2 8 7     Add the ones.
            6 + 7 = 13
```

```
  1
  4 3 6     13 = 1 ten and 3
+ 2 8 7
      3
```

```
  1
  4 3 6     Add the tens.
+ 2 8 7     1 + 3 + 8 = 12
    3       There are 12 tens.
```

```
  1 1
  4 3 6     12 tens = 1 hundred and 2 tens
+ 2 8 7
    2 3
```

```
  1 1
  4 3 6     Add the hundreds.
+ 2 8 7     1 + 4 + 2 = 7
  7 2 3     There are 7 hundreds.
```

745 − 179 = ____?____

Use play money or other objects to follow this example.

  7 4 5   Start at the right.
− 1 7 9   Subtract the ones.
            Can't subtract 9 from 5.

    3 15
  7 4̸ 5̸   Regroup the 4 tens and 5.
− 1 7 9   4 tens and 5 = 3 tens and 15

    3 15
  7 4̸ 5̸   Subtract the ones. 15 − 9 = 6
− 1 7 9   Subtract the tens.
      6   Can't subtract 7 from 3.

    13
  6 3̸ 15
  7̸ 4̸ 5̸   Regroup the 7 hundreds and 3 tens.
− 1 7 9   7 hundreds and 3 tens = 6 hundreds and 13 tens
      6

    13
  6 3̸ 15
  7̸ 4̸ 5̸   Subtract the tens. 13 − 7 = 6
− 1 7 9   There are 6 tens.
  5 6 6   Subtract the hundreds. 6 − 1 = 5
            There are 5 hundreds.

Do these problems. Watch the signs.

1. 435
  +256

2. 379
  −182

3. 607
  +284

4. 200
  +500

5. 317
  −248

6. 379
  +256

7. 345
  −213

8. 315
  +100

9. 594
  − 57

10. 594
   + 57

11. 594
   −257

12. 594
   −200

13. 314
   −107

14. 310
   −169

15. 247
   +253

16. 247
   +200

506 − 148 = _____?

  5 0 6   Start at the right.
− 1 4 8   Subtract the ones.
            Can't subtract 8 from 6.

  5 0 6   Can't regroup 0 tens and 6.
− 1 4 8

  49 16
  5̶ 0̶ 6   5 hundreds is the same
− 1 4 8   as 50 tens.
            Regroup 50 tens and 6.
            50 tens and 6 =
            49 tens and 16.

  49 16
  5̶ 0̶ 6̶   Subtract the ones.
− 1 4 8   Subtract the tens.
  3 5 8   Subtract the hundreds.

LESSON 20

Do these problems. Watch the signs.

1. 402   2. 777   3. 654   4. 800
  −176   +222   +101   −455

5. 486   6. 500   7. 308   8. 203
  +264   −375   −205   − 57

9. 6 + 9 + 1 = ■

10. 8 − 4 + 6 = ■

11. 3 + 9 + 4 − 7 = ■

12. 7 + 2 − 3 + 4 = ■

13. 5 − 5 + 5 − 5 = ■

14. 6 + 8 + 9 + 8 = ■

Roll a Problem Game

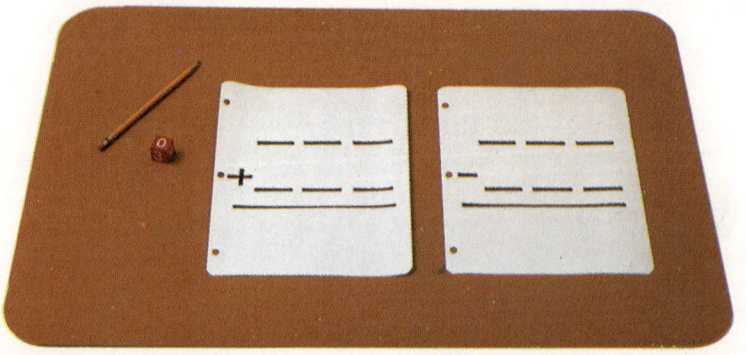

LESSON 21

Do these problems. Watch the signs.

1. 435
   +217

2. 755
   −694

3. 804
   +102

4. 705
   −349

5. 212
   +349

6. 825
   −312

7. 212
   +379

8. 208
   −199

9. 723
   +239

10. 325
   +184

11. 359
   −260

12. 954
   −675

Number correct ▪

41

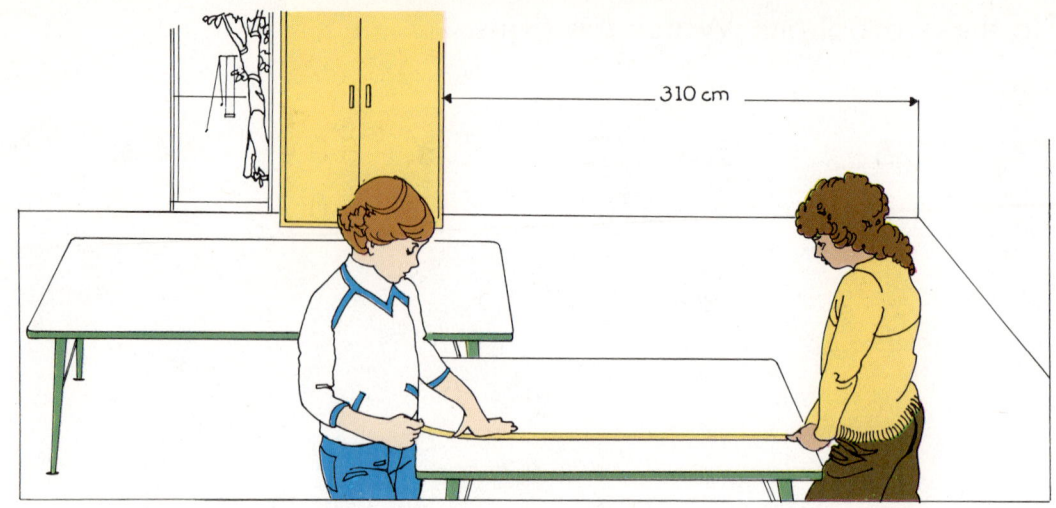

One table is 166 centimeters long. The other table is 137 centimeters long. It is 310 centimeters from the cabinet to the wall.

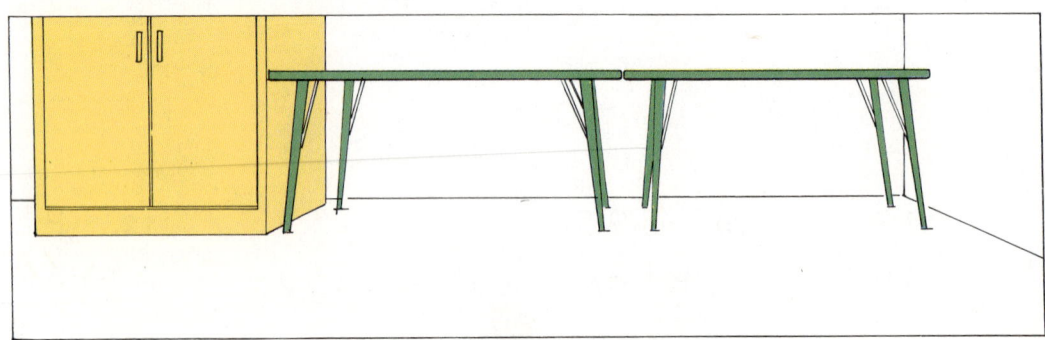

The two tables are put end to end next to the cabinet.

1. How many centimeters long are they together?

2. How far is it from the table on the right to the wall?

3. Could you squeeze into that space?

The Hill School has 342 pupils.
The Valley School has 419 pupils.

1. How many pupils are there in the two schools altogether?

2. How many more pupils does the Valley School have?

3. Today, 58 pupils are absent from the Hill School. How many pupils are at the school?

4. Which of the two school buildings is larger?

Checkbook Game

Keith's class estimated and compared prices.
Keith made this chart to show his results.

Item	Estimate	Actual Price	
		Good-Buy Market	Big-Food Market
dozen eggs (Grade A Large)	90¢	89¢	93¢
whole-wheat bread (Grain-Time brand)	50¢	65¢	63¢
toothpaste (medium size) Presto brand	75¢	68¢	71¢
Totals	215¢	222¢	227¢

Make a chart like this. Estimate and compare prices.
Then use your own chart to answer these questions.

1. Which store had a total price closer to your estimate?

2. Which store charged more for the 3 items?

3. Did every item cost more in the more expensive store?

Do these problems. Watch the signs.

1. $\begin{array}{r} 300 \\ -125 \\ \hline \end{array}$
2. $\begin{array}{r} 425 \\ +395 \\ \hline \end{array}$
3. $\begin{array}{r} 136 \\ -85 \\ \hline \end{array}$
4. $\begin{array}{r} 843 \\ -616 \\ \hline \end{array}$

5. $\begin{array}{r} 35 \\ 32 \\ +41 \\ \hline \end{array}$
6. $\begin{array}{r} 15 \\ 39 \\ +24 \\ \hline \end{array}$
7. $\begin{array}{r} 64 \\ 27 \\ +59 \\ \hline \end{array}$
8. $\begin{array}{r} 17 \\ 98 \\ 68 \\ +32 \\ \hline \end{array}$

Discuss the Thinking Story®

LESSON 23

Add.

1. 7
   8
   + 6
   ———

2. 7 6
   1 3
   + 4
   ———

3. 3 8
   2 5
   + 3 6
   ———

4. 2 5
   2 5
   + 2 5
   ———

5. 2 9
   3 6
   2 1
   + 1 4
   ———

6. 7 3
   1 7
   1 9
   + 2 5
   ———

7. 3 0
   2 0
   1 0
   + 6 0
   ———

8. 2 5
   2 5
   2 5
   + 2 5
   ———

9.   4 0
   1 2 0
     3 0
   + 1 4 0
   ———

10.   9 2
    2 4 0
    1 7 8
    + 4 1 5
    ———

11.   2 8
    1 0 9
      9 3
    + 1 7 7
    ———

12. 3 6 6
    7 7 4
    + 2 4 0
    ———

Number correct ▪

Jonathan brought 25 cups to the party. Anita brought 50 cups. Mary Ann brought 15 cups.

1. How many cups did they bring altogether?

2. 120 children will be at the party. How many more cups are needed?

3. Miss Nakamura must drive from Apple Town to Berry Point to Cherry City to Date Falls and back to Apple Town. How far is that?

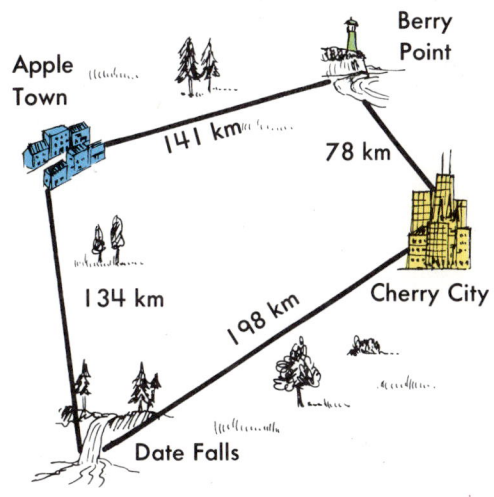

4. Mr. Ryan drives from Apple Town to Date Falls to Cherry City to Berry Point to Apple Town. How far is that?

Four Rolls of Four Cubes Game

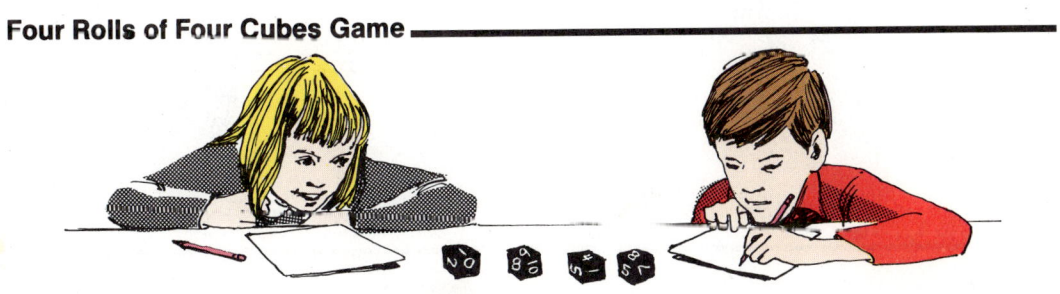

LESSON 24

Do these problems. Watch the signs.

1. 4083   2. 1000   3. 4893   4.   584
   +2196   - 750   - 962   +1208

5. 4761   6. 5000   7.   750   8. 1750
   -2819   -1234   + 250   +1250

9.   750   10.   29   11. 315   12. 480
     250   35   708   565
   + 350   62   95   249
               + 47   + 116   +197

Roll a Problem Game

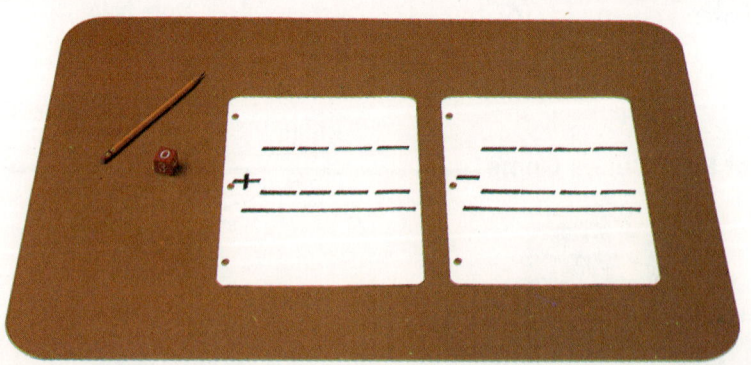

Do these problems. Watch the signs.

1. 4783
  +2651

2. 8074
  −2356

3. 5000
  +2500

4. 3417
  −2846

5. 6004
  +2333

6. 3871
  −2566

7. 8525
  +2475

8. 8943
  − 356

9. 7583
  −2583

10. 8000
   −2386

11. 3489
   −2438

12. 6173
   +3827

LESSON 25

Number correct ■

Complete the table. Show about how many years ago these famous people were born.

	Name	Year of Birth	Born About This Many Years Ago
1.	Joan of Arc	1412	■
2.	Jane Austen	1775	■
3.	Geronimo	1829	■
4.	Pablo Casals	1876	■
5.	Lise Meitner	1878	■
6.	Albert Einstein	1879	■
7.	Helen Keller	1880	■
8.	Tsung-Dao Lee	1926	■
9.	Martin Luther King, Jr.	1929	■
10.	Barbara Jordan	1936	■

Choose three of these people and find out why they are famous.

Complete the table. Show about how many years ago each thing was invented.

	Invention	Inventor	Year Invented	About How Many Years Ago?
1.	Lightning rod	Benjamin Franklin	1752	
2.	Telephone	Alexander Graham Bell	1876	
3.	Radio	Guglielmo Marconi	1895	
4.	Lawn mower	J. A. Burr	1899	
5.	Airplane	Orville and Wilbur Wright	1903	

6. Benjamin Franklin was born in 1706. About how old was he when he invented the lightning rod?

Brenda and David ran for school president.
Brenda got 1134 votes. David got 1078 votes.

1. Who won?

2. By how many votes?

3. How many people voted?

It is 4420 kilometers from Portland to Boston. It is 2780 kilometers from Boston to Miami. Miss Ortiz drove from Portland to Boston to Miami.

4. How far did Miss Ortiz drive?

5. How far is it back to Portland, if Miss Ortiz drives back the same way she came?

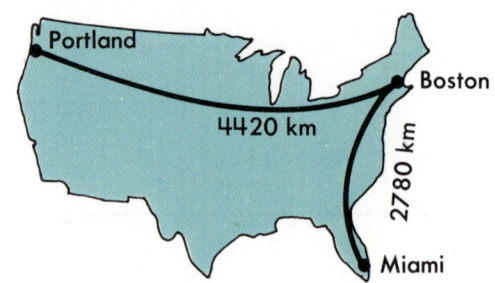

George Washington was born in 1732. Abraham Lincoln was born in 1809.

6. Which man was heavier?

7. How many kilograms heavier?

Discuss the Thinking Story®

Write T if the statement is true.
Write F if it is false.

1. $18 > 20$
2. $7 > 5$
3. $107 < 54$
4. $2869 > 2895$
5. $5097 < 5196$
6. $2743 = 2743$
7. $4096 = 4906$
8. $1111 < 222$
9. $980 < 1025$
10. $4010 = 4001$

11. $78 < 54$
12. $81 < 2$
13. $701 > 45$
14. $6982 < 5982$
15. $2000 > 1999$
16. $873 = 378$
17. $3425 < 3462$
18. $6311 > 6315$
19. $3020 < 3008$
20. $900 = 9000$

LESSON 27

Draw the right sign. Draw <, >, or =.

1. 8 ● 11
2. 612 ● 613
3. 5738 ● 5738
4. 483 ● 438
5. 8259 ● 8260
6. 1000 ● 100
7. 900 ● 1000
8. 8209 ● 8209
9. 1764 ● 1734
10. 6015 ● 6020

11. 752 ● 752
12. 2001 ● 2010
13. 35 ● 62
14. 5341 ● 2376
15. 345 ● 543
16. 222 ● 1110
17. 345 ● 345
18. 921 ● 899
19. 696 ● 701
20. 3121 ● 3121

Draw the right sign. Draw <, >, or =. Compare methods of solving. Which do you think are the easiest?

LESSON 28

1. 246 + 40 ◯ 546 + 140
2. 3000 + 2000 ◯ 3001 + 2001
3. 102 + 86 ◯ 586 + 240
4. 100 − 7 ◯ 200 − 7
5. 43 − 0 ◯ 53 − 10
6. 7 + 43 ◯ 43 + 72
7. 18 − 9 ◯ 19 − 10
8. 126 − 100 ◯ 126 − 10
9. 720 − 39 ◯ 720 − 49
10. 116 + 49 ◯ 47 + 116

11. 3 + 82 ◯ 2 + 83
12. 12 − 3 ◯ 14 − 1
13. 8 + 43 ◯ 43 + 8
14. 21 − 8 ◯ 28 − 1
15. 157 + 861 ◯ 57 + 61
16. 1000 − 3 ◯ 1000 − 43
17. 156 − 56 ◯ 166 − 66
18. 34 + 27 ◯ 27 + 34
19. 4259 + 675 ◯ 4259 + 575
20. 1085 − 200 ◯ 1085 + 200

Tony had 89¢. His mother gave him 68¢.

1. Can Tony buy the book?

2. Can he buy the car?

3. Can he buy 2 cars?

4. How wide is the doorway?

5. How wide is the piano from front to back?

6. Will the piano fit through the door?

7. Will Buffo fit through the door?

Inequality Game

Do these problems. Watch the signs.

1. $5 + 7 = \blacksquare$

2. $10 + 4 = \blacksquare$

3. $8 + 9 = \blacksquare$

4. $16 - 9 = \blacksquare$

5. $10 - 7 = \blacksquare$

6. $15 - 9 = \blacksquare$

7. $\begin{array}{r} 23 \\ +54 \\ \hline \end{array}$

8. $\begin{array}{r} 47 \\ +26 \\ \hline \end{array}$

9. $\begin{array}{r} 48 \\ -7 \\ \hline \end{array}$

10. $\begin{array}{r} 48 \\ -26 \\ \hline \end{array}$

11. $\begin{array}{r} 82 \\ -39 \\ \hline \end{array}$

12. $\begin{array}{r} 7 \\ +28 \\ \hline \end{array}$

13. $\begin{array}{r} 100 \\ -25 \\ \hline \end{array}$

14. $\begin{array}{r} 27 \\ 92 \\ +46 \\ \hline \end{array}$

15. $\begin{array}{r} 36 \\ 23 \\ +154 \\ \hline \end{array}$

16. $\begin{array}{r} 95 \\ 105 \\ 216 \\ +150 \\ \hline \end{array}$

17. $\begin{array}{r} 8756 \\ -3849 \\ \hline \end{array}$

18. $\begin{array}{r} 2046 \\ +3598 \\ \hline \end{array}$

LESSON 29

Find the perimeter.

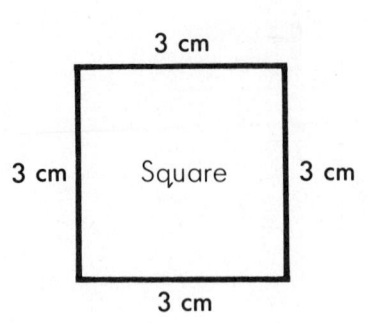

1.

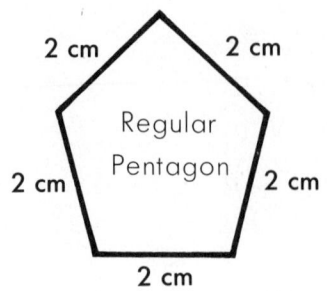

2.

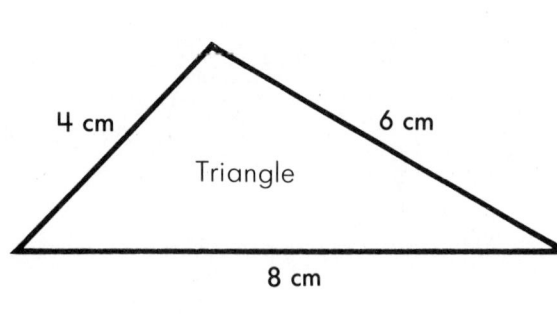

3.

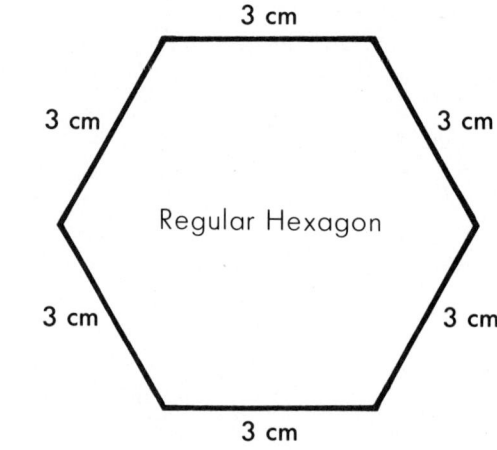

4.

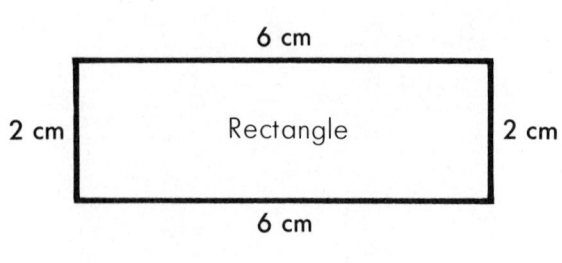

5.

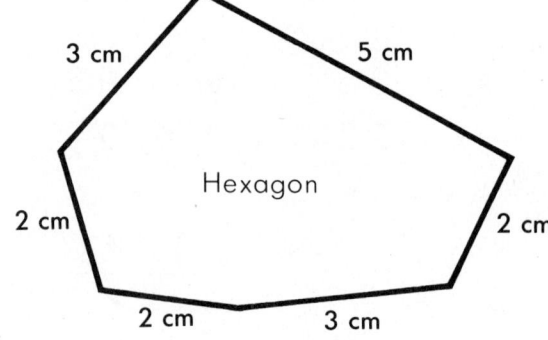

6.

1. How long a fence does Mrs. McGee need to go around her garden?

2. Mr. Wing gave Mrs. McGee 25 meters of fence. How many more meters of fence does she need?

3. What is the shape of Mrs. McGee's garden?

4. Miss Bradley jogs around the park one time. How far does she jog?

5. What is the shape of the park?

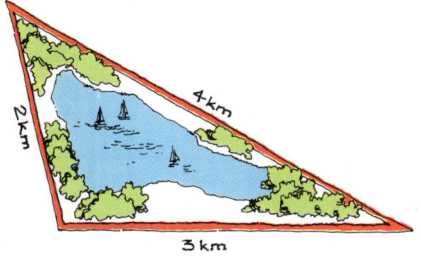

6. Mr. Zalesky built a house. He lived in it for 6 years. Then Miss Ortega lived in it for 12 years. Then she sold it to Mr. Howe. Mr. Howe has lived in it for 11 years. How old is the house?

LESSON 30

In each problem, 2 of the answers are clearly wrong and 1 is correct. Choose the correct answer. Explain why your answers make sense.

1. $48 + 27 =$
   - a. 45
   - b. 25
   - c. 75

2. $276 + 28 =$
   - a. 304
   - b. 84
   - c. 204

3. $206 + 209 =$
   - a. 215
   - b. 415
   - c. 615

4. $329 + 329 =$
   - a. 258
   - b. 358
   - c. 658

5. $612 + 398 =$
   - a. 110
   - b. 1010
   - c. 9010

6. $371 + 629 =$
   - a. 500
   - b. 1000
   - c. 10,000

7. $912 + 162 =$
   - a. 74
   - b. 174
   - c. 1074

8. $5763 + 2194 =$
   - a. 5757
   - b. 757
   - c. 7957

9. $4328 + 3672 =$
   - a. 4000
   - b. 500
   - c. 8000

10. $1009 + 3986 =$
    - a. 4995
    - b. 995
    - c. 9995

In each problem, 2 of the answers are clearly wrong and 1 is correct. Choose the correct answer. Explain why your answers make sense.

1. 3705 − 1698 =	**a.** 107 **b.** 5007 **c.** 2007	**5.** 5000 − 2500 =	**a.** 250 **b.** 2500 **c.** 9500
2. 750 + 750 =	**a.** 150 **b.** 750 **c.** 1500	**6.** 8003 − 2986 =	**a.** 5017 **b.** 8017 **c.** 9017
3. 2250 + 2250 =	**a.** 500 **b.** 4500 **c.** 8500	**7.** 17 + 8983 =	**a.** 2000 **b.** 9000 **c.** 4000
4. 5000 − 250 =	**a.** 250 **b.** 2500 **c.** 4750	**8.** 864 − 468 =	**a.** 396 **b.** 5396 **c.** 96

Make 1000 Game

I pick 687 to start with.

I'll add 286 and get to 973.

61

LESSON 31

What time is it? How many minutes after the hour?

1.  8:05

   5 minutes after 8

2. 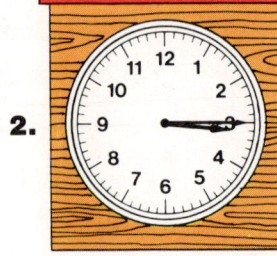 3:15

   ■ minutes after ■

3.

   ■ minutes after ■

4.

   ■ minutes after ■

5.

   ■ minutes after ■

6.

   ■ minutes after ■

7.

   ■ minutes after ■

8.

   ■ minutes after ■

What time is it? How many minutes before the next hour?

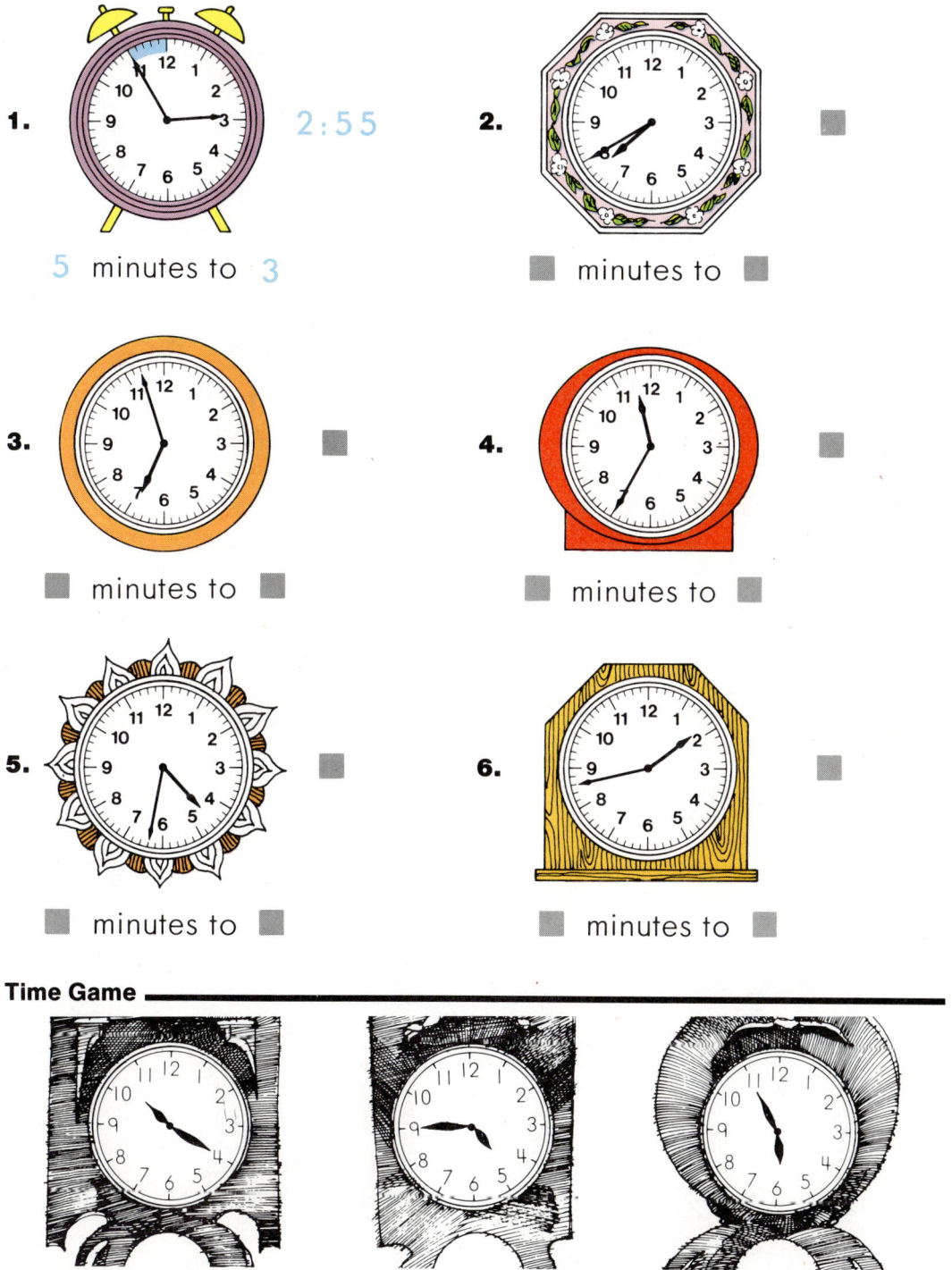

1. 2:55
   5 minutes to 3

2. ▨ minutes to ▨

3. ▨ minutes to ▨

4. ▨ minutes to ▨

5. ▨ minutes to ▨

6. ▨ minutes to ▨

Time Game

Which clocks show the same time?

LESSON 32

64

Tell the time in three ways.

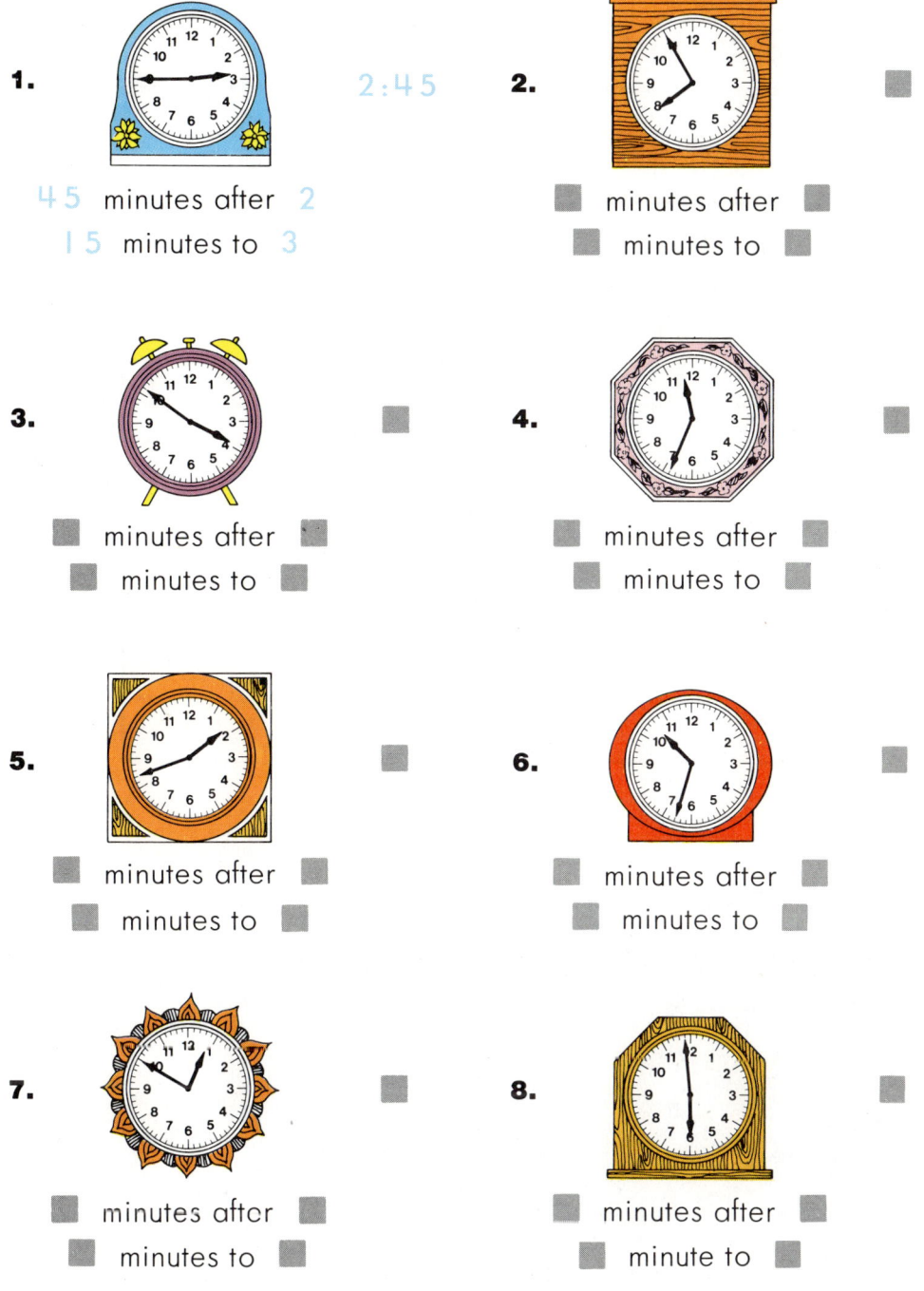

1. 2:45
   45 minutes after 2
   15 minutes to 3

2. ⬛:⬛
   ⬛ minutes after ⬛
   ⬛ minutes to ⬛

3. ⬛:⬛
   ⬛ minutes after ⬛
   ⬛ minutes to ⬛

4. ⬛:⬛
   ⬛ minutes after ⬛
   ⬛ minutes to ⬛

5. ⬛:⬛
   ⬛ minutes after ⬛
   ⬛ minutes to ⬛

6. ⬛:⬛
   ⬛ minutes after ⬛
   ⬛ minutes to ⬛

7. ⬛:⬛
   ⬛ minutes after ⬛
   ⬛ minutes to ⬛

8. ⬛:⬛
   ⬛ minutes after ⬛
   ⬛ minute to ⬛

Study the chart. Then make up three problems and solve them.

How Deep Are Some Bodies of Water?

Body of Water	Greatest Depth (meters)
Pacific Ocean	11,034
Atlantic Ocean	8,648
Indian Ocean	7,725
Arctic Ocean	5,450
Mediterranean Sea	5,150
Caribbean Sea	6,836
Red Sea	2,176

Do these problems. Watch the signs.

1. ■ − 3 = 7
2. ■ + 8 = 16
3. 4 + ■ = 12
4. ■ + 7 = 13
5. 10 − ■ = 3
6. 8 + ■ = 13

Draw the right sign. Draw <, >, or =.

7. 350 + 20 ● 375 + 25
8. 63 + 20 ● 64 + 21
9. 35 + 35 ● 39 + 40
10. 87 + 26 ● 26 + 87

11. 3 7
     6 2
    +4 8
    ─────

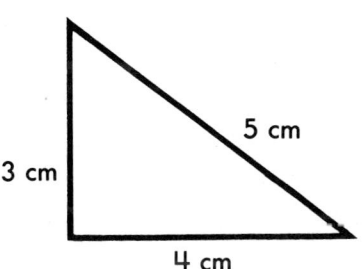

12. 3 7 0
     5 4 5
     6 9 8
    + 8 5
    ──────

13. Perimeter is ■ centimeters.
14. What is the shape?

LESSON 34

Count up or down. Fill in the missing numbers.

1. | 7 | 8 | ■ | ■ | ■ | ■ | 13 | ■ |

2. | 363 | 362 | ■ | ■ | ■ | 358 | ■ |

3. | 1096 | 1097 | ■ | ■ | ■ | 1101 |

4. | 3905 | 3906 | ■ | ■ | ■ | ■ |

Do these problems. Watch the signs.

5. 5 + 5 = ■

6. 8 + 7 = ■

7. 16 − 10 = ■

8. 12 − 5 = ■

9. 4 + 4 = ■

10. 9 + 7 = ■

11. 15 − 5 = ■

12. 14 − 8 = ■

13. 7 + 7 = ■

14. 13 − 4 = ■

Do these problems. Watch the signs.

15. 58
    −37

16. 58
    +37

17. 83
    −46

18. 249
    +138

19. 493
    +576

20. 1247
    −1058

Add.

21. 37
    58
    +43

22. 256
    709
    432
    + 88

23. 321
    713
    +186

Do these problems. Watch the signs.

24. $5 + \blacksquare = 11$

27. $\blacksquare - 7 = 8$

25. $\blacksquare + 7 = 12$

28. $20 - \blacksquare = 12$

26. $6 + \blacksquare = 15$

29. $19 - \blacksquare = 10$

30. Miss Annino had 17 pencils. She gave out some. She has 9 pencils left. How many did she give out?

31. How much money does Rose need to buy the 3 books?

32. Juan was born in 1971. Mr. Cerda was born in 1940. How many centimeters taller than Juan is Mr. Cerda?

33. Emiko wants to buy a record for 69¢. She has 30¢. How much more money does she need?

34.

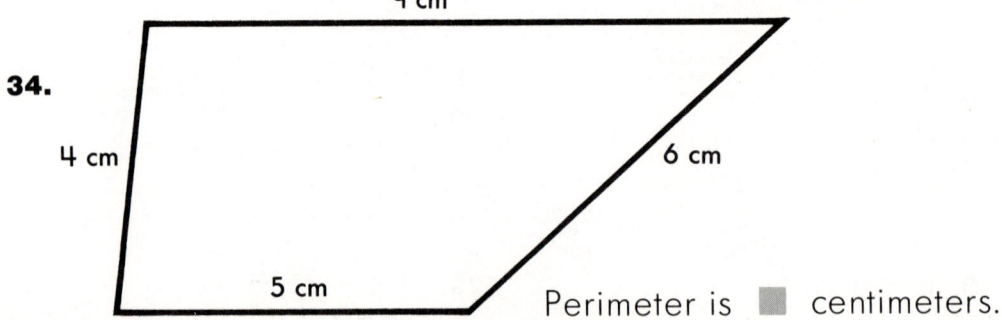

Perimeter is ■ centimeters.

Draw the right sign. Draw <, >, or =.

35. 43 ● 34

36. 1011 ● 1011

37. 83 + 2746 ● 88 + 2747

38. 86 − 43 ● 87 − 44

Tell the time in three ways.

39.    ■ : ■
■ minutes after ■
■ minutes to ■

40.    ■ : ■
■ minutes after ■
■ minutes to ■

LESSON 35

Use this code chart to solve the puzzle.

A	B	C	D	E	F	G	H	I	J	K	L	M
1	2	3	4	5	6	7	8	9	10	11	12	13
N	O	P	Q	R	S	T	U	V	W	X	Y	Z
14	15	16	17	18	19	20	21	22	23	24	25	26

Where should you leave your dog when you go shopping?

22 − 13   7 + 7   1820 − 1819

80 − 78   92 − 91   9 + 9   50 − 39   3 + 6   1 + 13   556 − 549

67 − 55   7 + 8   886 − 866

Make up your own puzzles. Then ask a friend to solve them.

Mr. Barclay is going to paint both walls.

1. On which wall do you think he will use more paint?
2. Which wall is longer?
3. Which wall has a larger area?

Nellie the cow is hungry.

4. Which patch of grass has more grass for Nellie to eat?
5. Which patch of grass is longer?
6. Which patch of grass has a larger area?

Cindy is trying to toss the ball through a hole.

7. Which hole is the easiest to get the ball through?
8. Which hole is the hardest to get the ball through?
9. Which hole has the largest area?
10. Which hole has the smallest area?

LESSON 36

1. Michelle has a sheet of paper. She wants more room to write. So she cuts her sheet into 2 pieces. Now does she have more room to write?

Every day Mr. Ross jogs once around the outside of Peach Park. He jogs 6 kilometers north, 1 kilometer east, 6 kilometers south, and then 1 kilometer west.

2. Draw an outline of Peach Park.

Every day Miss Lee jogs once around the outside of Plum Park. She jogs 3 kilometers north, 3 kilometers west, 3 kilometers south, and then 3 kilometers east.

3. Draw an outline of Plum Park.

4. Who jogs farther each day, Mr. Ross or Miss Lee?

5. Which park has a larger area, Peach Park or Plum Park?

Discuss the Thinking Story®

What is the area?

1.

1 cm
1 cm

1 square centimeter

2.

■ square centimeters

3.

■ square centimeters

4.

■ square centimeters

5.

■ square centimeters

6.

■ square centimeters

7.

■ square centimeters

8.

■ square centimeters

LESSON 37

75

What is the area?

1.

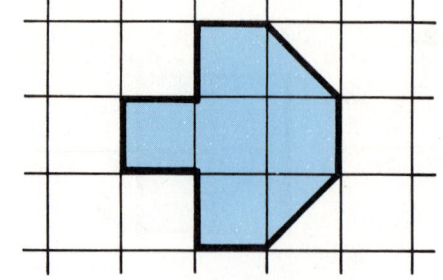

6 square centimeters

2.

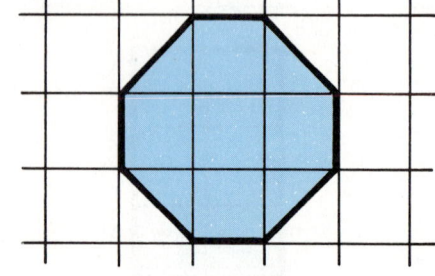

■ square centimeters

3.

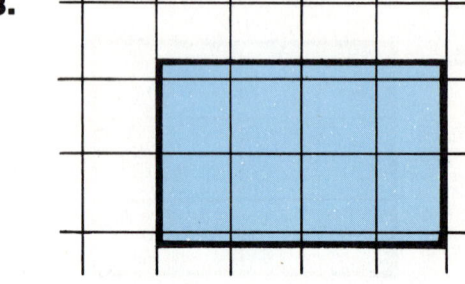

About ■ square centimeters

4.

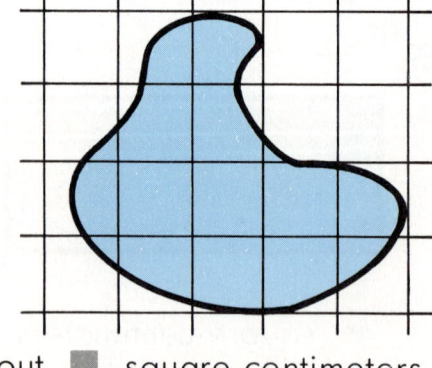

About ■ square centimeters

5.

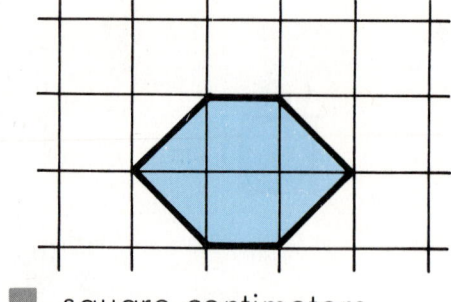

■ square centimeters

6.

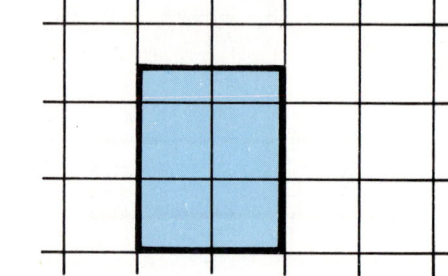

About ■ square centimeters

7.

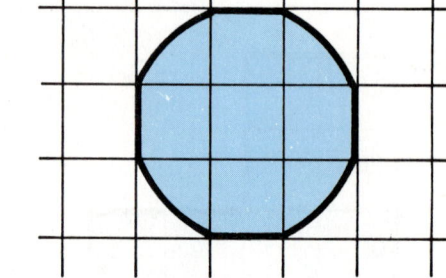

About ■ square centimeters

8.

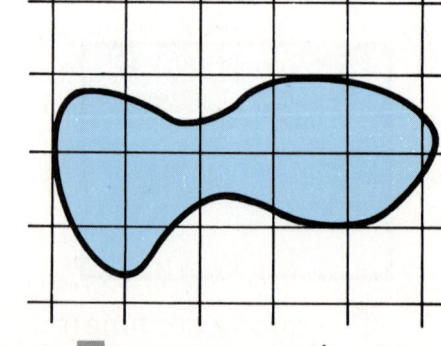

About ■ square centimeters

   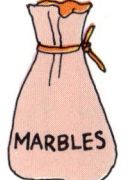 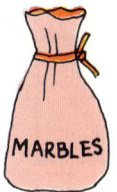

LESSON 38

1. There are 2 marbles in each bag. How many marbles are there?

    $5 \times 2 = \blacksquare$

2. There are 6 crayons in each box. How many crayons are there?

    $3 \times 6 = \blacksquare$

3. Each triangle has 3 sides. How many sides are there altogether?

    $7 \times 3 = \blacksquare$

4. There are 4 cans in each box. How many cans are there?

    $5 \times 4 = \blacksquare$

1. Each rectangle has 4 sides.
   How many sides are there altogether? $6 \times 4 =$

 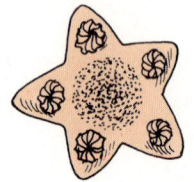  

2. Each star has 5 points. How
   many points are there altogether? $4 \times 5 =$

3. There are 3 people in each row. There are
   4 rows. How many people are seated? $4 \times 3 =$

4. Each child has 3 dollars. How
   many dollars do they have altogether? $3 \times 3 =$

Estimate the area of the blue part of each rectangle.

LESSON 39

1.

5 cm
5 cm

2.

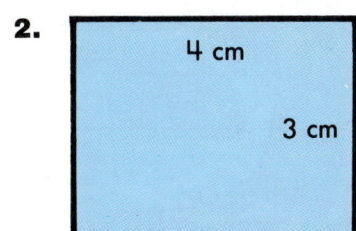

4 cm
3 cm

3.

6 cm
2 cm

4.

6 cm
3 cm

5.

6 cm
3 cm

6.

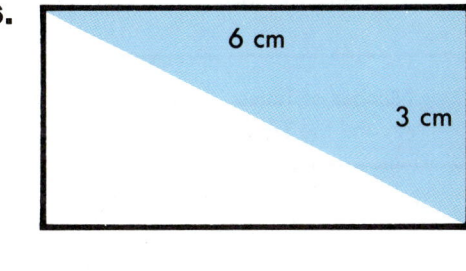

6 cm
3 cm

7.

6 cm
3 cm

8.

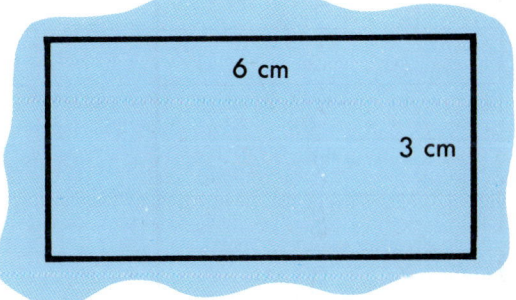

6 cm
3 cm

79

Mr. Nosho told Portia about the Super Duper Racetrack. "If you drive around it one time, you will go exactly 4 kilometers," he said. "But most races are more than one time around."

"If a race is 2 times around, how many kilometers is that?" Portia wondered. She also wondered about longer races.

Help Portia by copying and filling in this chart.

Number of Times Around the Track	Number of Kilometers
1	4
2	■
3	■
4	■
5	■
6	■
7	■
8	■
9	■
10	■

Each bag has 5, 6, or 7 peanuts.
Andy bought 3 bags.

1. What is the smallest number of peanuts Andy might have?

2. What is the largest number of peanuts Andy might have?

3. How many peanuts would you guess Andy has?

Gina caught 4 fish. Every fish weighed between 2 and 3 kilograms.

4. Can Gina have 14 kilograms of fish altogether?

5. Can she have 3 kilograms?

6. Can she have 10 kilograms?

7. Can she have 9 kilograms?

Multacktoe

15	16	6
25	4	5
10	0	2

Card 1

12	1	10
0	4	20
8	9	15

Card 2

Multiply.

1. 2 × 1 = ■
2. 2 × 2 = ■
3. 3 × 2 = ■
4. 5 × 4 = ■
5. 4 × 4 = ■

6. 3 × 3 = ■
7. 4 × 3 = ■
8. 5 × 3 = ■
9. 6 × 3 = ■
10. 7 × 3 = ■

Roger wanted to buy candy and fruit for Puggy's birthday party. He made a chart to help him choose what to buy.

Copy and fill in the chart.

Number	Peanuts 10¢	Banana 7¢	Chocolate 5¢	Apple 8¢	Mint 2¢
1					
2					
3				24¢	
4					
5					
6					

1. How much will 5 apples cost?

2. How much will 6 bags of peanuts cost?

3. How much would 6 of each item cost altogether?

4. Write that amount in dollars and cents.

5. Roger does not want to spend more than $2.00. Can he buy 6 of each item?

LESSON 41

Multiply.

1. 6 × 5 = ■
2. 3 × 2 = ■
3. 4 × 10 = ■
4. 7 × 5 = ■

5. 8 × 6 = ■
6. 7 × 3 = ■
7. 3 × 7 = ■
8. 2 × 6 = ■

Carolyn has 7 nickels. She wants to buy a kite that costs 95¢.

9. How much money does Carolyn have in cents?

10. How much more does she need to buy the kite?

Do these problems. Watch the signs.

11. 324
    +479

12. 821
    −731

13. 601
    +399

14. 900
    −500

Think about the problem. Then write which number sentence tells you the answer.

1. Gloria wants to buy 15 oranges. Each package has 3 oranges. How many packages must she buy?

   a. $5 \times 3 = 15$ b. $3 \times 15 = 45$

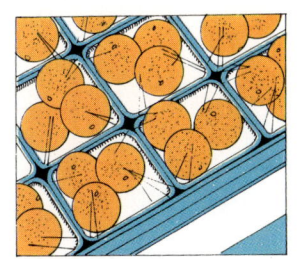

2. Ron has 28¢. How many marbles can he buy?

   a. $28 - 7 = 21$ b. $4 \times 7 = 28$

3. 1 pear costs 9¢. How much will 8 pears cost?

   a. $8 + 9 = 17$ b. $8 \times 9 = 72$

Multiplication Table Game

Multiplication Table

X	0	1	2	3	4	5	6	7	8	9	10
0	0	0	0	0	0	0	0	0	0	0	0
1	0	1	2	3	4	5	6	7	8	9	10
2	0	2	4	6	8	10	12	14	16	18	20
3	0	3	6	9	12	15	18	21	24	27	30
4	0	4	8	12	16	20	24	28	32	36	40
5	0	5	10	15	20	25	30	35	40	45	50
6	0	6	12	18	24	30	36	42	48	54	60
7	0	7	14	21	28	35	42	49	56	63	70
8	0	8	16	24	32	40	48	56	64	72	80
9	0	9	18	27	36	45	54	63	72	81	90
10	0	10	20	30	40	50	60	70	80	90	100

Find the answers in the multiplication table.

1. $7 \times \blacksquare = 49$
2. $5 \times \blacksquare = 30$
3. $4 \times \blacksquare = 36$
4. $7 \times 8 = \blacksquare$
5. $6 \times 7 = \blacksquare$

6. $\blacksquare \times 9 = 81$
7. $\blacksquare \times 3 = 21$
8. $\blacksquare \times 9 = 63$
9. $4 \times 8 = \blacksquare$
10. $8 \times 8 = \blacksquare$

Multiply.

1. $7 \times 5 = \blacksquare$ 7. $5 \times 7 = \blacksquare$

2. $8 \times 7 = \blacksquare$ 8. $7 \times 8 = \blacksquare$

3. $4 \times 9 = \blacksquare$ 9. $9 \times 4 = \blacksquare$

4. $3 \times 8 = \blacksquare$ 10. $8 \times 3 = \blacksquare$

5. $10 \times 6 = \blacksquare$ 11. $6 \times 10 = \blacksquare$

6. $6 \times 7 = \blacksquare$ 12. $7 \times 6 = \blacksquare$

13. $\begin{array}{r} 9 \\ \times 9 \\ \hline \end{array}$ 14. $\begin{array}{r} 8 \\ \times 8 \\ \hline \end{array}$ 15. $\begin{array}{r} 9 \\ \times 8 \\ \hline \end{array}$ 16. $\begin{array}{r} 8 \\ \times 9 \\ \hline \end{array}$ 17. $\begin{array}{r} 7 \\ \times 7 \\ \hline \end{array}$

18. $\begin{array}{r} 7 \\ \times 9 \\ \hline \end{array}$ 19. $\begin{array}{r} 9 \\ \times 7 \\ \hline \end{array}$ 20. $\begin{array}{r} 5 \\ \times 8 \\ \hline \end{array}$ 21. $\begin{array}{r} 8 \\ \times 5 \\ \hline \end{array}$ 22. $\begin{array}{r} 5 \\ \times 5 \\ \hline \end{array}$

LESSON 43

What is the area?

1.

2.

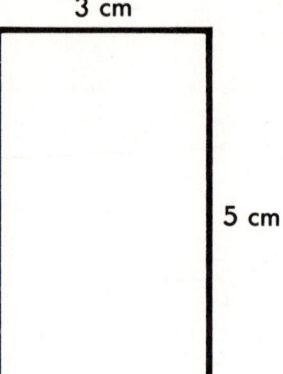

3.

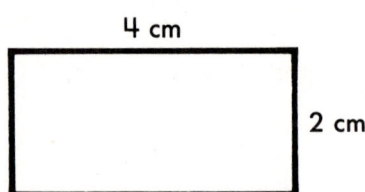

4.

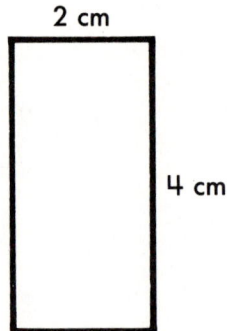

5. Rita has 10 nickels. How much money does she have in cents?

6. Joe has 5 dimes. How much money does he have in cents?

Discuss the Thinking Story

Manolita dreamed about a magic number machine. When she put something into the machine, 5 times as many came out.

The chart shows what Manolita dreamed she put into the machine. Tell what she dreamed came out.

	In		Out
1.	3 turtles	3 × 5	15 turtles
2.	6 bananas	6 × 5	■
3.	9 dollars	9 × 5	■
4.	7 flowers	7 × 5	■
5.	8 books	8 × 5	■
6.	9 cats	9 × 5	■

LESSON 44

Manolita dreamed about a machine that makes pencils. The machine could make 4 pencils every hour. Fill in the chart. Show how many pencils the machine could make in 1 hour, in 2 hours, and so on.

Number of Hours	Number of Pencils
1	4
2	■
3	■
4	■
5	■
6	■
7	■
8	■
9	■
10	■

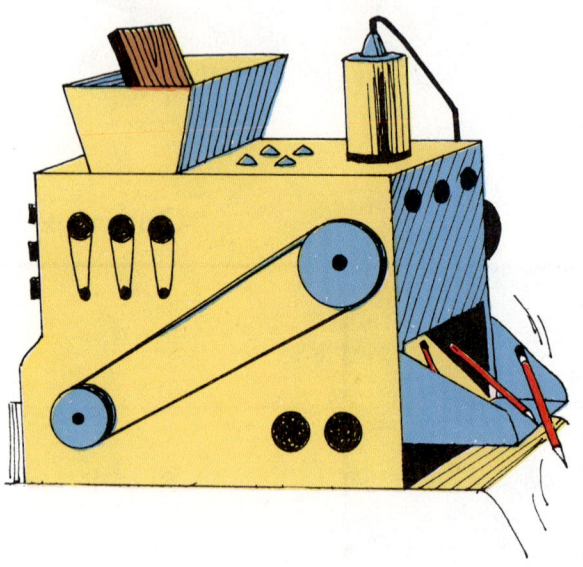

Shopping Game

Multiply.

1. $5 \times 10 = \blacksquare$
2. $4 \times 10 = \blacksquare$
3. $10 \times 10 = \blacksquare$
4. $12 \times 10 = \blacksquare$
5. $19 \times 10 = \blacksquare$
6. $10 \times 21 = \blacksquare$
7. $50 \times 10 = \blacksquare$
8. $81 \times 10 = \blacksquare$
9. $10 \times 35 = \blacksquare$
10. $10 \times 45 = \blacksquare$

11. $7 \times 10 = \blacksquare$
12. $9 \times 10 = \blacksquare$
13. $11 \times 10 = \blacksquare$
14. $10 \times 15 = \blacksquare$
15. $20 \times 10 = \blacksquare$
16. $10 \times 48 = \blacksquare$
17. $80 \times 10 = \blacksquare$
18. $10 \times 78 = \blacksquare$
19. $78 \times 10 = \blacksquare$
20. $18 \times 10 = \blacksquare$

LESSON 45

Multiply.

1. 90 × 10 = ◼
2. 91 × 10 = ◼
3. 92 × 10 = ◼
4. 99 × 10 = ◼
5. 100 × 10 = ◼

6. 10 × 100 = ◼
7. 10 × 101 = ◼
8. 102 × 10 = ◼
9. 110 × 10 = ◼
10. 273 × 10 = ◼

Do these problems. Watch the signs.

11. 37
    +43
    ———

12. 872
    +365
    ———

13. 379
    −287
    ———

14. 600
    −450
    ———

15. 750
    −750
    ———

16. 897
    −225
    ———

17. 6242
    +3758
    ————

18. 310
     430
    +180
    ———

Multiply.

1. 7 × 100 = ⬛
2. 10 × 100 = ⬛
3. 20 × 100 = ⬛
4. 100 × 90 = ⬛
5. 3 × 1000 = ⬛
6. 10 × 1000 = ⬛
7. 10 × 73 = ⬛
8. 80 × 10 = ⬛
9. 40 × 10 = ⬛
10. 10 × 10 = ⬛
11. 100 × 10 = ⬛
12. 1000 × 10 = ⬛

13. 8 × 1000 = ⬛
14. 14 × 100 = ⬛
15. 100 × 57 = ⬛
16. 99 × 100 = ⬛
17. 8 × 1000 = ⬛
18. 50 × 10 = ⬛
19. 10 × 300 = ⬛
20. 83 × 10 = ⬛
21. 83 × 100 = ⬛
22. 1000 × 83 = ⬛
23. 6 × 100 = ⬛
24. 60 × 10 = ⬛

LESSON 46

1. Miss Eppler has thirteen $10 bills. Does she have enough money to buy the television?

2. There are 7 boxes of balloons. Each box has 100 balloons. There are 629 children. Can each child get a balloon?

Do these problems. Watch the signs.

3. $7 + 3 + 2 + 8 - 10 = \blacksquare$

4. $6 + 6 + 6 + 6 + 6 = \blacksquare$

5. $4 + 3 + 5 + 2 - 7 = \blacksquare$

6. $3 + 4 - 2 + 1 + 7 - 6 = \blacksquare$

7. $5 + 3 + 2 - 8 + 3 - 5 = \blacksquare$

Lynne bought things for her birthday party. The chart shows what she bought. Write the missing amounts.

	Item	How Many	Unit Price	Total Price
1.	Whistle	3	7¢	
2.	Party Hat	10	9¢	
3.	Noisemaker	3	10¢	
4.	Balloon	4	6¢	

5. How many people do you think Lynne expected at the party?

6. Which costs more, a whistle or a balloon?

7. How much money did Lynne spend?

8. Write that in dollars and cents.

LESSON 47

Multiply.

1. 8 × 1 = ▢
2. 10 × 3 = ▢
3. 2 × 6 = ▢
4. 2 × 10 = ▢
5. 2 × 9 = ▢
6. 0 × 8 = ▢

7. 8 × 7 = ▢
8. 5 × 0 = ▢
9. 9 × 1 = ▢
10. 6 × 2 = ▢
11. 7 × 2 = ▢
12. 10 × 7 = ▢

13. 9 × 2
14. 2 × 6
15. 10 × 2
16. 4 × 2
17. 2 × 5

18. 7 × 8
19. 10 × 3
20. 2 × 7
21. 4 × 10
22. 8 × 2

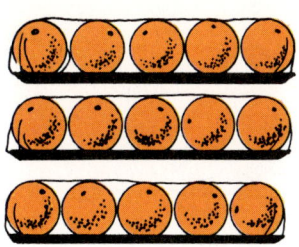
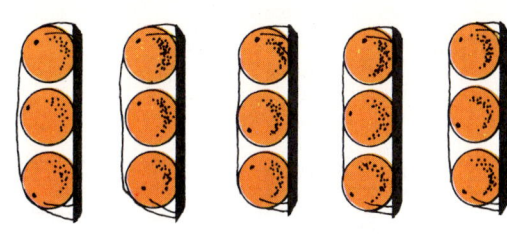

1. $3 \times 5 = \blacksquare$

2. $5 \times 3 = \blacksquare$

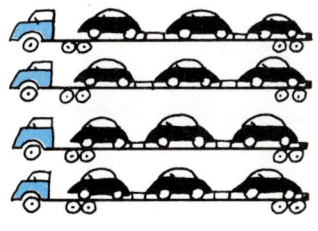

3. $4 \times 3 = \blacksquare$

4. $3 \times 4 = \blacksquare$

5. $3 \times 7 = \blacksquare$

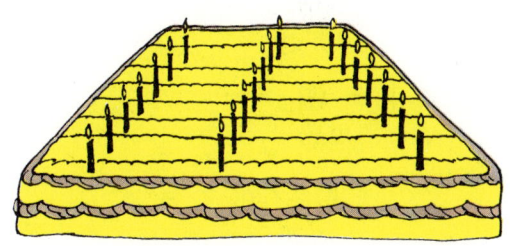

6. $7 \times 3 = \blacksquare$

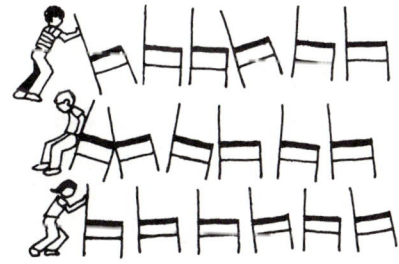

7. $6 \times 3 = \blacksquare$

8. $3 \times 6 = \blacksquare$

Multiply.

1. $3 \times 5 = \blacksquare$
2. $10 \times 7 = \blacksquare$
3. $5 \times 7 = \blacksquare$
4. $2 \times 8 = \blacksquare$
5. $4 \times 5 = \blacksquare$
6. $5 \times 1 = \blacksquare$

7. $5 \times 3 = \blacksquare$
8. $5 \times 2 = \blacksquare$
9. $0 \times 10 = \blacksquare$
10. $6 \times 5 = \blacksquare$
11. $9 \times 5 = \blacksquare$
12. $5 \times 4 = \blacksquare$

13. 8 × 7
14. 10 × 9
15. 8 × 3
16. 3 × 9
17. 5 × 4

18. 7 × 1
19. 9 × 3
20. 5 × 5
21. 8 × 5
22. 3 × 7

Multiply.

1. $9 \times 1 = $ ▨
2. $9 \times 2 = $ ▨
3. $9 \times 3 = $ ▨
4. $9 \times 8 = $ ▨
5. $7 \times 9 = $ ▨

6. $4 \times 9 = $ ▨
7. $9 \times 6 = $ ▨
8. $9 \times 9 = $ ▨
9. $5 \times 9 = $ ▨
10. $9 \times 10 = $ ▨

Add.

11. $9 + 9 = $ ▨
12. $8 + 8 = $ ▨
13. $7 + 7 = $ ▨
14. $6 + 6 = $ ▨
15. $5 + 5 = $ ▨

Add the Products Game

4×2 is 8, so I add 8 to my score.

Multiply.

1. 9   2. 5   3. 8   4. 5   5. 7
   ×3   ×9   ×1   ×4   ×3

6. 9   7. 3   8. 2   9. 8   10. 9
   ×8   ×3   ×9   ×2   ×9

11. 8 × 5 = ▇   17. 6 × 1 = ▇

12. 6 × 9 = ▇   18. 7 × 9 = ▇

13. 7 × 8 = ▇   19. 2 × 7 = ▇

14. 4 × 9 = ▇   20. 6 × 5 = ▇

15. 3 × 8 = ▇   21. 10 × 6 = ▇

16. 5 × 7 = ▇   22. 0 × 9 = ▇

1. Copy and fill in the chart.

How Many Legs?

Number of Each	🧒	🐎	🕷
1	2	4	8
2			
3			
4			
5			
6			
7			
8			
9			
10			

2. How many horseshoes are needed to shoe 7 horses?

3. How many sneakers are there on 5 basketball players?

Multiply.

1. 8 × 8 = ■
2. 7 × 2 = ■
3. 4 × 8 = ■
4. 5 × 9 = ■
5. 10 × 10 = ■
6. 9 × 4 = ■
7. 8 × 7 = ■
8. 4 × 4 = ■

9. 6 × 2 = ■
10. 6 × 3 = ■
11. 6 × 4 = ■
12. 6 × 5 = ■
13. 6 × 8 = ■
14. 6 × 9 = ■
15. 7 × 4 = ■
16. 9 × 8 = ■

Do these problems. Watch the signs.

17. 8376 − 3475
18. 2258 + 3769
19. 6210 + 3256
20. 7000 − 6000

Multiply.

1. $2 \times 7 =$ ◼
2. $4 \times 7 =$ ◼
3. $8 \times 7 =$ ◼
4. $2 \times 6 =$ ◼
5. $4 \times 6 =$ ◼
6. $8 \times 6 =$ ◼
7. $9 \times 2 =$ ◼
8. $9 \times 4 =$ ◼
9. $9 \times 8 =$ ◼
10. $6 \times 2 =$ ◼
11. $6 \times 4 =$ ◼
12. $6 \times 8 =$ ◼

13. $5 \times 2 =$ ◼
14. $5 \times 4 =$ ◼
15. $5 \times 8 =$ ◼
16. $2 \times 8 =$ ◼
17. $4 \times 8 =$ ◼
18. $8 \times 8 =$ ◼
19. $2 \times 4 =$ ◼
20. $4 \times 4 =$ ◼
21. $8 \times 4 =$ ◼
22. $2 \times 3 =$ ◼
23. $4 \times 3 =$ ◼
24. $8 \times 3 =$ ◼

LESSON 51

Multiply.

1. 9 × 7
2. 9 × 6
3. 9 × 9
4. 8 × 9
5. 5 × 9

6. 5 × 6
7. 5 × 10
8. 0 × 8
9. 7 × 2
10. 9 × 3

11. 6 × 3
12. 1 × 7
13. 5 × 3
14. 3 × 7
15. 7 × 7

Discuss the Thinking Story®

Multacktoe

36	6	16
28	0	72
12	100	40

Card 1

18	1	20
56	0	63
30	8	24

Card 2

Miss Green lives in East City. Every day she drives 3 kilometers to Centerville and then back home.

1. How many kilometers does she drive in 1 day?

2. How many kilometers does she drive in 5 days?

3. Miss Green stops at a gas station 2 kilometers from home. How far is the gas station from Centerville?

4. How many people live in East City?

Multiply.

1.   6
  ×3

2.   8
  ×7

3.   9
  ×6

4.   6
  ×8

5.   7
  ×9

6.   7
  ×4

7.   6
  ×2

8.   5
  ×3

9.   3
  ×5

10.   6
  ×7

11. 6 × 5 = ■

12. 4 × 8 = ■

13. 8 × 6 = ■

14. 6 × 4 = ■

15. 2 × 2 = ■

16. 3 × 3 = ■

17. 4 × 4 = ■

18. 5 × 5 = ■

19. 6 × 6 = ■

20. 8 × 8 = ■

21. 9 × 9 = ■

22. 10 × 10 = ■

What is the area? Write the number of square centimeters.

LESSON 53

1. 1 cm × 1 cm

2. 2 cm × 2 cm

3. 3 cm × 3 cm

4. 4 cm × 4 cm

5. 5 cm × 5 cm

6. 6 cm × 6 cm

7. 7 cm × 7 cm

8. 8 cm × 8 cm

107

1. The Bears scored 4 touchdowns and nothing else.
   Each touchdown is 6 points.
   How many points did the Bears score?

2. The Lions scored 8 field goals and no touchdowns.
   Each field goal is 3 points.
   How many points did the Lions score?

3. Who won?

4. By how much?

Do these problems. Watch the signs.

5. 9 − 2 = ■
6. 14 − 7 = ■
7. 19 − 5 = ■
8. 20 − 10 = ■
9. 16 − 9 = ■

10. 8 + 7 = ■
11. 6 + 9 = ■
12. 10 + 5 = ■
13. 8 + 8 = ■
14. 7 + 0 = ■

Multiply.

1. 7 × 8 = ◼
2. 3 × 7 = ◼
3. 7 × 5 = ◼
4. 7 × 10 = ◼
5. 7 × 6 = ◼
6. 7 × 7 = ◼
7. 4 × 7 = ◼
8. 6 × 7 = ◼

9. 7 × 0 = ◼
10. 1 × 7 = ◼
11. 8 × 7 = ◼
12. 7 × 9 = ◼
13. 5 × 7 = ◼
14. 7 × 4 = ◼
15. 7 × 100 = ◼
16. 7 × 2 = ◼

17. 9
    × 7
    ___

18. 7
    × 3
    ___

19. 7
    × 1
    ___

20. 10
    × 7
    ___

LESSON 54

Multiply.

1. 6 × 9 = ◼
2. 5 × 4 = ◼
3. 8 × 8 = ◼
4. 6 × 7 = ◼
5. 9 × 8 = ◼
6. 3 × 10 = ◼
7. 8 × 7 = ◼
8. 4 × 8 = ◼
9. 3 × 9 = ◼
10. 5 × 8 = ◼

11. 7 × 5 = ◼
12. 4 × 7 = ◼
13. 8 × 6 = ◼
14. 8 × 3 = ◼
15. 9 × 9 = ◼
16. 0 × 7 = ◼
17. 10 × 5 = ◼
18. 8 × 1 = ◼
19. 7 × 7 = ◼
20. 6 × 6 = ◼

Number correct ◼

Multiply.

1. $2 \times 0 = \blacksquare$
2. $5 \times 2 = \blacksquare$
3. $3 \times 5 = \blacksquare$
4. $8 \times 2 = \blacksquare$
5. $8 \times 10 = \blacksquare$
6. $9 \times 4 = \blacksquare$
7. $6 \times 8 = \blacksquare$
8. $9 \times 7 = \blacksquare$

9. $2 \times 3 = \blacksquare$
10. $9 \times 0 = \blacksquare$
11. $1 \times 8 = \blacksquare$
12. $5 \times 10 = \blacksquare$
13. $6 \times 6 = \blacksquare$
14. $7 \times 2 = \blacksquare$
15. $2 \times 6 = \blacksquare$
16. $3 \times 9 = \blacksquare$

17. 8×5
18. 10×8
19. 3×1
20. 9×9
21. 4×5

22. 6×3
23. 1×4
24. 4×8
25. 5×5
26. 4×3

LESSON 55

Multiply.

27. 8 × 6 = ▪

28. 6 × 9 = ▪

29. 8 × 7 = ▪

30. 2 × 7 = ▪

31. 10 × 6 = ▪

32. 6 × 0 = ▪

33. 4 × 6 = ▪

34. 3 × 7 = ▪

35. 8 × 8 = ▪

36. 6 × 5 = ▪

37. 7 × 7 = ▪

38. 9 × 2 = ▪

39. 4 × 4 = ▪

40. 4 × 2 = ▪

41. 3 × 3 = ▪

42. 6 × 7 = ▪

43. 8 × 3

44. 7 × 4

45. 1 × 1

46. 5 × 9

47. 2 × 2

48. 8 × 9

49. 10 × 10

50. 5 × 7

Number correct ▪

1. How much will 5 pencils cost?

2. How much will 2 pens cost?

3. John has 7 nickels.
   How much money is that in cents?

4. Maya has 6 dimes. Can she buy 2 notebooks?

5. Josh has 25¢.
   How much will he have left if he buys 2 erasers?

6. Laura has 30¢. How many pencils can she buy?

1. Each person has $8.
   How much do they have altogether?

2. Each woman weighs 55 kilograms.
   How much do the 2 women weigh together?

3. Each man is 2 meters tall. If they lie end to end,
   how long a line will the 3 men make?

4. Each man can jump a stream that is 2 meters wide.
   How wide a stream can the 3 men jump?

Discuss the Thinking Story®

Use objects to act out these problems.

1. There are 24 candies and 4 children. How many candies are there for each child?

   $24 \div 4 = $ ■

2. There are 12 coins in 3 rows. How many coins are in each row?

   $12 \div 3 = $ ■

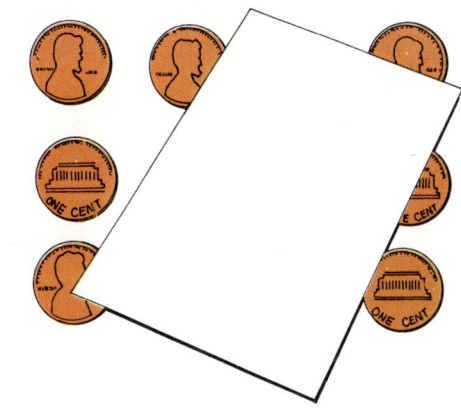

3. There are 35 cabbage plants. There are 5 rows. How many plants are there in each row?

   $35 \div 5 = $ ■

1. The 3 new pencils weigh 18 grams altogether. How many grams does each pencil weigh?

    18 ÷ 3 = ■

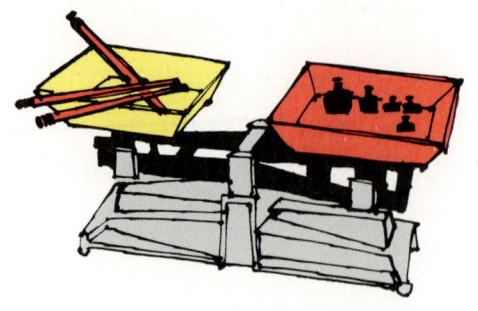

2. There are 10 fish in 2 tanks. Each tank has the same number of fish. How many fish are in each tank?

    10 ÷ 2 = ■

3. Betty, Sue, and Grant found 24¢. They want to share it equally. How many cents should each child get?

    24 ÷ 3 = ■

4. Frank has 10¢. He only has nickels. How many nickels does Frank have?

    10 ÷ 5 = ■

Do these problems. Watch the signs.

1. 345
  +722

2. 609
  −345

3. 812
  −799

4. 400
  +500

Multiply.

5. 4
  ×5

6. 6
  ×4

7. 8
  ×7

8. 3
  ×6

9. 10
  ×10

10. 7
  ×6

11. 9
  ×1

12. 4
  ×8

13. 7
  ×2

14. 5
  ×9

Missing Factor Puzzle

LESSON 58

Do these problems.

1. $7 \times \blacksquare = 56$
2. $56 \div 7 = \blacksquare$
3. $7\overline{)56}$

4. $\blacksquare \times 9 = 36$
5. $36 \div 9 = \blacksquare$
6. $9\overline{)36}$

7. $\blacksquare \times 8 = 48$
8. $48 \div 8 = \blacksquare$
9. $8\overline{)48}$

10. Cathy wants to buy 18 tennis balls. They come in cans of 3. How many cans should she buy?

    $\blacksquare \times 3 = 18$ $18 \div 3 = \blacksquare$

11. Ray needs $35. He can earn $7 a week mowing lawns. In how many weeks can Ray earn the money he needs?

    $\blacksquare \times 7 = 35$ $35 \div 7 = \blacksquare$

Divide.

1. $32 \div 8 =$ ▪
2. $21 \div 3 =$ ▪
3. $7 \div 1 =$ ▪
4. $56 \div 7 =$ ▪
5. $49 \div 7 =$ ▪
6. $30 \div 10 =$ ▪

7. $72 \div 8 =$ ▪
8. $64 \div 8 =$ ▪
9. $12 \div 4 =$ ▪
10. $21 \div 7 =$ ▪
11. $18 \div 2 =$ ▪
12. $45 \div 9 =$ ▪

13. $4\overline{)16}$
14. $9\overline{)36}$
15. $6\overline{)24}$
16. $7\overline{)42}$

17. $7\overline{)63}$
18. $6\overline{)36}$
19. $4\overline{)36}$
20. $3\overline{)27}$

21. $9\overline{)81}$
22. $2\overline{)8}$
23. $8\overline{)56}$
24. $5\overline{)35}$

LESSON 59

Do these problems.

1. $3 \times \blacksquare = 12$
2. $5 \times \blacksquare = 20$
3. $5 \times \blacksquare = 40$
4. $7 \times \blacksquare = 49$
5. $8 \times \blacksquare = 32$
6. $8 \times \blacksquare = 24$
7. $3 \times \blacksquare = 15$

8. $\blacksquare \times 3 = 12$
9. $5 \times \blacksquare = 30$
10. $5 \times \blacksquare = 50$
11. $8 \times \blacksquare = 64$
12. $4 \times \blacksquare = 32$
13. $4 \times \blacksquare = 24$
14. $7 \times \blacksquare = 35$

Multigo Game

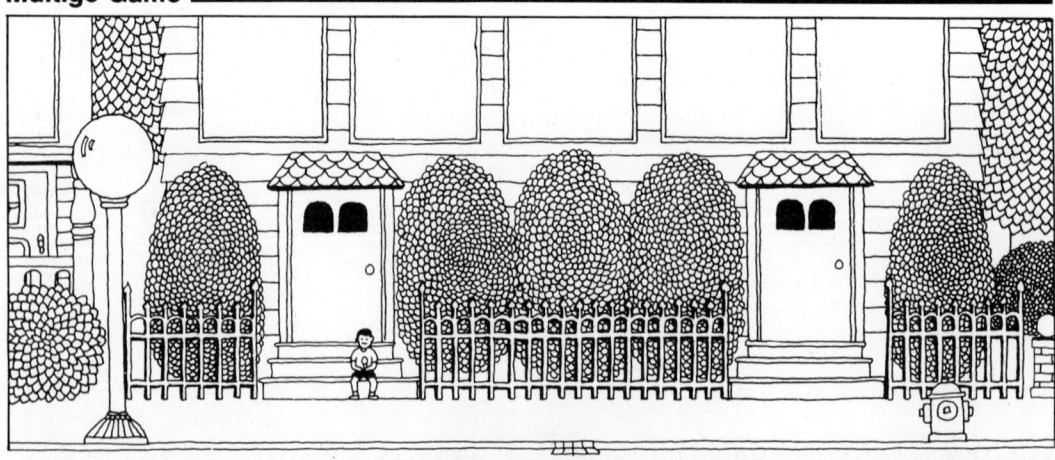

Do these problems. Watch the signs.

1. 3 × 2 = ⬛
2. 5 × 2 = ⬛
3. 7 × 2 = ⬛
4. 9 × 2 = ⬛
5. 12 ÷ 2 = ⬛
6. 10 ÷ 2 = ⬛
7. 3 × 4 = ⬛
8. 5 × 4 = ⬛
9. 8 × 7 = ⬛
10. 24 ÷ 6 = ⬛
11. 48 ÷ 6 = ⬛
12. 24 ÷ 3 = ⬛

13. 4 × 2 = ⬛
14. 6 × 2 = ⬛
15. 8 × 2 = ⬛
16. 10 × 2 = ⬛
17. 6 ÷ 2 = ⬛
18. 8 ÷ 2 = ⬛
19. 12 ÷ 3 = ⬛
20. 20 ÷ 5 = ⬛
21. 56 ÷ 8 = ⬛
22. 9 × 3 = ⬛
23. 9 × 4 = ⬛
24. 9 × 5 = ⬛

Divide.

1. 3)24   2. 4)24   3. 6)24   4. 8)24

5. 3)27   6. 9)81   7. 8)72   8. 7)42

9. 8)16   10. 5)25   11. 8)64   12. 7)35

13. 4)28   14. 7)49   15. 5)10   16. 8)56

17. 2)18   18. 3)18   19. 6)18   20. 9)18

21. 6)48   22. 9)54   23. 5)40   24. 8)32

25. 4)24   26. 6)54   27. 2)6   28. 9)45

Missing Divisor Game

Copy these problems.

28 ÷ ■ = 7   10 ÷ ■ = 5

24 ÷ ■ = 3   54 ÷ ■ = 9

■) 63̄ = 7   ■) 15̄ = 5   ■) 30̄ = 6

Do these problems.

1. 5) 25̄ (quotient ■)
2. 6) 48̄ (quotient ■)
3. 8) 64̄ (quotient ■)

4. ■) 42̄ = 7
5. ■) 49̄ = 7
6. ■) 16̄ = 2

7. 2) ■ = 6
8. 7) ■ = 9
9. 8) ■ = 4

LESSON 61

Use sticks or other objects to divide.

1. $4\overline{)7}$ (1 R3)
2. $3\overline{)8}$
3. $5\overline{)20}$
4. $6\overline{)20}$

5. $5\overline{)24}$
6. $8\overline{)30}$
7. $9\overline{)54}$
8. $9\overline{)56}$

JoAnne and her 2 friends want to share 20 baseball cards equally.

9. How many baseball cards should each of the 3 children get?

10. How many baseball cards would be left over?

Mrs. Sartor has 17 balloons to divide equally among 4 children.

11. How many balloons should each child get?

12. How many balloons will be left over?

Miss Franklin has 40 shells to divide equally among 5 children.

1. How many shells will each child get?

2. How many shells will be left over?

Mr. Bailey has 40 bananas for Choco. Choco eats 5 bananas each day.

3. How many days will the bananas last?

4. How much does Choco weigh?

Mrs. McIntosh needs 65 party hats for a party. The hats come in packages of 8.

5. How many packages should Mrs. McIntosh buy?

6. Will she have any extra party hats?

7. How many extra?

LESSON 62

Do these problems. Watch the signs.

1. 8
  + 6

2. 8
  − 6

3. 8
  × 6

4. 9
  × 7

5. 9
  − 7

6. 4) 32

7. 6) 36

8. 9) 36

9. 7) 56

10. 243
   + 378

11. 594
   − 368

12. 803
   − 246

13. 185
   + 68

14. $8 + 7 =$ ■

15. $8 - 7 =$ ■

16. $17 - 9 =$ ■

17. $18 \div 9 =$ ■

18. $3 \times 9 =$ ■

19. $6 \times 7 =$ ■

20. $5 + 9 =$ ■

21. $15 - 7 =$ ■

22. $24 \div 8 =$ ■

23. $24 \div 6 =$ ■

24. $63 \div 7 =$ ■

25. $14 \div 2 =$ ■

Do these problems. Work from left to right. Watch the signs.

1. $3 + 5 - 8 \times 4 \times 7 + 2 =$ ◼
2. $5 + 2 \times 8 - 6 \div 10 + 4 =$ ◼
3. $4 - 3 \times 7 \times 8 + 4 \div 6 =$ ◼
4. $10 - 4 \times 5 + 6 \div 9 + 6 =$ ◼
5. $43 - 3 \div 8 \times 5 - 1 \div 4 =$ ◼
6. $7 + 6 - 4 \times 9 + 9 \times 0 =$ ◼
7. $8 \div 4 \times 4 \div 4 \times 4 \div 4 \times 4 =$ ◼
8. $17 - 3 + 3 - 3 + 3 - 3 + 3 =$ ◼

Discuss the Thinking Story®

1. One year ago Christopher weighed 30 kilograms. Now he weighs 37 kilograms. How many kilograms did he gain last year?

2. Taro, Alice, and Dan want to share 12 cookies equally. How many cookies should each child get?

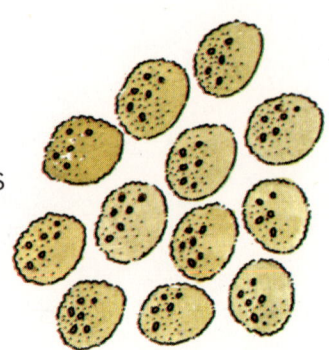

3. Dolores had 24 balloons. Some of them burst. Now she has 4 balloons. How many burst?

4. Apples cost 8¢ each. How much will 4 apples cost?

5. Yo-yos cost 39¢ each. How much will 2 yo-yos cost?

6. A bag of peanuts costs 10¢. John has 45¢. How many bags can he buy?

1. Jorge saves 5¢ each day. How much money will he save in 7 days?

2. Tad, Phillip, and Donna had a race. Each child finished the race in about 20 seconds. About how long did the race take?

3. Mrs. Tyler drove from her home to the library and back. She drove a total of 18 kilometers. About how far is it from her home to the library?

4. What's wrong here?

LESSON 64

Do these problems. Watch the signs.

1. 50 ÷ 10 = ■
2. 60 ÷ 6 = ■
3. 5 × 10 = ■
4. 6 × 10 = ■
5. 40 ÷ 8 = ■
6. 7 × 7 = ■
7. 6 × 5 = ■
8. 8 × 7 = ■

9. 40 ÷ 4 = ■
10. 60 ÷ 10 = ■
11. 4 × 10 = ■
12. 40 ÷ 5 = ■
13. 5 × 8 = ■
14. 6 × 8 = ■
15. 9 × 3 = ■
16. 42 ÷ 7 = ■

Guess the Cube Game

The product is 24.

Then her number is 4.

And her number is 6.

Do these problems. Watch the signs.

1.   256
  − 134

2.   372
  + 216

3.   429
  + 236

4.   700
  − 250

5.   873
  − 225

6.   184
  + 632

7.   927
  − 356

8.   313
  +   97

9.   244
  + 378

10.   417
  − 278

11.   803
  − 597

12.   575
  + 325

13.   63
    54
    88
  + 25

14.   471
    386
  + 198

15.   249
    249
    251
  + 251

16.   107
    104
    102
  + 105

The function rule for this function machine is ×4.

1. Suppose 3 is put into this function machine. What number will come out?

2. Suppose 7 is put into this function machine. What number will come out?

The function rule for this function machine is −7.

3. If 16 is put in, what number will come out?

4. If 7 is put in, what number will come out?

Sam made a chart. He wrote each number that he put into this function machine. He also wrote each number that came out. Then he found the function rule.

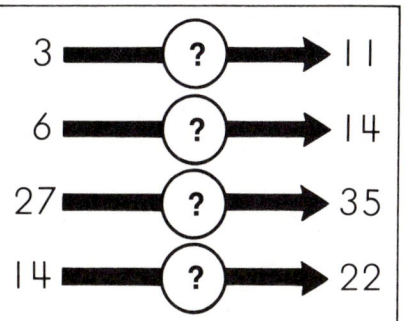

Function rule is __+ 8__.

Find a function rule for each set of numbers.

1.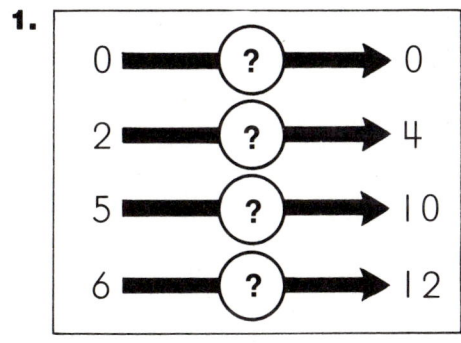

Function rule is

2.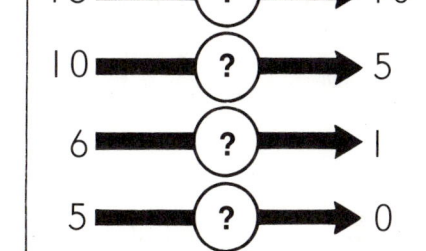

Function rule is ▪

3.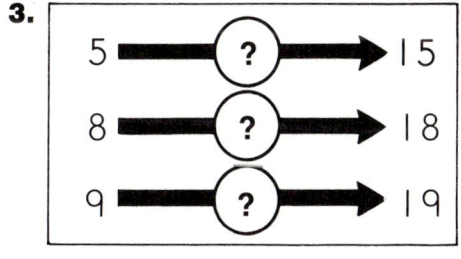

Function rule is ▪

4.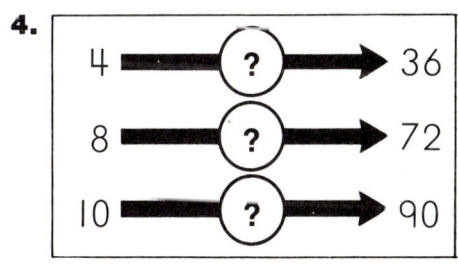

Function rule is ▪

Find the value of *n*.

1.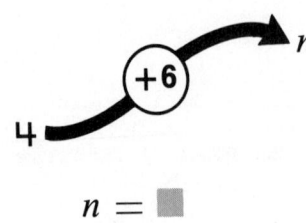

   $n = \blacksquare$

2.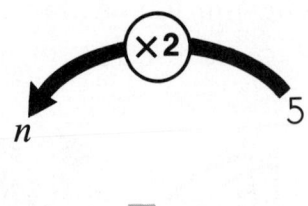

   $n = \blacksquare$

3.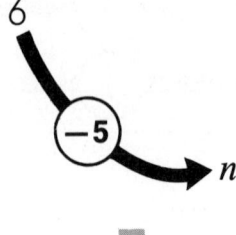

   $n = \blacksquare$

4.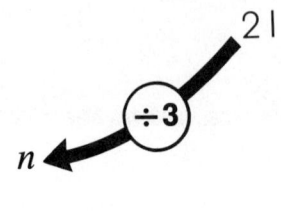

   $n = \blacksquare$

Find the value of *n*. Then find the value of *m*.

5.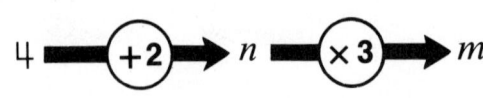

   $n = \blacksquare$

   $m = \blacksquare$

6.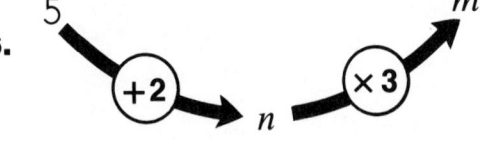

   $n = \blacksquare$

   $m = \blacksquare$

7.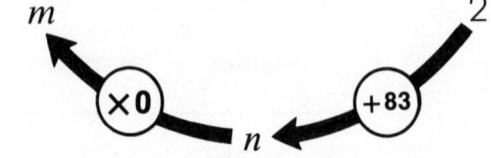

   $n = \blacksquare$

   $m = \blacksquare$

Find the values of *n*, *x*, and *y*.

1.

n = ▪

2.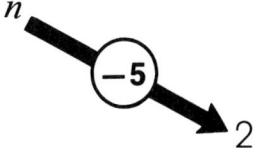

n = ▪

3.

n = ▪

4.

x = ▪

5.

y = ▪

6. 21 ⟶ ÷3 ⟶ *n*

n = ▪

7.

x = ▪

8.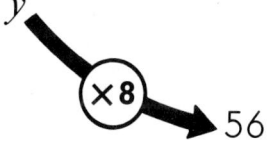

y = ▪

Beaver Pond Game

Write the inverse arrow operation.

1.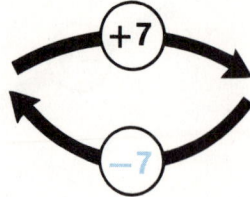
2.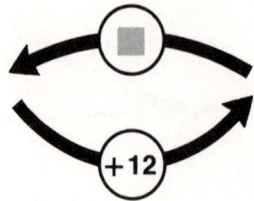

3.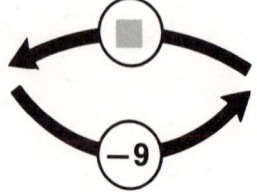
4.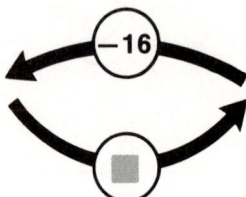

5.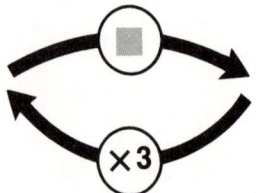
6.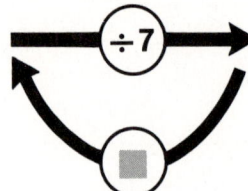

7.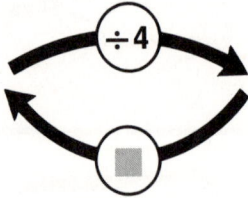
8.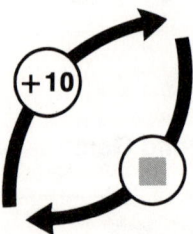

9.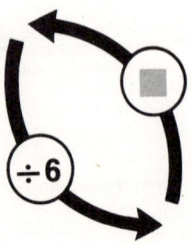
10.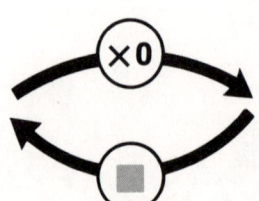

Use inverse arrow operations to find the value of *n*.

1. 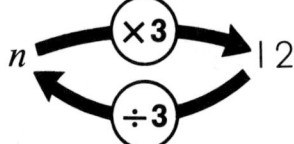 $n = $ ▪

2. 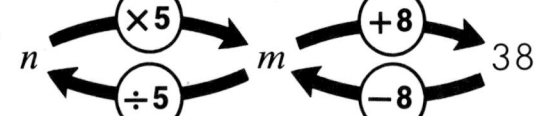 $n = $ ▪

3.  $n = $ ▪

4. 13 ←(−7)— *n* $n = $ ▪

5.  $n = $ ▪

6.  $n = $ ▪

7. 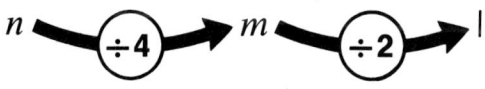 $n = $ ▪

8.  $n = $ ▪

1. If $x = 3$, what is y? ■

2. If $y = 3$, what is x? ■

3. If $x = 6$, what is y? ■

4. If $y = 6$, what is x? ■

5. If $x = 6$, what is y? ■

6. If $y = 6$, what is x? ■

7. If $x = 9$, what is y? ■

8. If $y = 9$, what is x? ■

9. If $x = 56$, what is y? ■

10. If $x = 42$, what is y? ■

11. If $y = 63$, what is x? ■

12. If $y = 35$, what is x? ■

13. If x is 6, what is y? ■

14. If x is 9, what is y? ■

15. If y is 32, what is x? ■

16. If y is 64, what is x? ■

Do these problems. Watch the signs.

17. 7245
    $+1672$

18. 3472
    $+1189$

19. 3212
    -1777

20. 6000
    -3500

Do these problems. Watch the signs.

1. $3 \times 6 = \blacksquare$
2. $12 - 7 = \blacksquare$
3. $8 \times 4 = \blacksquare$
4. $8 - 4 = \blacksquare$
5. $4 + 8 = \blacksquare$
6. $20 \div 5 = \blacksquare$
7. $8 \div 4 = \blacksquare$
8. $8 + 4 = \blacksquare$

9.
```
  122
+  64
```

10.
```
  1734
+  580
```

11.
```
  122
-  64
```

12.
```
  875
  875
  225
+ 145
```

13.
```
  4826
- 1270
```

14.
```
   548
+ 1349
```

15.
```
  7205
- 6347
```

Divide.

16. $5 \overline{)25}$
17. $6 \overline{)32}$
18. $7 \overline{)42}$
19. $2 \overline{)9}$

Multiply.

1. 10 × 9 = ■
2. 16 × 10 = ■
3. 7 × 100 = ■
4. 28 × 100 = ■

5. 10 × 72 = ■
6. 100 × 10 = ■
7. 25 × 1000 = ■
8. 100 × 100 = ■

Find a function rule.

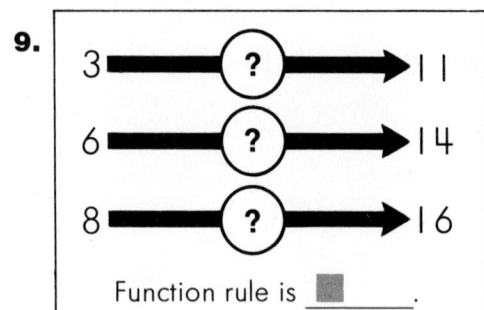

9.
3 → ? → 11
6 → ? → 14
8 → ? → 16
Function rule is _____.

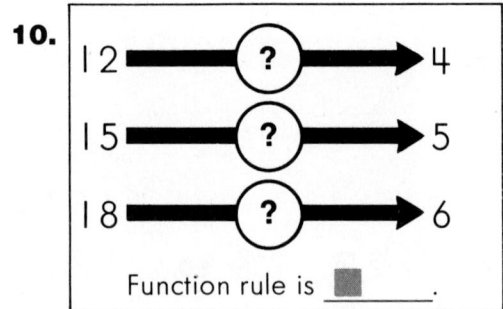

10.
12 → ? → 4
15 → ? → 5
18 → ? → 6
Function rule is _____.

Find the values of x and y.

11. 6 →(×7)→ y y = ■

12. x →(÷4)→ 8 x = ■

13. 6 →(−1)→ x x = ■

14. x →(×2)→ n →(+4)→ 12 x = ■

140

1. There are 8 cans in each box. How many cans are there in 6 boxes?

2. Susan has $1.00. Can she buy 2 kilograms of onions?

Mr. Kimoto's garden is a square. Each side is 5 meters long.

3. What is the area of Mr. Kimoto's garden?

4. How long is the fence that goes around the garden?

5. Michael can ride 1 kilometer in about 4 minutes. About how long will it take him to ride 4 kilometers?

6. Miss Lin lives 20 kilometers from work. Miss Aguilar lives 15 kilometers from work. Which woman is older?

LESSON 70

Do these problems. Watch the signs.

1. $6 + 4 = \blacksquare$
2. $7 - 2 = \blacksquare$
3. $8 + 7 = \blacksquare$

4. $9 + 6 = \blacksquare$
5. $14 - 7 = \blacksquare$
6. $16 - 8 = \blacksquare$

7. $\begin{array}{r} 43 \\ +18 \\ \hline \end{array}$
8. $\begin{array}{r} 25 \\ -17 \\ \hline \end{array}$
9. $\begin{array}{r} 428 \\ +397 \\ \hline \end{array}$
10. $\begin{array}{r} 382 \\ -176 \\ \hline \end{array}$

11. $\begin{array}{r} 2150 \\ -741 \\ \hline \end{array}$
12. $\begin{array}{r} 8674 \\ +9182 \\ \hline \end{array}$
13. $\begin{array}{r} 9182 \\ -8674 \\ \hline \end{array}$
14. $\begin{array}{r} 137 \\ 69 \\ +55 \\ \hline \end{array}$

15. $10 \times 7 = \blacksquare$
16. $100 \times 5 = \blacksquare$
17. $7 \times 1000 = \blacksquare$

18. $10 \times 100 = \blacksquare$
19. $100 \times 18 = \blacksquare$
20. $26 \times 1000 = \blacksquare$

Multiply.

21. 6 **22.** 7 **23.** 8 **24.** 9 **25.** 8
× 4   × 3   × 5   × 6   × 7

26. 7 × 0 = ■　　**30.** 9 × 1 = ■

27. 8 × 2 = ■　　**31.** 7 × 9 = ■

28. 6 × 8 = ■　　**32.** 3 × 9 = ■

29. 7 × 6 = ■　　**33.** 3 × 8 = ■

Divide.

34. 3)̅2̅4̅　　**35.** 6)̅2̅5̅　　**36.** 8)̅1̅6̅　　**37.** 2)̅1̅1̅

38. 48 ÷ 8 = ■　　**42.** 21 ÷ 7 = ■

39. 20 ÷ 5 = ■　　**43.** 56 ÷ 8 = ■

40. 36 ÷ 6 = ■　　**44.** 16 ÷ 2 = ■

41. 24 ÷ 6 = ■　　**45.** 60 ÷ 10 = ■

Find a function rule.

46.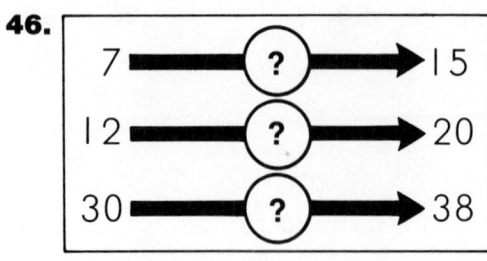

47.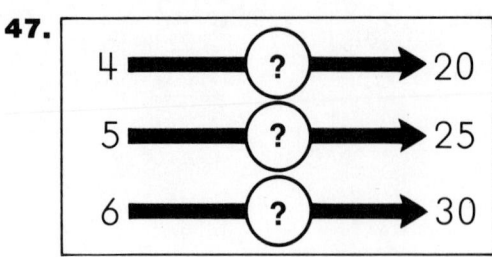

Function rule is ■   Function rule is ■

Find the value of x.

48. $x \longrightarrow (\div 3) \longrightarrow 7$ $x = $ ■

49. $x \longrightarrow (+4) \longrightarrow 14$ $x = $ ■

50. $6 \longleftarrow (-7) \longleftarrow x$ $x = $ ■

51. $x \longrightarrow (\times 5) \longrightarrow 30$ $x = $ ■

52. $x \longrightarrow (\times 2) \longrightarrow n \longrightarrow (+5) \longrightarrow 25$ $x = $ ■

53. $10 \longleftarrow (-11) \longleftarrow n \longleftarrow (\times 3) \longleftarrow x$ $x = $ ■

54. Marco has 55¢. How much more does he need to buy a book that costs 79¢?

55. Alia has 9 nickels. How much is that in cents?

56. Pears cost 8¢ each. How much will 3 pears cost?

57. There are 12 crayons. The 3 children want to share them equally. How many crayons should each child get?

Millers Park has the shape of a rectangle. It is 7 kilometers long and 3 kilometers wide.

58. What is the area of Millers Park?

59. How far is it to walk once around the park?

LESSON 71

Use this code to solve the puzzles.

A	B	C	D	E	F	G	H	I	J	K	L	M
1	2	3	4	5	6	7	8	9	10	11	12	13
N	O	P	Q	R	S	T	U	V	W	X	Y	Z
14	15	16	17	18	19	20	21	22	23	24	25	26

What is a rectangle?

$18 - 17$ 2×7 $9 \div 9$ $37 - 23$ $56 \div 8$ 3×4 $35 \div 7$

4×5 4×2 $4 \div 4$ 2×10 $64 \div 8$ $8 \div 8$ $38 - 19$

$18 \div 9$ $40 \div 8$ $30 \div 6$ 7×2

3×3 $9 + 5$ $7 \div 7$ $8 + 6$

$6 \div 6$ $24 \div 8$ $18 \div 6$ 9×1 2×2 $20 \div 4$ $7 + 7$ 10×2

146

A	B	C	D	E	F	G	H	I	J	K	L	M
1	2	3	4	5	6	7	8	9	10	11	12	13
N	O	P	Q	R	S	T	U	V	W	X	Y	Z
14	15	16	17	18	19	20	21	22	23	24	25	26

What is a polygon?

$10 \div 10$ 4×4 $4 \div 4$ 6×3 9×2 3×5 4×5

5×4 $64 \div 8$ 1×1 10×2 $32 \div 4$ $6 - 5$ $27 - 8$

6×2 $35 \div 7$ $42 \div 7$ $42 - 22$

$48 \div 6$ $21 - 6$ $7 + 6$ $45 \div 9$

Make up your own puzzles. Ask a friend to solve them.

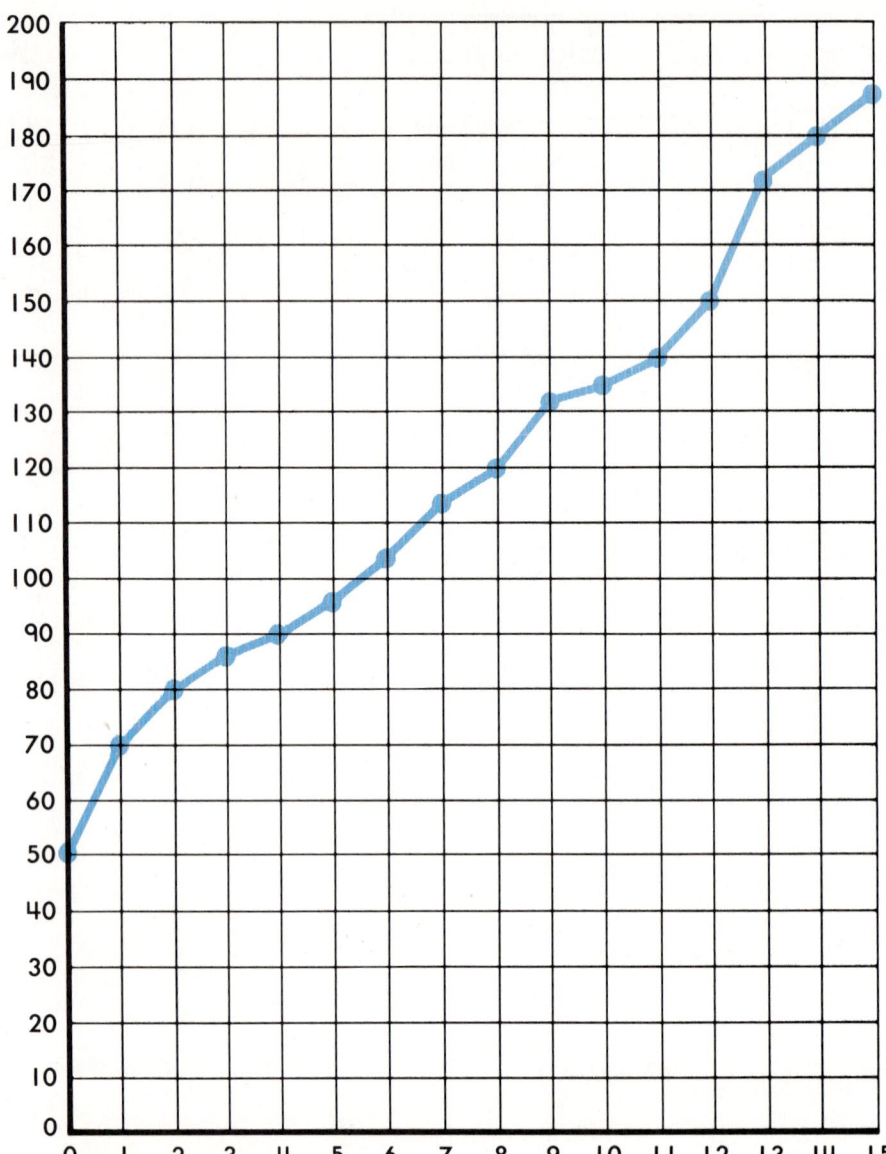

Use the graph to answer these questions.

About how tall was Todd on his

1. first birthday?

2. fifth birthday?

3. eighth birthday?

4. fourteenth birthday?

About how many centimeters did Todd grow between his

5. first and fifth birthdays?

6. fifth and eighth birthdays?

7. eighth and fourteenth birthdays?

8. first and fourteenth birthdays?

Discuss the Thinking Story®

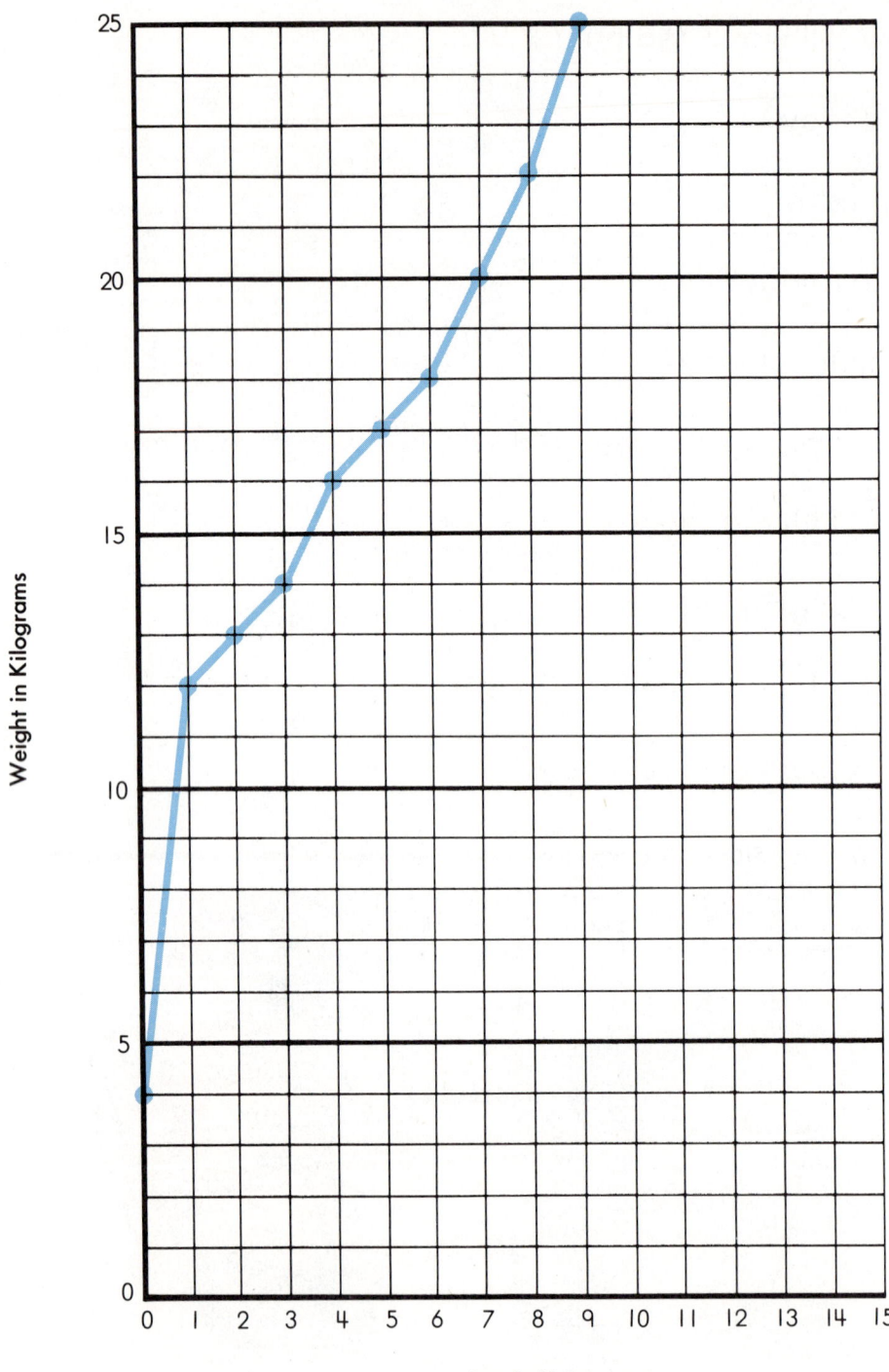

Use the graph to answer these questions.

About how much did Wendy weigh on her

1. first birthday?

2. third birthday?

3. seventh birthday?

4. ninth birthday?

5. About how much do you think Wendy weighed when she was $7\frac{1}{2}$ years old?

6. About how old do you think Wendy was when she weighed 24 kilograms?

Do these problems. Watch the signs.

7. 3
   × 4

8. 6
   × 5

9. 7
   + 3

10. 8
    − 5

11. 8
    × 7

12. 479
    + 635

13. 856
    + 342

14. 503
    − 327

15. 654
      327
    + 98

LESSON 74

Brad wanted to find out about how hot water cools. He left a glass of hot water in the room. Every 15 minutes he measured the temperature of the water. He made this chart. Make a line graph to show how the water cooled.

Number of Minutes After Start	Temperature
0	80°C
15	55°C
30	42°C
45	35°C
60	31°C
75	27°C
90	25°C
105	23°C
120	22°C
135	21°C
150	21°C
165	20°C
180	20°C
195	20°C
210	20°C
225	20°C
240	20°C

About what do you think the temperature of the room was?

■ °C

Do these problems. Watch the signs.

1. $5 \times 6 = \blacksquare$
2. $7 \times 8 = \blacksquare$
3. $9 \times 9 = \blacksquare$
4. $3 \times 2 = \blacksquare$
5. $7 \times 0 = \blacksquare$

6. $6 \div 2 = \blacksquare$
7. $27 \div 9 = \blacksquare$
8. $36 \div 9 = \blacksquare$
9. $48 \div 6 = \blacksquare$
10. $36 \div 4 = \blacksquare$

11. $756 + 352$
12. $937 - 638$
13. $729 + 389$
14. $600 - 599$

Divide.

15. $6\overline{)30}$
16. $7\overline{)49}$
17. $2\overline{)12}$
18. $2\overline{)13}$

19. $5\overline{)35}$
20. $4\overline{)30}$
21. $9\overline{)81}$
22. $9\overline{)85}$

LESSON 75

The meter, centimeter, and kilometer are units of length.

There are 100 centimeters in 1 meter.
100 cm = 1 m

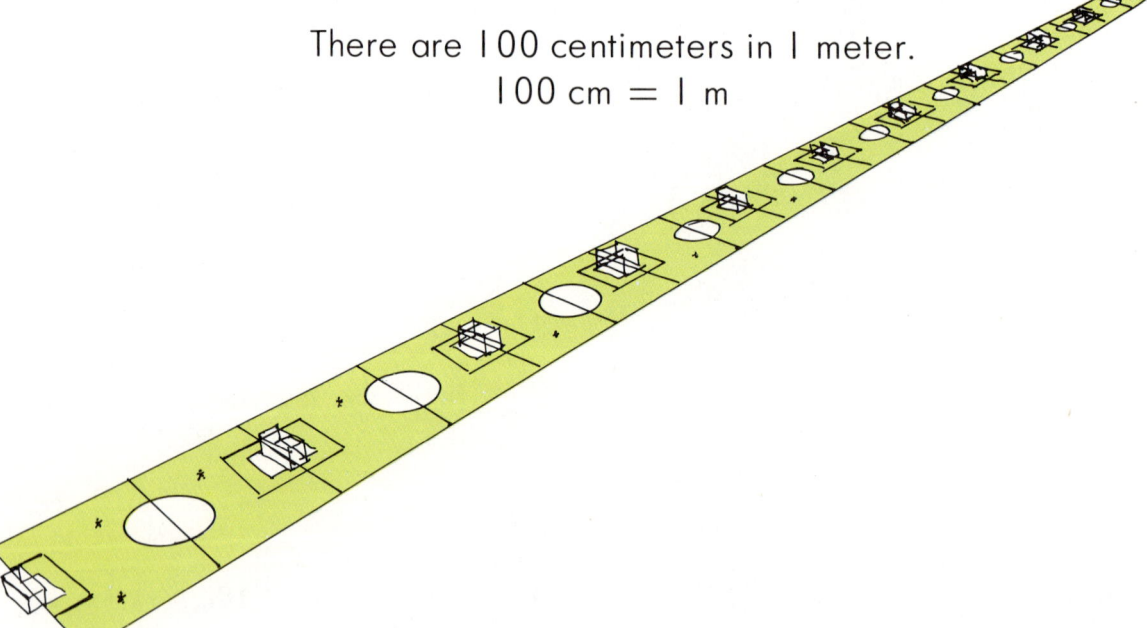

10 soccer fields end to end would be about 1 kilometer long.
There are 1000 meters in 1 kilometer.
1000 m = 1 km

The gram and the kilogram are units of weight.

There are 1000 grams in 1 kilogram.
1000 g = 1 kg

Do these problems.

1. 1 m = ■ cm
2. 2 m = ■ cm
3. 7 m = ■ cm
4. 1 km = ■ m
5. 3 km = ■ m
6. 10 km = ■ m
7. 1 kg = ■ g
8. 4 kg = ■ g
9. 6 kg = ■ g
10. ■ cm = 3 m
11. ■ m = 5 km
12. ■ g = 5 kg

Write the name of the unit that makes sense. Write *kilometers, meters, centimeters, kilograms,* or *grams.*

1. About 2 ■ tall
3. About 130 ■ tall
2. Weighs about 75 ■
4. Weighs about 27 ■

5. About 2 ■ across
7. About 30 ■ long
6. Weighs about 3 ■
8. Weighs about 500 ■

9. About 18 ■ long
10. Weighs about 6 ■

Find the Distance Game

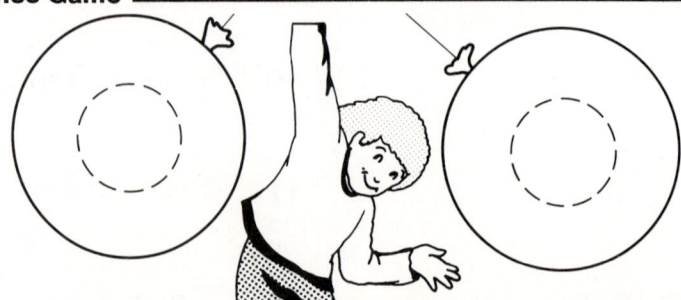

Estimate the length. Then measure to check.

LESSON 76

1.

2.

3.

4.

5.

1. The poles are 12 meters apart. About how long is the rope?

2. Billy weighs 25 kilograms. When he holds Chompers, the scale shows 34 kilograms. How much does Chompers weigh?

3. Marilyn is 129 centimeters tall. Jeb is 133 centimeters tall. How much taller is Jeb than Marilyn?

Measuring

The inch, foot, yard, and mile are units of length.

There are 12 inches in 1 foot.
12 in. = 1 ft.

There are 3 feet in 1 yard.
There are 36 inches in 1 yard.

It takes about 15 or 20 minutes to walk 1 mile.
There are 5280 feet in 1 mile.

The pound and ounce are units of weight.

There are 16 ounces in 1 pound.

1. 1 foot = ■ inches
2. 2 feet = ■ inches
3. 1 yard = ■ feet
4. 10 yards = ■ feet
5. 1 yard = ■ inches
6. 2 yards = ■ inches

7. 4 yards = ■ inches
8. 1 mile = ■ feet
9. 2 miles = ■ feet
10. 1 pound = ■ ounces
11. 2 pounds = ■ ounces
12. 10 pounds = ■ ounces

Write the name of the unit that makes sense. Write *inches, feet, yards, miles, ounces,* or *pounds*.

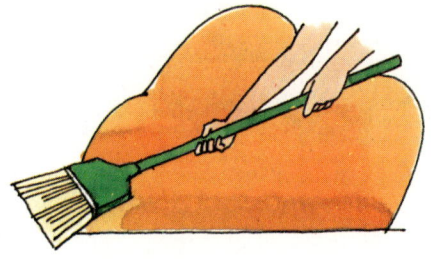

1. About 18 ■ long

3. About 1 ■ long

2. Weighs about 3500 ■

4. Weighs about 12 ■

5. About 6 ■ tall

7. About 1 ■ long

6. Weighs about 180 ■

8. About 2 ■ thick

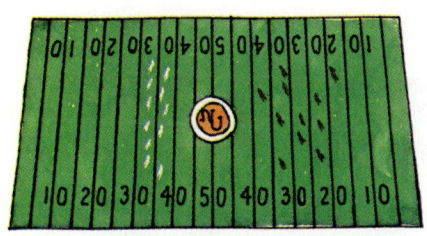

9. About 100 ■ long

11. About 7 ■ long

10. About 50 ■ wide

12. Weighs about 4 ■

161

Estimate the length. Then measure to check.

1.

2.

3.

4.

5.

Sasha can reach up to a height of 6 feet.

1. If she stands on the stool, can she reach the top shelf?

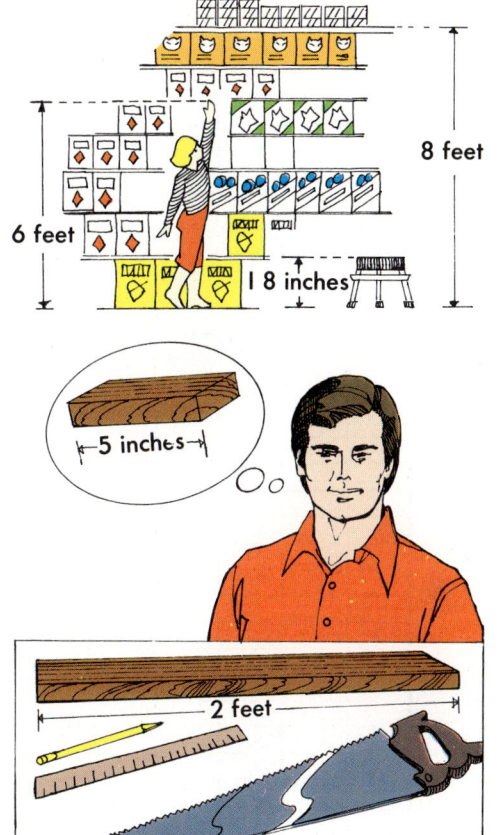

The board is 2 feet long. Mr. Wright needs pieces that are 5 inches long.

2. How many 5-inch pieces can he get from the board?

3. How long will the leftover piece be?

4. Mr. Hakim needs 1 pound of cream cheese for a cake. Each package is 8 ounces. How many packages should he buy?

Measuring

LESSON 79

Copy and complete this graph of the multiples of 5.

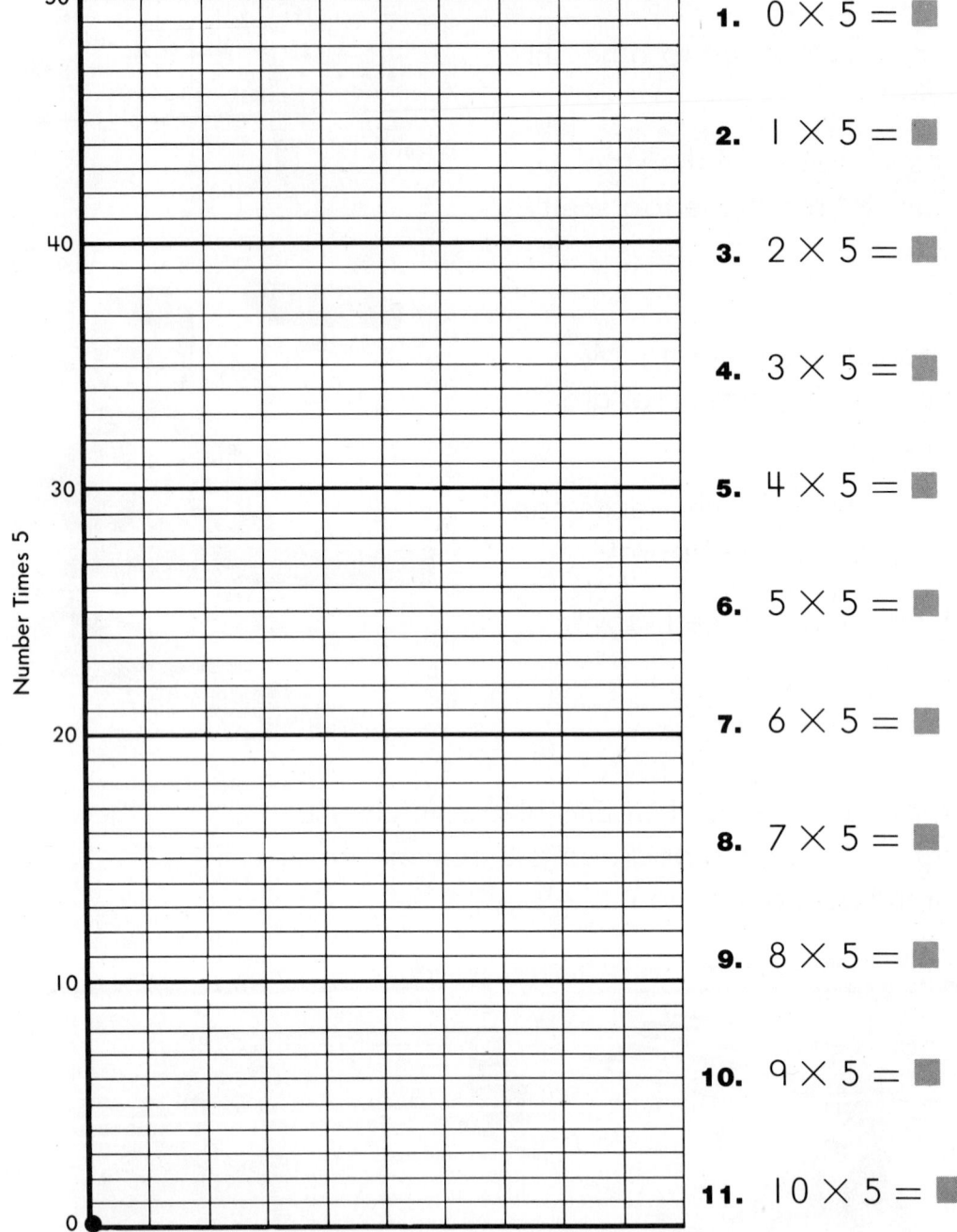

1. $0 \times 5 = \blacksquare$
2. $1 \times 5 = \blacksquare$
3. $2 \times 5 = \blacksquare$
4. $3 \times 5 = \blacksquare$
5. $4 \times 5 = \blacksquare$
6. $5 \times 5 = \blacksquare$
7. $6 \times 5 = \blacksquare$
8. $7 \times 5 = \blacksquare$
9. $8 \times 5 = \blacksquare$
10. $9 \times 5 = \blacksquare$
11. $10 \times 5 = \blacksquare$

Do these problems. Watch the signs.

1. $6 \times 3 = \blacksquare$
2. $7 \times 2 = \blacksquare$
3. $8 \div 2 = \blacksquare$
4. $4 \times 7 = \blacksquare$
5. $27 \div 3 = \blacksquare$

6. $16 \div 4 = \blacksquare$
7. $5 \times 5 = \blacksquare$
8. $6 \times 6 = \blacksquare$
9. $7 \div 7 = \blacksquare$
10. $14 \div 2 = \blacksquare$

11. 235
    +765
    ----

12. 2350
    +7650
    -----

13. 800
    -401
    ----

14. 279
    -186
    ----

15. 269
    + 35
    ----

16. 2136
    + 725
    -----

17. 9712
    - 341
    -----

18.   57
      87
     106
    +113

LESSON 80

Ruth is making a chart and a graph to show the length of different numbers of ice-cream sticks.

Copy and complete the chart and the graph.

Number of Sticks	Total Length (centimeters)
1	11
2	▪
3	▪
4	▪
5	▪
6	▪
7	▪
8	▪
9	▪

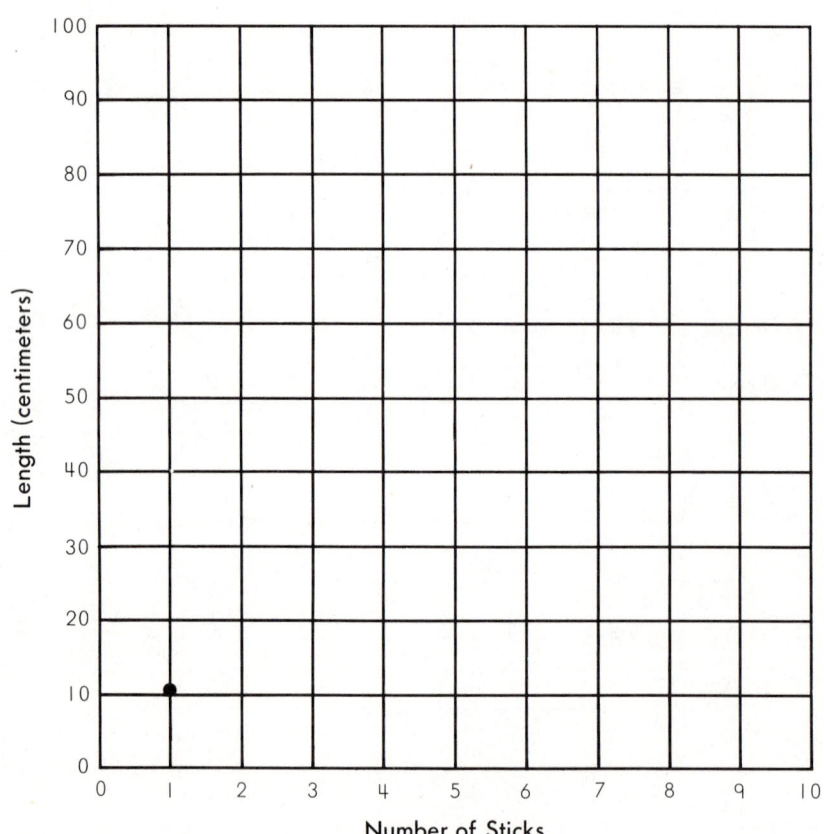

Now make a chart and a graph to show the weight of different numbers of cubes.

Multiply.

1. 6
  × 5

2. 8
  × 7

3. 9
  × 9

4. 8
  × 0

5. 8
  × 3

Divide.

6. $27 \div 9 =$ ▮

7. $60 \div 10 =$ ▮

8. $72 \div 8 =$ ▮

9. $20 \div 5 =$ ▮

10. $30 \div 6 =$ ▮

11. $50 \div 10 =$ ▮

12. $4\overline{)32}$

13. $7\overline{)63}$

14. $8\overline{)64}$

15. $2\overline{)14}$

Do these problems. Watch the signs.

16. 5
  + 4

17. 7
  − 2

18. 8
  + 3

19. 6
  + 5

20. 9
  − 8

21. 16
  − 8

22. 10
  + 8

23. 9
  + 9

24. 7
  − 6

25. 8
  + 4

LESSON 81

Draw the right sign. Draw <, >, or =.

1. 8 ● 7
2. 9 ● 5 + 5
3. 4 + 8 ● 10 + 2
4. 3 × 5 ● 4 × 6
5. 10 + 7 ● 9 + 9
6. 18 − 9 ● 13 − 3
7. 24 ÷ 3 ● 24 ÷ 4
8. 36 ÷ 9 ● 36 ÷ 6
9. 15 − 8 ● 12 − 5
10. 42 ÷ 7 ● 42 ÷ 6
11. 5 × 7 ● 6 × 6
12. 6 × 8 ● 7 × 7
13. 7 × 8 ● 8 × 7
14. 12 ÷ 3 ● 24 ÷ 6
15. 9 × 6 ● 8 × 7
16. 5 × 9 ● 6 × 8

Discuss the Thinking Story

Draw the right sign. Draw $<$, $>$, or $=$.

1. $9 \times 9 \bullet 10 \times 8$
2. $8 \times 8 \bullet 9 \times 7$
3. $72 \div 8 \bullet 48 \div 6$
4. $12 \div 4 \bullet 24 \div 8$
5. $6 + 9 \bullet 8 + 8$
6. $36 + 39 \bullet 38 + 38$
7. $12 - 7 \bullet 13 - 8$
8. $15 - 6 \bullet 13 - 8$
9. $24 \div 4 \bullet 48 \div 8$
10. $6 + 7 \bullet 7 + 6$
11. $5 + 9 \bullet 8 + 4$
12. $13 - 9 \bullet 14 - 10$
13. $12 - 5 \bullet 11 - 6$
14. $7 \times 6 \bullet 9 \times 7$
15. $0 \times 9 \bullet 1 \times 1$
16. $32 \div 8 \bullet 35 \div 7$

Try to Make an Equality Game

LESSON 82

Do these problems.

1. $4 and 5¢ = ☐ ¢
2. $ ☐ and ☐ ¢ = 24¢
3. 37¢ = $ ☐ and ☐ ¢
4. 5¢ = $ ☐ and ☐ ¢
5. $1.1 = $ ☐ and ☐ ¢
6. $1.5 = $ ☐ and ☐ ¢
7. $4.5 = $ ☐ and ☐ ¢
8. $ ☐ and ☐ ¢ = $9.2
9. $13.7 = $ ☐ and ☐ ¢
10. $10.5 = $ ☐ and ☐ ¢

11. $1 and 0¢ = ☐ ¢
12. $8 and 0¢ = ☐ ¢
13. ☐ ¢ = $7 and 6¢
14. $9 and 4¢ = ☐ ¢
15. $10 and 4¢ = ☐ ¢
16. $10 and 6¢ = $ ☐
17. $ ☐ = $6 and 1¢
18. $ ☐ = $6 and 3¢
19. $ ☐ = $3 and 3¢
20. $ ☐ and ☐ ¢ = $8.0

21. There are $5 worth of dimes in a roll. How many dimes are there

   a. in 1 roll? ☐
   b. in 2 rolls? ☐

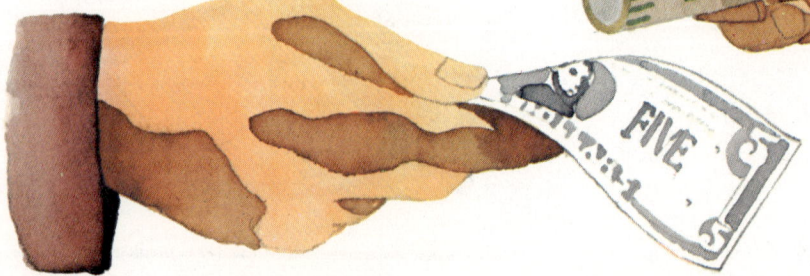

Dollars and Dimes Game

LESSON 83

_____ ¢ = $ _____ and _____ ¢
_____ ¢ = $ _____ and _____ ¢
_____ ¢ = $ _____ and _____ ¢
_____ ¢ = $ _____ and _____ ¢
_____ ¢ = $ _____ and _____ ¢

Totals: $ _____ and _____ ¢

Total money = $ _____ and _____ ¢

Isaac has 3 one-dollar bills and 14 dimes.

1. Does Isaac have enough money to buy the book?

2. Does he have enough money to buy 2 baseballs?

3. Does he have enough to buy the book and 2 baseballs?

LESSON 84

There are 10 decimeters in 1 meter.
10 dm = 1 m

Do these problems.

1. 2 m = ■ dm
2. 37 dm = ■ m and ■ dm
3. 40 m = ■ dm
4. 4.5 m = ■ m and ■ dm
5. ■ m and ■ dm = 9.2 m
6. ■ m and ■ dm = 12.0 m
7. ■ dm = 100 m

8. 4 m and 5 dm = ■ dm
9. ■ dm = 7 m and 6 dm
10. 800 dm = ■ m
11. 7 m and 4 dm = ■ m
12. ■ m = 6 m and 1 dm
13. ■ m = 10 m and 0 dm
14. 3000 dm = ■ m

Do these problems.

Metric Unit Game

1. 10 dm = ◼ m
2. 20 dm = ◼ m
3. 15 dm = ◼ m
4. 37 dm = ◼ m
5. ◼ dm = 3.7 m
6. 5.4 m = ◼ dm
7. 60 dm = ◼ m
8. 4.8 m = ◼ dm
9. 64 dm = ◼ m
10. 10 m = ◼ dm
11. 37 dm = ◼ m and ◼ dm
12. ◼ dm = 6 m and 2 dm
13. ◼ m = 6 m and 2 dm
14. 6.8 m = ◼ m and ◼ dm
15. 6.8 m = ◼ dm
16. 10.2 m = ◼ m and ◼ dm
17. 20.2 m = ◼ m and ◼ dm

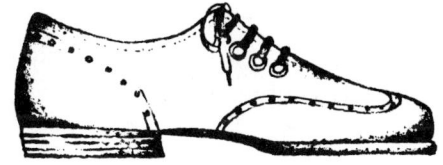
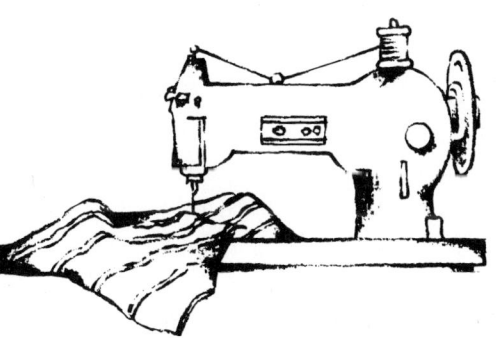

173

LESSON 85

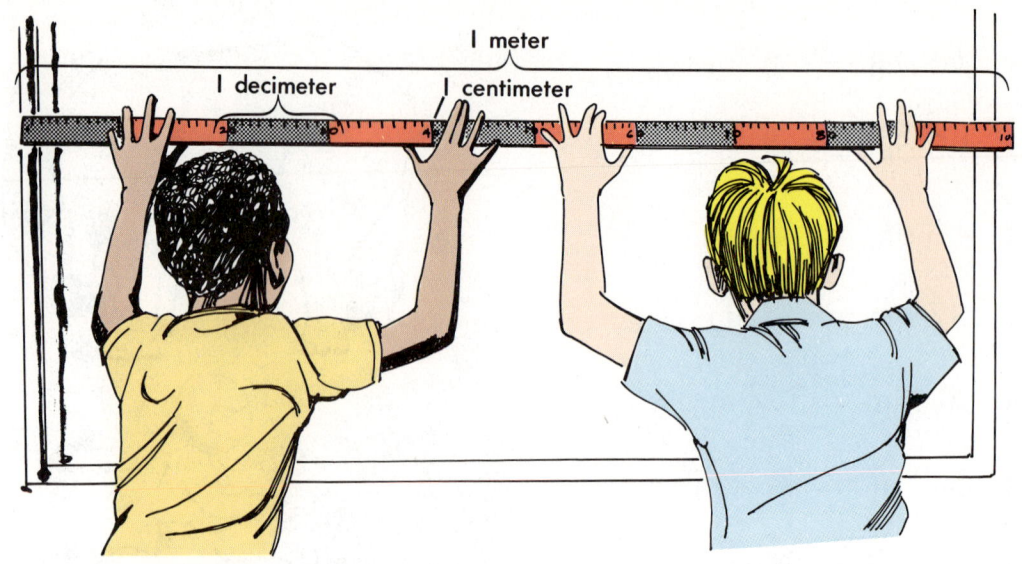

1 meter = 10 decimeters = 100 centimeters

Do these problems.

1. 300 cm = ■ m
2. 600 cm = ■ m
3. 1000 cm = ■ m
4. ■ cm = 9 m
5. 100 cm = ■ m
6. 1200 cm = ■ m

7. 800 cm = ■ m
8. ■ cm = 5 m
9. 2000 cm = ■ m
10. ■ cm = 10 m
11. ■ cm = 1 m
12. ■ cm = 23 m

Do these problems.

1. 1 m and 73 cm = ▇ cm
2. 5 m and 43 cm = ▇ cm
3. 12 m and 17 cm = ▇ cm
4. 2 m and 10 cm = ▇ cm
5. 2 m and 9 cm = ▇ cm
6. ▇ m and ▇ cm = 1040 cm
7. ▇ m and ▇ cm = 430 cm
8. ▇ m and ▇ cm = 1234 cm
9. ▇ m and 61 cm = 261 cm
10. 4 m and ▇ cm = 452 cm
11. ▇ m and ▇ cm = 925 cm
12. 22 m and 14 cm = ▇ cm
13. ▇ m and 8 cm = 308 cm
14. 4 m and 5 cm = ▇ cm

Measuring the Classroom

Do these problems.

1. 200¢ = $ ■
2. ■ ¢ = $10
3. 1300¢ = $ ■
4. $1 and 73¢ = ■ ¢
5. $ ■ and 69¢ = 269¢
6. $7 and 81¢ = ■ ¢
7. $5 and 10¢ = ■ ¢
8. $ ■ and ■ ¢ = 807¢
9. ■ ¢ = $6 and 5¢
10. ■ ¢ = $6 and 50¢

11. ■ ¢ = $6 and 55¢
12. ■ ¢ = $5
13. 2000¢ = $ ■
14. ■ ¢ = $15
15. $5 and ■ ¢ = 507¢
16. $ ■ and ■ ¢ = 357¢
17. $5 and 4¢ = ■ ¢
18. $5 and 9¢ = ■ ¢
19. $5 and 90¢ = ■ ¢
20. $ ■ and ■ ¢ = 2034¢

21. Look at the items in the store window. Which pairs of items can be bought for less than $1?

Do these problems. Watch the signs.

1. 3 × 9 = ⬛
2. 32 ÷ 4 = ⬛
3. 63 ÷ 7 = ⬛
4. 7 × 8 = ⬛
5. 2 × 5 = ⬛
6. 60 ÷ 10 = ⬛
7. 7 × 6 = ⬛
8. 24 ÷ 3 = ⬛

9. 4 × 7 = ⬛
10. 7 × 5 = ⬛
11. 6 × 6 = ⬛
12. 72 ÷ 8 = ⬛
13. 36 ÷ 4 = ⬛
14. 9 × 9 = ⬛
15. 6 × 4 = ⬛
16. 6 × 8 = ⬛

17. 320
    −205
    ─────

18. 4230
    +5985
    ─────

19. 6050
    −3296
    ─────

20. 367
     484
     872
    +906

LESSON 87

Rewrite to show less than 100¢.

1. $1 and 120¢ = $ 2 and 20 ¢
2. $1 and 150¢ = $ ■ and ■ ¢
3. $1 and 250¢ = $ ■ and ■ ¢
4. $3 and 250¢ = $ ■ and ■ ¢
5. $10 and 129¢ = $ ■ and ■ ¢
6. $4 and 105¢ = $ ■ and ■ ¢
7. $4 and 205¢ = $ ■ and ■ ¢
8. $9 and 100¢ = $ ■ and ■ ¢

Discuss the Thinking Story®

Patti has a dollar bill and 350¢.

1. Does she have enough money to buy a baseball bat that costs $6?

2. Does she have enough to buy 10 pens that cost 39¢ each?

3. Does she have enough to buy 2 cans of tennis balls that cost $2 each?

Dollars and Cents Game

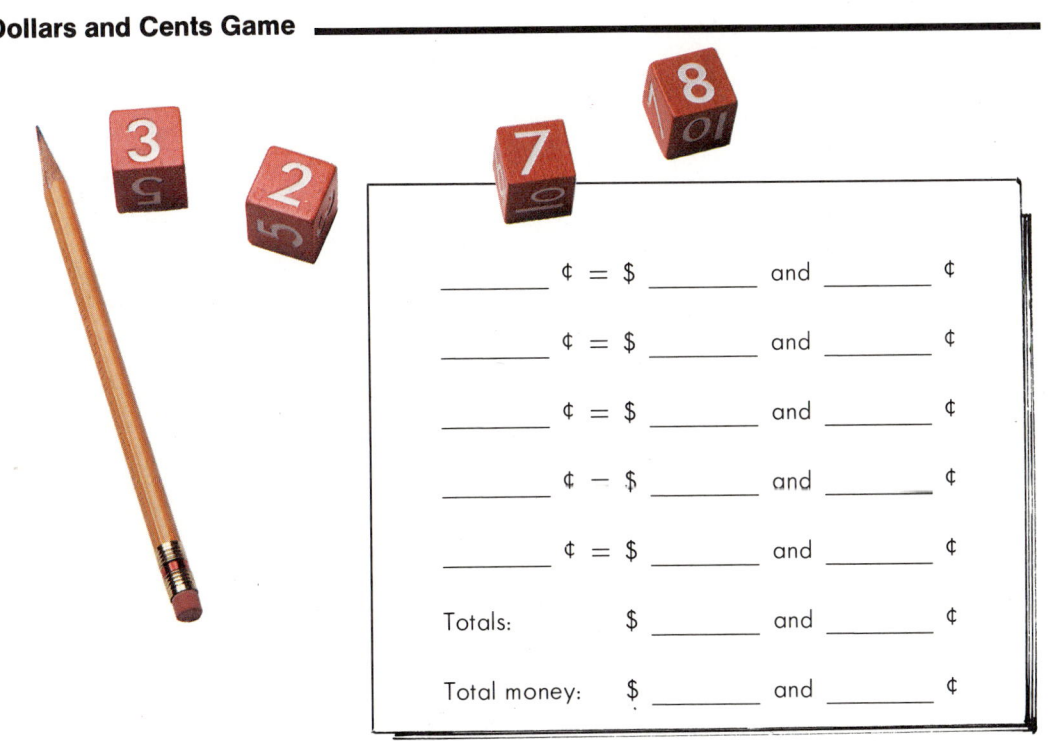

_____ ¢ = $ _____ and _____ ¢

_____ ¢ = $ _____ and _____ ¢

_____ ¢ = $ _____ and _____ ¢

_____ ¢ = $ _____ and _____ ¢

_____ ¢ = $ _____ and _____ ¢

Totals: $ _____ and _____ ¢

Total money: $ _____ and _____ ¢

LESSON 88

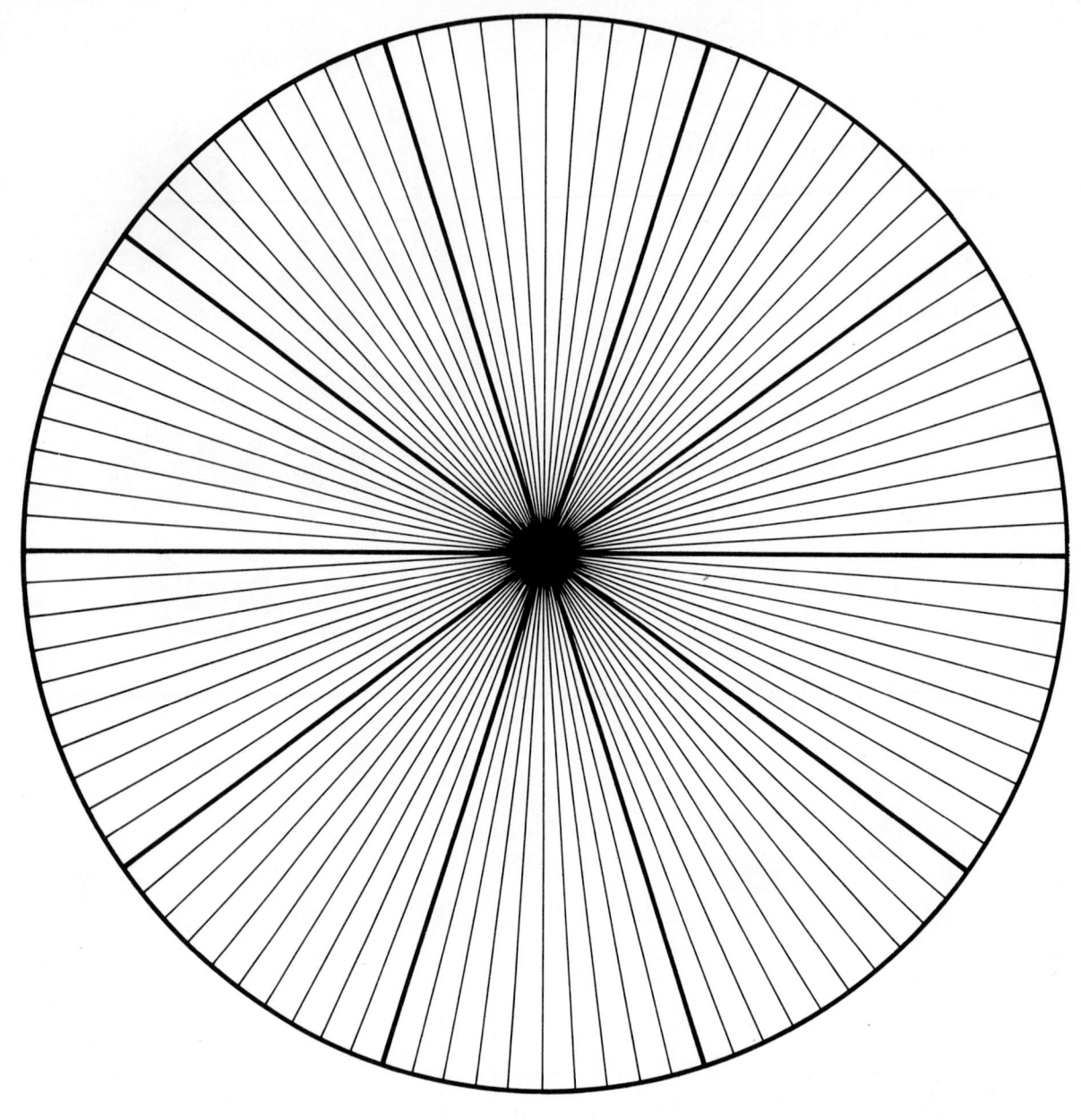

Complete each statement.

1. There are 10 hundredths in 1 tenth.

2. 0.1 = 0.10   3. 1 dime = ▇ cents   4. 1 dm = ▇ cm

5. There are ▇ hundredths in 5 tenths.

6. 0.5 = ▇   7. 5 dimes = ▇ cents   8. 5 dm = ▇ cm

9. There are 80 hundredths in ▇ tenths.

10. ▇ = 0.80   11. ▇ dimes = 80 cents   12. ▇ dm = 80 cm

13. There are 30 hundredths in ▇ tenths.

14. ▇ = 0.30   15. ▇ ¢ = 30¢   16. ▇ dm = 30 cm

17. There are 60 hundredths in ▇ tenths.

18. ▇ = 0.60   19. ▇ ¢ = 60¢   20. ▇ dm = 60 cm

LESSON 89

Draw the correct sign. Draw <, >, or =.

1. 34 ● 46
2. 3.4 ● 4.6
3. 6.43 ● 6.5
4. 5.7 ● 5.70
5. 1 ● 0.1
6. 31.20 ● 31.26
7. 5.4 ● 50.4
8. 6.30 ● 7.2
9. 2.1 ● 1.21
10. 70.0 ● 7.00
11. 0.7 ● 1.02
12. 0.3 ● 0.03
13. 5.2 ● 5.08
14. 12.1 ● 1.21
15. 70.04 ● 7.4
16. 5.4 ● 5.04
17. 3.7 ● 3.70
18. 2.10 ● 1.3
19. 8.0 ● 3.2
20. 14.34 ● 14.44
21. 0.5 ● 0.10
22. 1.05 ● 1.50

Number correct ■

Do these problems. Watch the signs.

1. 6   2. 4   3. 9   4. 7   5. 5
   ×7   ×8   −6   ×3   −2

6. 7   7. 4   8. 8   9. 5   10. 10
   ×8   +9   ×8   ×7   + 6

11. 634   12. 300   13. 4724   14. 7100
    +269   −158   + 986   − 600

15. 24 ÷ 8 = ■   19. 18 − 9 = ■

16. 9 × 4 = ■   20. 45 ÷ 5 = ■

17. 6 × 9 = ■   21. 17 − 8 = ■

18. 48 ÷ 6 = ■   22. 10 × 8 = ■

LESSON 90

4.75 + 3.86 = ?

   4.75
+ 3.86   Line up the decimal points.
―――――

  1 1
   4.75
+ 3.86   Add.
―――――
   8.61

―――――――――――――――――――

6.39 + 2.4 = ?

   6.39
+ 2.4   Line up the decimal points.
―――――

   6.39
+ 2.40   If it helps, put in a zero (since
―――――   2.4 and 2.40 have the same value).

   6.39
+ 2.40   Add.
―――――
   8.79

Add.

1. 3.27
   +2.48

2. 7.63
   +1.54

3. 5.4
   +2.55

4. 8.31
   +4.24

5. 7.45
   +6.7

6. 1.30
   +2.74

7. 10.28
   +17.94

8. 12.34
   +19.8

9. 43.72
   +56.28

10. 2.4
   +1.65

11. 325.6
   + 35.3

12. 98.6
   +98.6

13. 4.3 + 1.5 = ■

14. 2.5 + 4 = ■

15. 25.6 + 30.2 = ■

16. 86.8 + 2.7 = ■

17. 9 + 5.6 = ■

18. 4.2 + 1.05 = ■

19. 3.4 + 10.4 = ■

20. 121.8 + 72.2 = ■

1. How much do the bicycle and the basket cost together?

2. It is 9.23 meters from the ground to the top of the house. The antenna is 1.60 meters tall. How far is it from the ground to the top of the antenna?

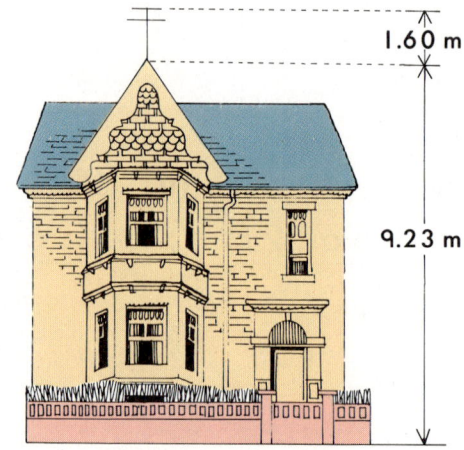

3. Lynda had $2.73. Then she earned $1.50. How much does she have now?

LESSON 91

23.79 − 10.82 = ?

```
  2 3 . 7 9
− 1 0 . 8 2      Line up the decimal points.
```

```
      2  17
  2 3 . 7 9
− 1 0 . 8 2      Subtract.
  1 2 . 9 7
```

4.6 − 3.25 = ?

```
  4 . 6
− 3 . 2 5        Line up the decimal points.
```

```
  4 . 6 0        If it helps, put in a zero (since
− 3 . 2 5        4.6 and 4.60 have the same value).
```

```
      5  10
  4 . 6 0
− 3 . 2 5        Subtract.
  1 . 3 5
```

187

Subtract.

1. 12.73   2. 5.45   3. 10.00   4. 43.85
   − 9.06   −2.9   − 2.50   −27.8

5. 63.5   6. 2.05   7. 5.09   8. 6.43
   −18.55   −1.38   −4.92   −2.31

9. 4.7   10. 10.00 11. 17.4   12. 12.07
   −4   − 0.03   −15.26   − 9.38

13. $7.0 - 3.5 =$ ■

14. $4.2 - 1.75 =$ ■

15. $5.6 - 1.43 =$ ■

16. $5.06 - 1.43 =$ ■

17. $8.30 - 4.17 =$ ■

18. $8.03 - 4.17 =$ ■

19. $0.9 - 0.85 =$ ■

20. $0.42 - 0.39 =$ ■

1. Miss Swenson has a pole that is 2.00 meters long. She wants to cut it so that it is 1.55 meters long. How long a piece must she cut off?

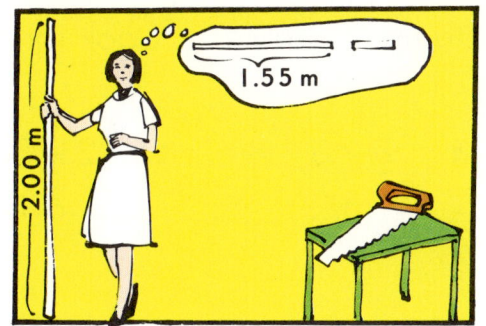

2. Sid is saving his money to buy a football. It costs $12. He has $5.65. How much more money does he need?

3. Mr. Rice bought some gum for 15 cents. He gave the storekeeper a $5 bill. How much change should the storekeeper give Mr. Rice?

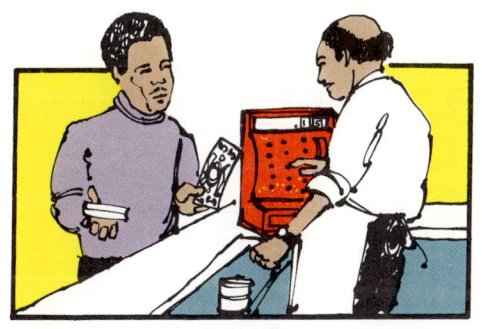

4. Before today, Andrea had ridden her bicycle a total of 274.8 kilometers. Now she has ridden her bicycle a total of 275.4 kilometers. How far did Andrea ride today?

Do these problems. Look for problems that are alike.

1. 823
  −159

2. 243
  + 61

3. 82.3
  −15.9

4. 307
  −180

5. 351
  + 39

6. 3.51
  +0.39

7. 3.07
  − 1.8

8. 8.23
  −1.59

9. 2.43
  +0.61

10. 35.1
  + 3.9

11. 24.3
  + 6.1

12. 823
  −159

13. 2.43
  +0.61

14. 61
  +243

15. 30.7
  − 18

Store Game

Draw the right sign. Draw <, >, or =.

1. 2.3 ● 2.7
2. 0.50 ● 1.2
3. 63 ● 7.4
4. 1.80 ● 1.08
5. 3.4 ● 3.07
6. 0.9 ● 4
7. 13.50 ● 13.47
8. 12 ● 12.0
9. 0.64 ● 1.0
10. 0.08 ● 3

11. 22 ● 2.02
12. 1.51 ● 1.15
13. 3.5 ● 4.5
14. 3.5 ● 0.45
15. 10.1 ● 10.01
16. 0.2 ● 4.06
17. 5 ● 5.00
18. 42.40 ● 42.36
19. 3.10 ● 2.3
20. 21.1 ● 2.11

1. One book is 25 centimeters long. How many meters long is a row of 5 books?

2. Each book costs 25¢. How much do 5 books cost?

3. Mr. Brown had $10. He spent some money at the football game. He has $5.73 left. How much did Mr. Brown spend?

Stan is 1.32 meters tall. Craig is 1.28 meters tall.

4. Who is taller?

5. How many meters taller?

6. How many centimeters taller?

Make up at least three problems. Solve them. Use them in the next lesson to try to stump the rest of the class.

Harder Checkbook Game

LESSON 94

1. Mrs. Wong made curtains for 1 window. She used 2.68 meters of cloth. How many meters of cloth will she need to make curtains for 4 more windows?

2. Mrs. Wong is buying 10.8 meters of cloth. The piece at the store is 14.5 meters long. What length of cloth will be left?

3. The cloth costs $35.26. Mrs. Wong gave the storekeeper two $20 bills. How much change should Mrs. Wong get?

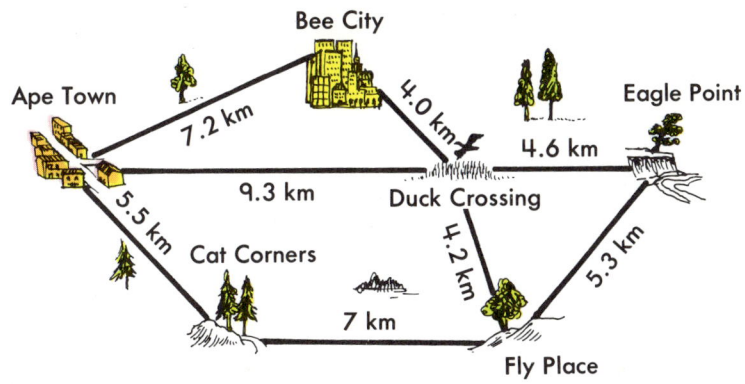

1. How far is it from Ape Town to Duck Crossing?

2. How far is it from Ape Town to Eagle Point?

3. How far is it from Ape Town to Fly Place if you go through Duck Crossing?

4. How far is it from Ape Town to Fly Place if you go through Cat Corners?

5. If you go from Fly Place to Ape Town, is it shorter to go through Duck Crossing or Cat Corners?

6. How much shorter?

7. Suppose you are going from Duck Crossing to Ape Town. How much farther would it be to go through Bee City?

Discuss the Thinking Story®

195

LESSON 95

Do these problems. Watch the signs.

1. 5.3
   − 2.1

2. 5.47
   − 3.6

3. 2.4
   − 1.87

4. 4.71
   + 5.62

5. 5.62
   + 4.71

6. 5.62
   − 4.71

7. 3.8
   + 1.2

8. 4.07
   − 3.7

9. 12.13
   − 8.6

10. 5.81 − 3.28 = ■

12. 4.2 − 1.75 = ■

11. 2.66 − 1.7 = ■

13. 5.4 + 8.17 = ■

Number correct ■

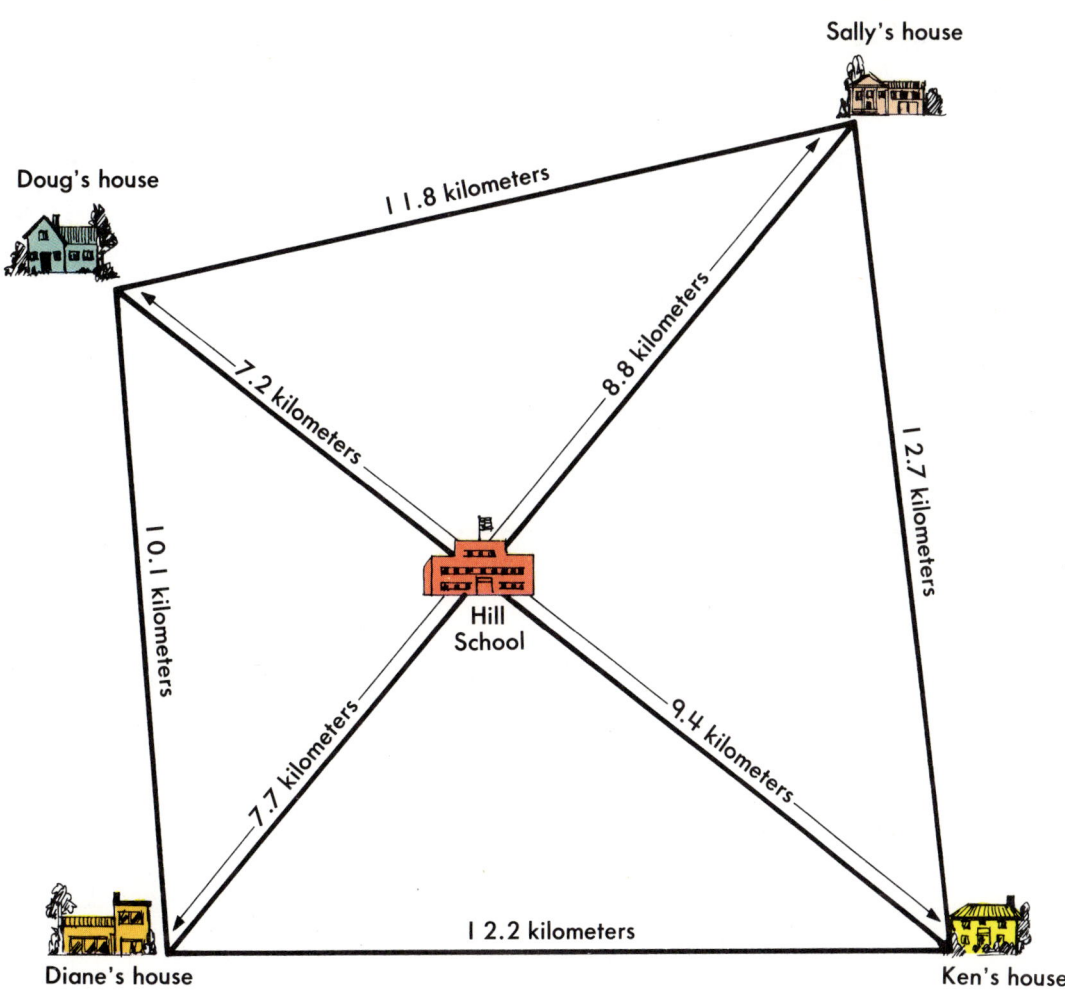

Make up 3 problems and solve them.

Coloring Halves, Thirds, and Fourths

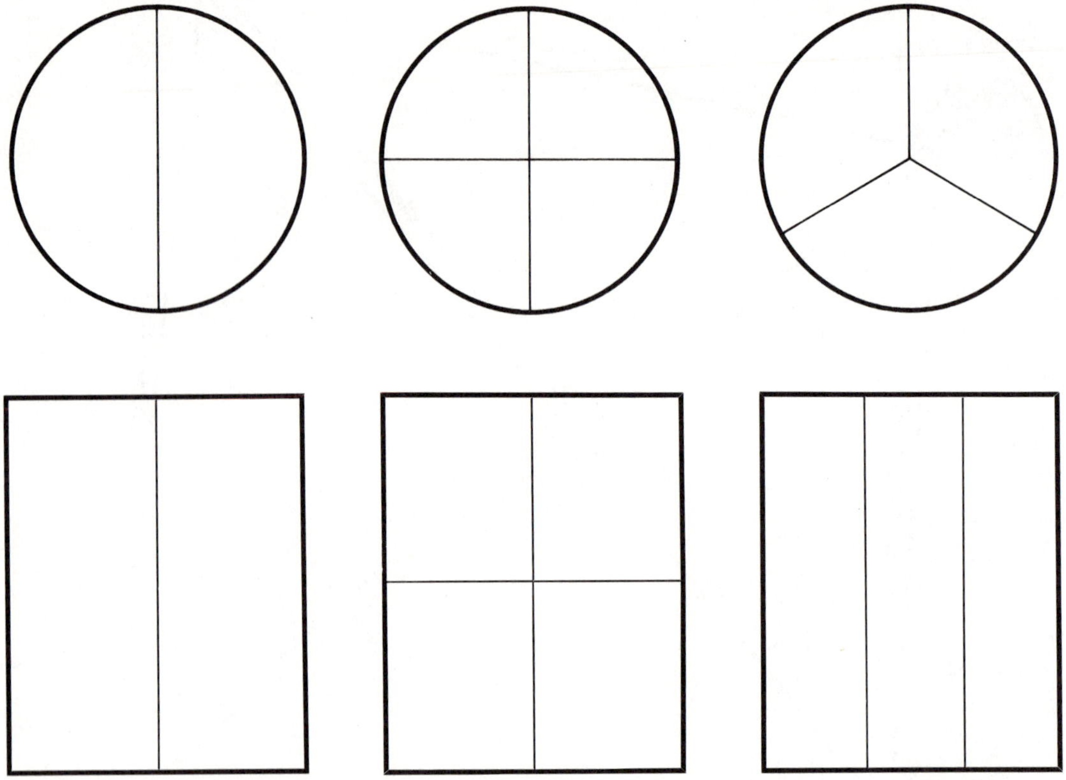

What fraction of each figure is colored?

1.

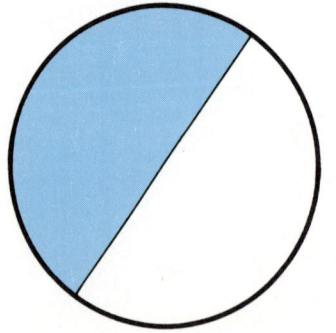

2.

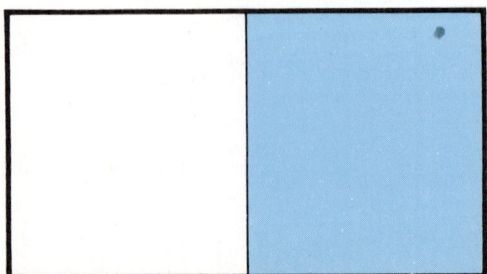

What fraction of each figure is colored?

1.

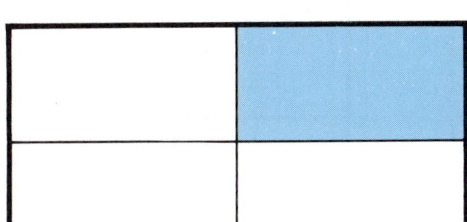

2.

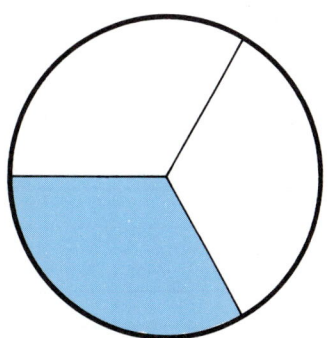

3.

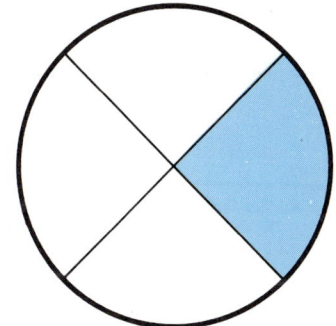

4.

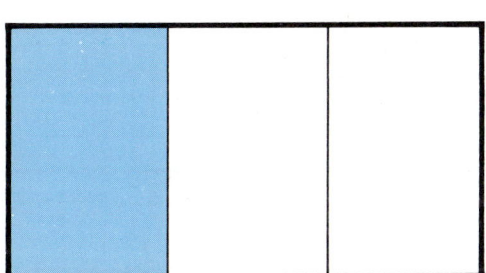

5.

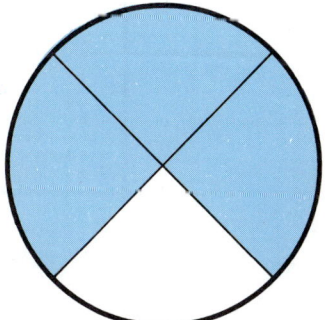

6.

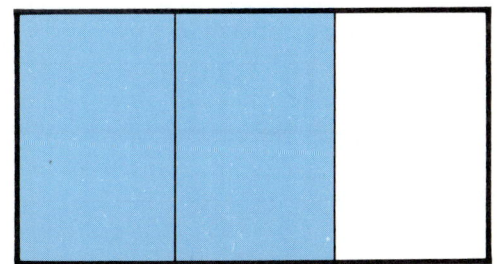

Tell how many parts the rectangle or line segment is divided into. Tell how many dividing lines were drawn.

	Number of Parts	Number of Dividing Lines
1.	2	1
2.		
3.		
4.		
5.		
6.		
7.		
8.		

1. Which is bigger, $\frac{1}{2}$ of the cake or $\frac{1}{3}$ of the cake?

2. Which is bigger, $\frac{1}{2}$ of the pie or $\frac{1}{5}$ of the pie?

3. Which is bigger, $\frac{1}{3}$ of the loaf or $\frac{1}{5}$ of the loaf?

4. Which is bigger, $\frac{1}{3}$ of the roast or $\frac{1}{4}$ of the roast?

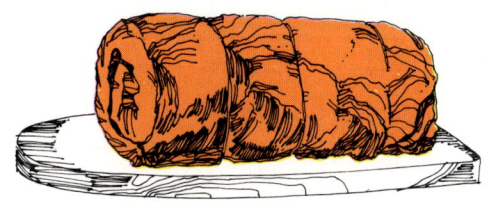

5. Which is bigger, $\frac{1}{2}$ of the small cake or $\frac{1}{4}$ of the big cake?

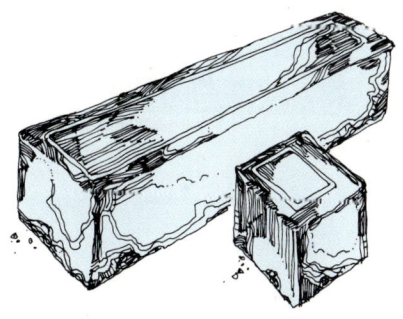

What fraction is colored?

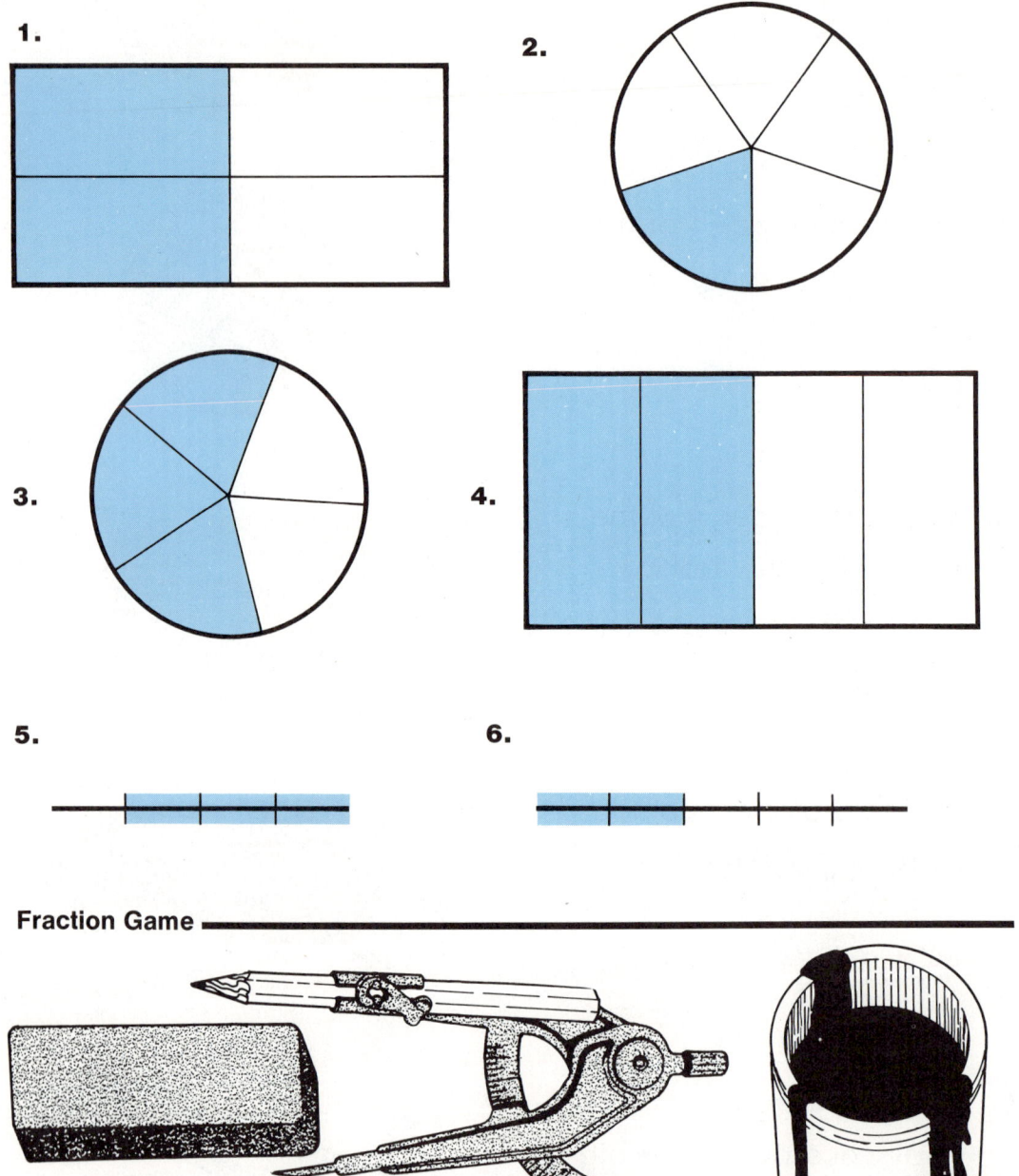

Fraction Game

Use objects to act out these problems.

Rosalie divided 15 coins into 3 equal piles.

1. How many coins are there in each pile?

2. $\frac{1}{3}$ of 15 is ▇ .

She divided 10 coins into 5 equal piles.

3. Draw the 5 piles.

4. How many coins are there in each pile?

5. $\frac{1}{5}$ of 10 is ▇ .

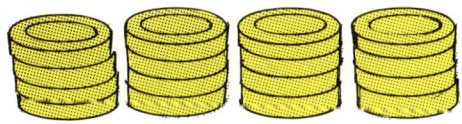 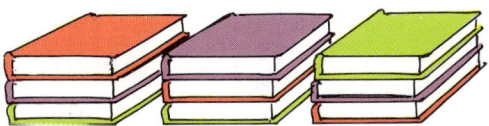

6. $\frac{1}{4}$ of 16 is ▇ .

7. $\frac{1}{3}$ of 9 = ▇ .

8. $\frac{1}{2}$ of 10 is ▇ .

10. $\frac{1}{4}$ of 12 is ▇ .

9. $\frac{1}{5}$ of 15 is ▇ .

11. $\frac{1}{3}$ of 12 is ▇ .

LESSON 98

What fraction of each circle is colored?

1.
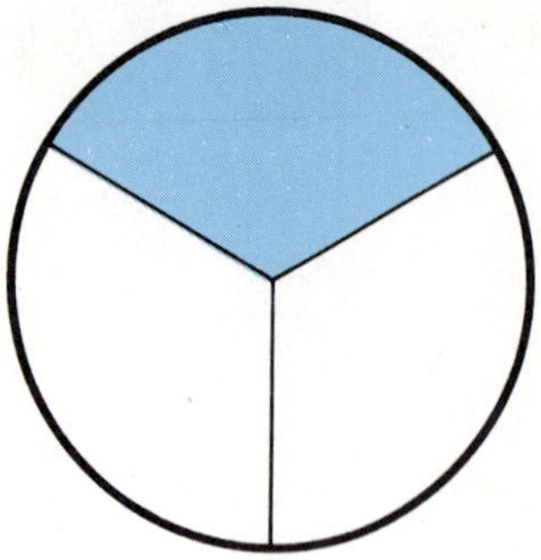

2.
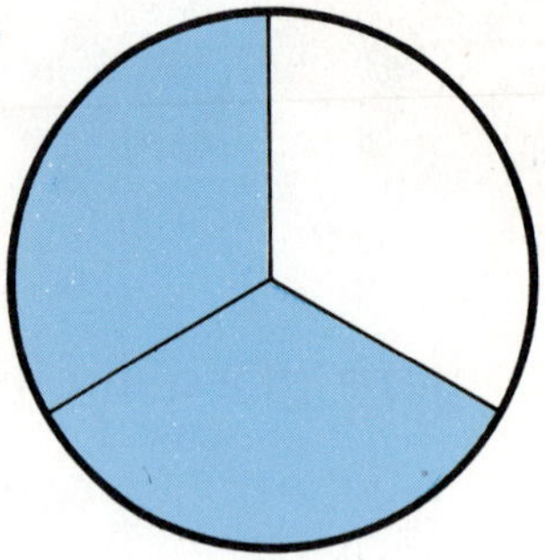

3.
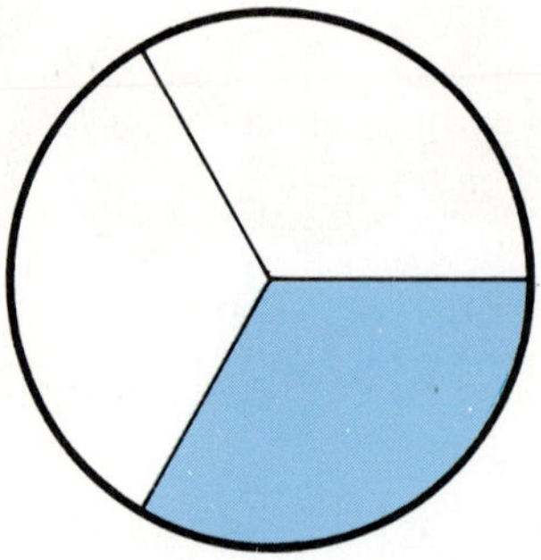

4.
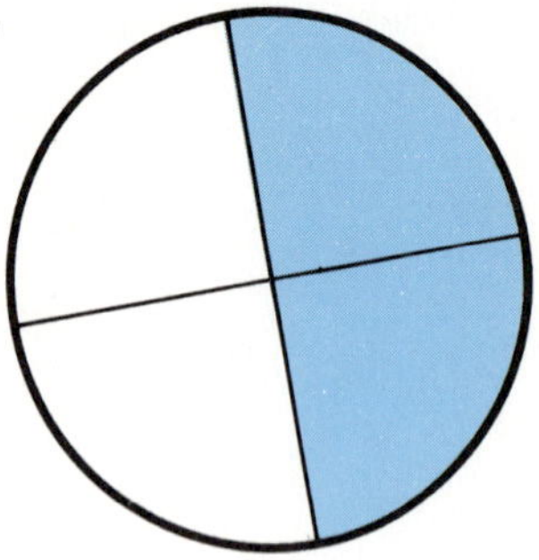

5.
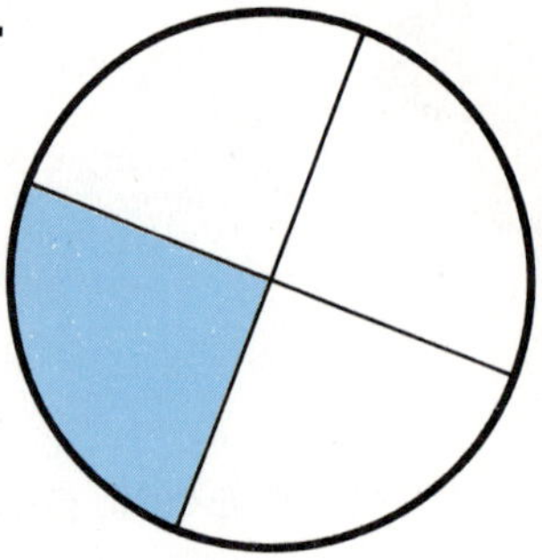

6.
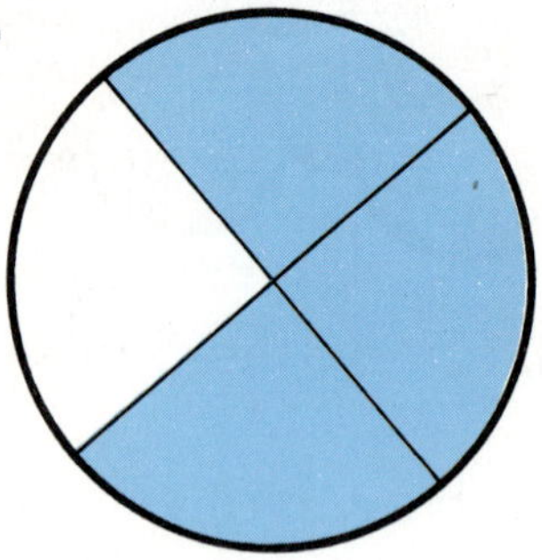

7.
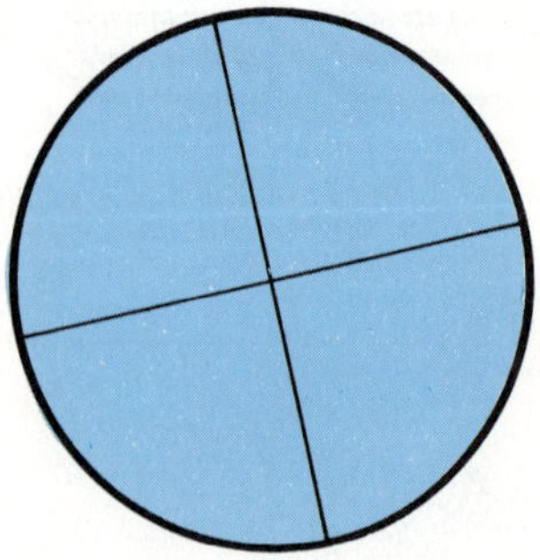

8.
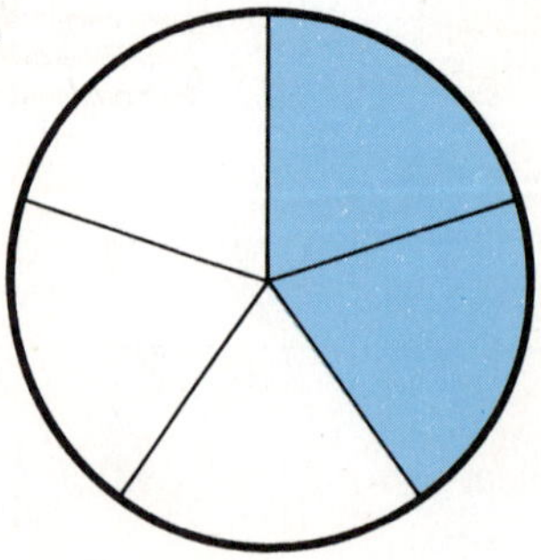

9.
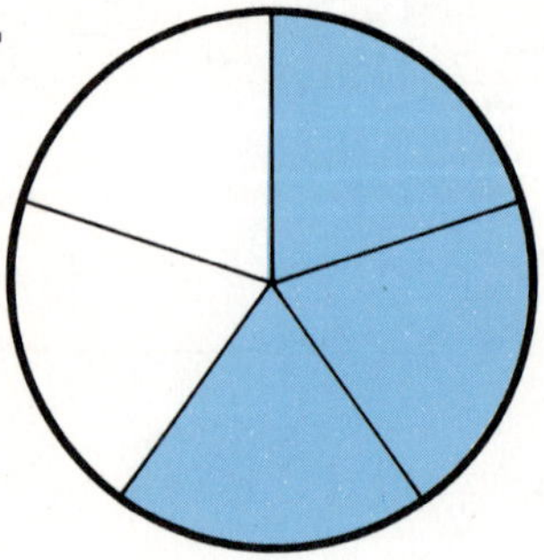

1. Copy or trace this figure 4 times.

    Color $\frac{1}{4}$ in 4 different ways.

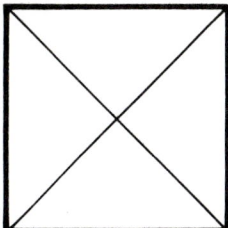

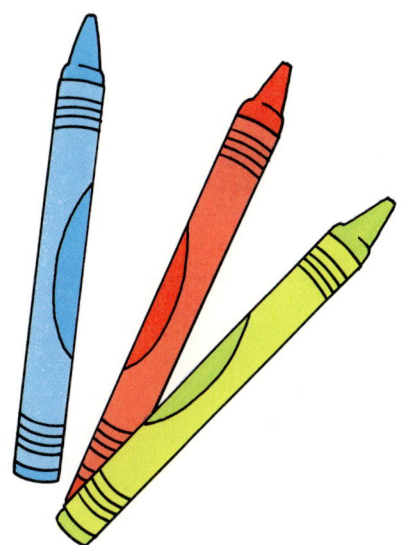

2. Copy or trace this figure 6 times.

    Color $\frac{2}{4}$ in 6 different ways.

Pouring Fractions

I think that's about $\frac{1}{4}$ full.

What fraction is colored?

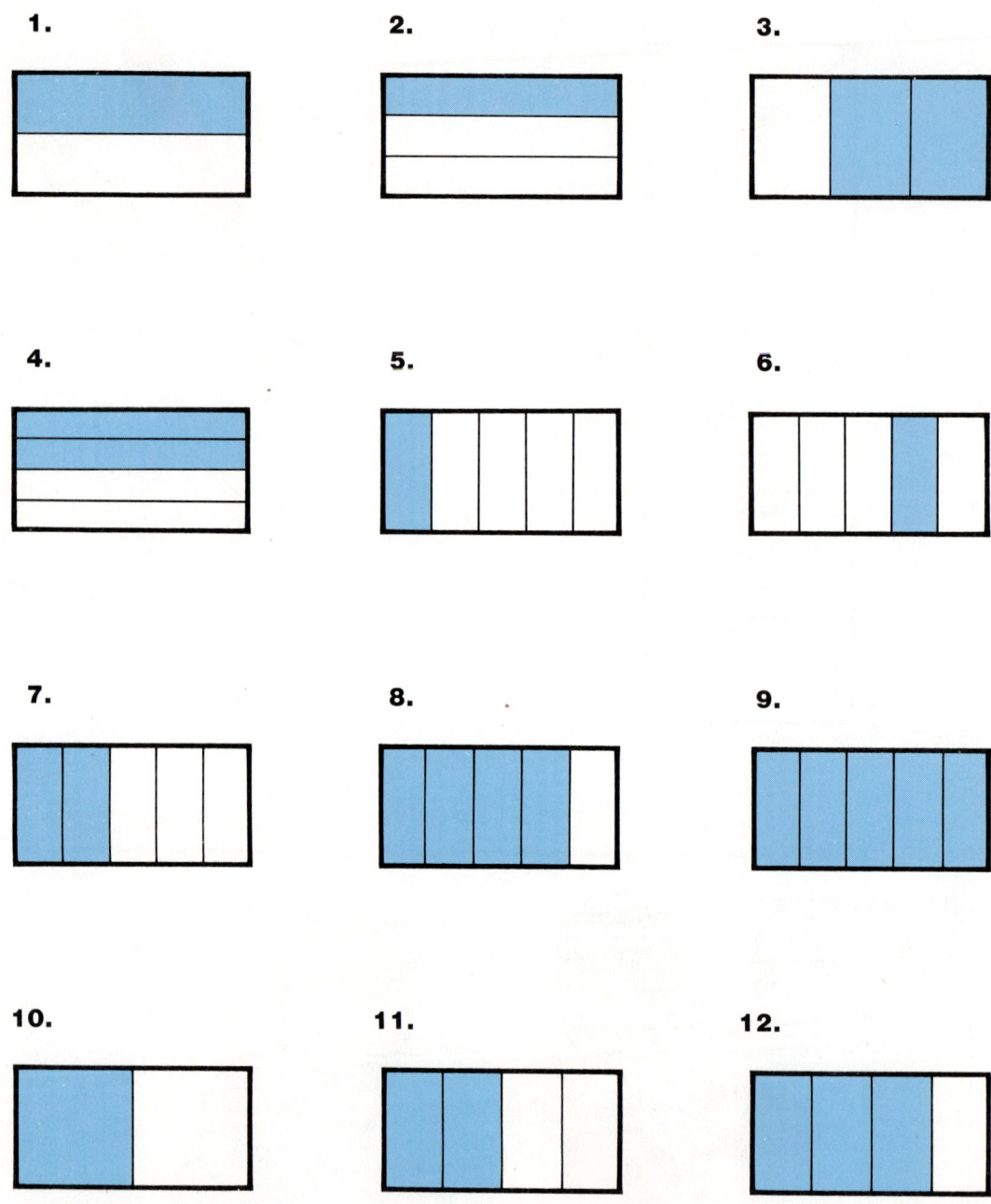

1. What is the area of the rectangle?

   ■ square centimeters

2. Copy or trace the rectangle. Color $\frac{1}{2}$ of it.

3. What is the area of the part you colored?

   ■ square centimeters

4. What is $\frac{1}{2}$ of 10?

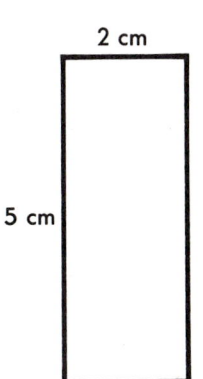

Use objects to help you do these problems.

5. $\frac{1}{4}$ of 20 is ■ .

6. $\frac{2}{4}$ of 20 is ■ .

7. $\frac{3}{4}$ of 20 is ■ .

8. $\frac{4}{4}$ of 20 is ■ .

9. $\frac{1}{2}$ of 10 is ■ .

10. $\frac{2}{2}$ of 10 is ■ .

11. $\frac{1}{5}$ of 30 is ■ .

12. $\frac{3}{5}$ of 30 is ■ .

Discuss the Thinking Story®

LESSON 100

1. In Wayne's class, $\frac{1}{3}$ of the children are boys. What fraction of the children are girls?

There are 20 children in Bev's class; $\frac{1}{2}$ of them are girls.

2. How many girls are in Bev's class?

3. How many boys are in Bev's class?

4. Keiko and her four friends want to share a pie equally. What fraction of the pie should each child get?

5. There are 60 minutes in 1 hour. How many minutes are there in $\frac{1}{4}$ of an hour?

What fraction is colored?

1.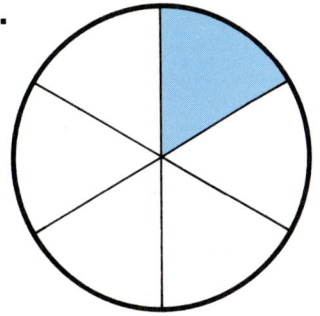
2.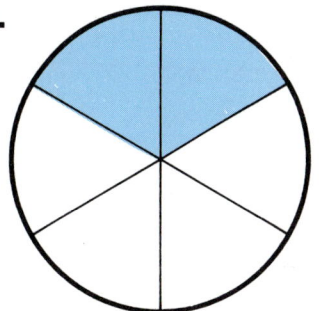
3.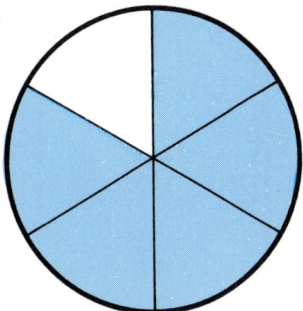

4.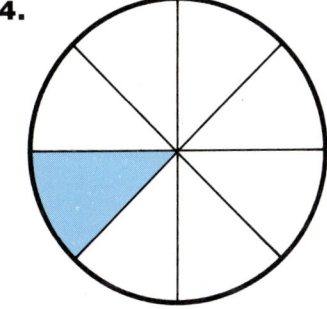
5.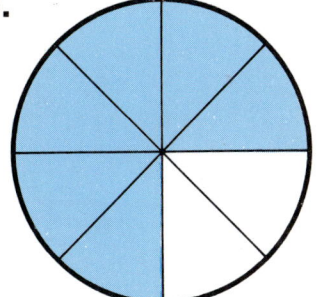
6.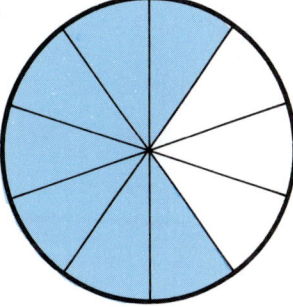

7.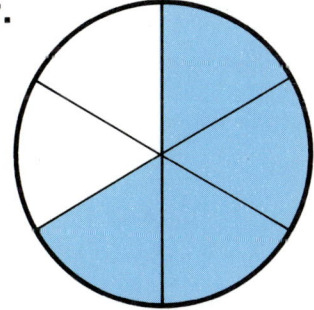
8.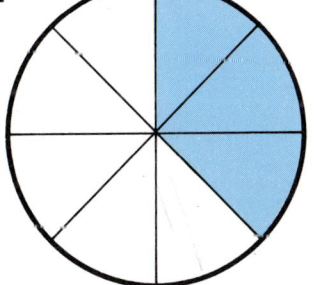
9.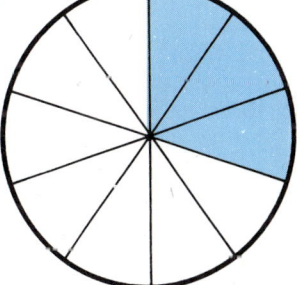

LESSON 101

Do these problems.

1. $\frac{1}{6}$ of 12 is ▪ .
2. $\frac{1}{6}$ of 18 is ▪ .
3. $\frac{2}{6}$ of 12 is ▪ .
4. $\frac{5}{6}$ of 18 is ▪ .
5. $\frac{1}{7}$ of 14 is ▪ .
6. $\frac{2}{7}$ of 14 is ▪ .
7. $\frac{3}{7}$ of 14 is ▪ .
8. $\frac{1}{7}$ of 7 is ▪ .
9. $\frac{1}{8}$ of 24 is ▪ .
10. $\frac{2}{8}$ of 24 is ▪ .

11. $\frac{1}{4}$ of 24 is ▪ .
12. $\frac{3}{4}$ of 24 is ▪ .
13. $\frac{1}{9}$ of 18 is ▪ .
14. $\frac{2}{9}$ of 18 is ▪ .
15. $\frac{3}{9}$ of 18 is ▪ .
16. $\frac{1}{3}$ of 18 is ▪ .
17. $\frac{1}{10}$ of 30 is ▪ .
18. $\frac{2}{10}$ of 30 is ▪ .
19. $\frac{3}{10}$ of 30 is ▪ .
20. $\frac{1}{10}$ of 20 is ▪ .

What fraction is colored?

1.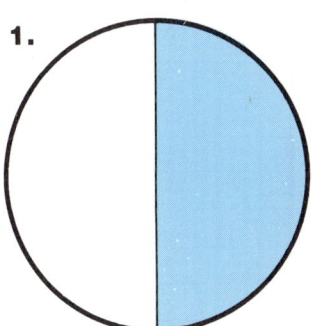
2.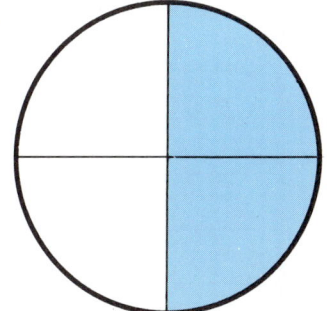
3.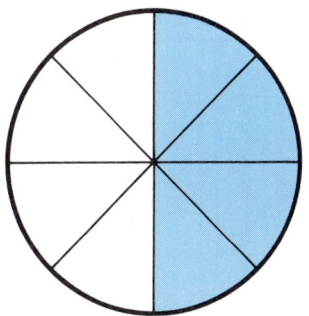

4.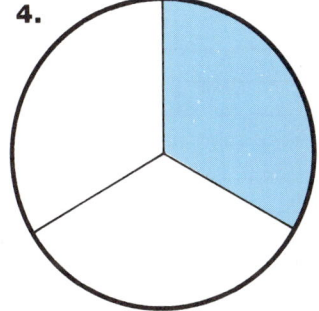
5.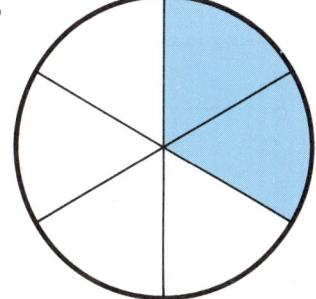
6.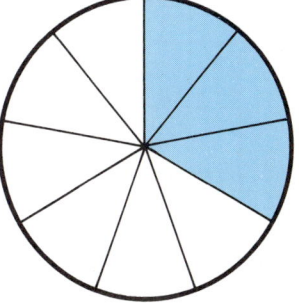

Folding Halves, Quarters, and Eighths

What fraction is colored?

1. 2. 3.

4. 5. 6.

7. 8. 9.

Do these problems. Watch the signs.

1. $6 \times 3 = \blacksquare$
2. $9 \times 7 = \blacksquare$
3. $40 \div 5 = \blacksquare$
4. $6 \times 9 = \blacksquare$
5. $48 \div 6 = \blacksquare$

6. $27 \div 9 = \blacksquare$
7. $7 \times 8 = \blacksquare$
8. $30 \div 10 = \blacksquare$
9. $5 \times 7 = \blacksquare$
10. $28 \div 4 = \blacksquare$

11.
```
  505
- 228
-----
```

12.
```
  674
+ 793
-----
```

13.
```
  4050
- 2175
------
```

14.
```
  3200
  2750
+ 1675
------
```

15.
```
  3.05
+ 0.68
------
```

16.
```
  3.7
+ 1.85
------
```

17.
```
  25.40
-  8.6
-------
```

18.
```
  12.6
-  4.35
-------
```

19. $6.2 + 5.4 = \blacksquare$
20. $10.5 - 2.5 = \blacksquare$
21. $3 - 1.5 = \blacksquare$
22. $3 + 1.5 = \blacksquare$

What fraction is colored?

1.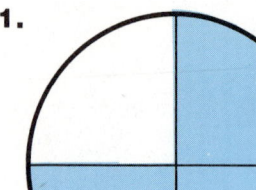

2.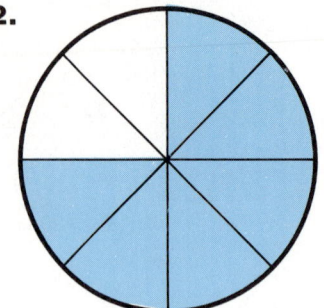

3.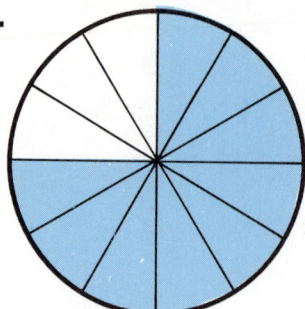

4.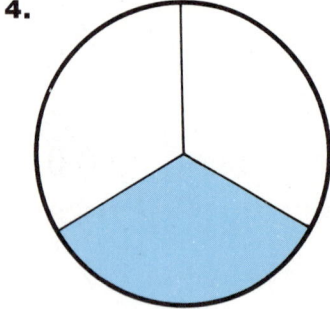

5.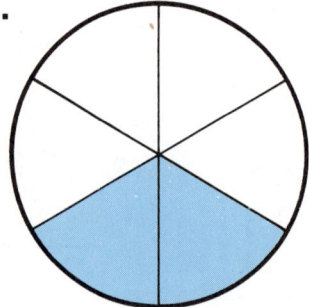

6.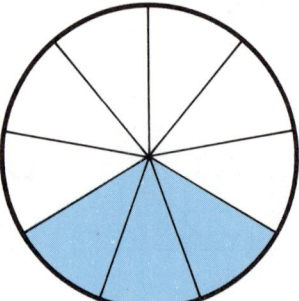

7.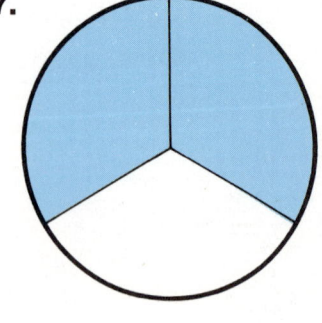

8.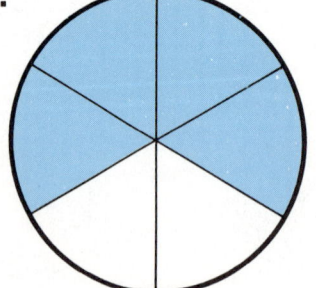

9.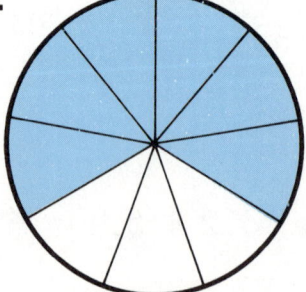

How many minutes?

1. 1 hour = ■ minutes

2. $\frac{1}{2}$ of an hour = ■ minutes

3. $\frac{2}{2}$ of an hour = ■ minutes

4. $\frac{2}{4}$ of an hour = ■ minutes

5. $\frac{3}{4}$ of an hour = ■ minutes

6. $\frac{4}{4}$ of an hour = ■ minutes

7. $\frac{1}{3}$ of an hour = ■ minutes

8. $\frac{2}{3}$ of an hour = ■ minutes

9. $\frac{3}{3}$ of an hour = ■ minutes

Which is longer?

10. $\frac{1}{2}$ of an hour or $\frac{2}{4}$ of an hour?

11. $\frac{1}{2}$ of an hour or $\frac{3}{4}$ of an hour?

12. $\frac{2}{2}$ of an hour or $\frac{4}{4}$ of an hour?

LESSON 104

Do these problems. Watch the signs.

1. 6 × 7 = ■
2. 8 × 9 = ■
3. 49 ÷ 7 = ■
4. 8 + 9 = ■
5. 6 × 8 = ■
6. 4 × 5 = ■

7. 3 × 1 = ■
8. 8 × 0 = ■
9. 28 ÷ 4 = ■
10. 16 − 7 = ■
11. 15 − 8 = ■
12. 8 × 7 = ■

Draw the right sign. Draw <, >, or =.

13. 2.54 ● 2.70
14. 0.6 ● 0.45
15. 12.1 ● 1.21
16. 1.05 ● 1.4

17. 2.5 ● 2.50
18. 6.67 ● 16.67
19. 10.5 ● 2.05
20. 35.6 ● 40.2

Do these problems. Watch the signs.

1. 587
   $+369$

2. 5.87
   $+3.69$

3. 587
   -369

4. 5.87
   -3.69

5. 53.20
   $+4.78$

6. 26.10
   -13.05

7. 3.45
   $+6.8$

8. 4.6
   -3.15

9. $12.8 - 4.6 =$ ■

10. $1.08 + 1.08 =$ ■

11. $32.6 - 24.25 =$ ■

12. $21 + 7.5 =$ ■

Do these problems.

13. $3 \text{ m} =$ ■ cm

14. $628 \text{ cm} =$ ■ m

15. ■ cm $= 5.71$ m

16. $628¢ = \$$ ■

17. $\$4.05 =$ ■ ¢

Try to Make an Inequality Game

Now, try to make an inequality.

$10 \times 2 < 6 \times 5$. That's true, so I get a point.

217

1. The book cost $8.76. Miss Appleton gave the storekeeper a $10 bill. How much change should she get?

2. Jim earned $2.50 today. Now he has $4.75. How much did he have before?

3. Each box is 1.5 m tall. How tall are the two boxes?

4. Danny saved $2.63 last week. He saved $3.49 this week. How much did he save in the two weeks?

Do these problems. Watch the signs.

LESSON 105

1. $5 \times 6 = \blacksquare$
2. $8 \times 8 = \blacksquare$
3. $6 \div 3 = \blacksquare$
4. $4 + 9 = \blacksquare$
5. $3 \times 8 = \blacksquare$

6. $12 - 7 = \blacksquare$
7. $2 \times 9 = \blacksquare$
8. $7 \times 8 = \blacksquare$
9. $56 \div 8 = \blacksquare$
10. $10 \times 5 = \blacksquare$

Draw the right sign. Draw $<$, $>$, or $=$.

11. 3.9 ● 4.3
12. 0.8 ● 6
13. 7.2 ● 7.20
14. 15.7 ● 10.0

15. 1.05 ● 1.3
16. 22.3 ● 2.23
17. 0.48 ● 0.61
18. 1.5 ● 1.5

Do these problems. Watch the signs.

19. 43
     +26

20. 57
     −44

21. 63
     −28

22. 47
     +86

23. 102
     − 83

24. 349
     +586

25. 2843
     +1376

26. 2843
     −1376

27. 4.6
     +2.3

28. 5.8
     −2.4

29. 1.7
     +3.4

30. 17.05
     +24.7

31. $3.46 - 1.72 = \blacksquare$

32. $4.70 + 10.26 = \blacksquare$

33. $6.2 - 3.05 = \blacksquare$

34. $11.7 - 4.8 = \blacksquare$

What fraction is colored?

35.

36.

37.
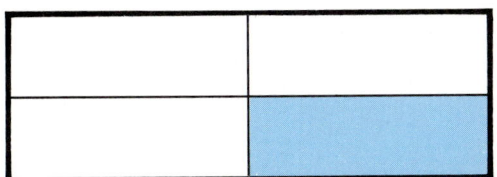

38.
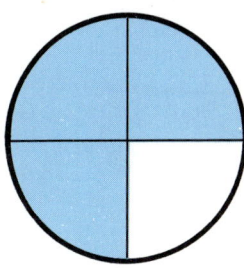

39.
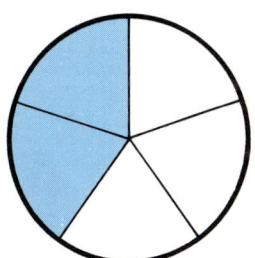

40.
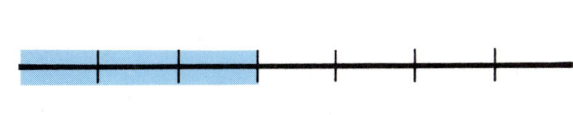

Copy or trace each figure. Color the fractions shown.

41. $\frac{1}{2}$
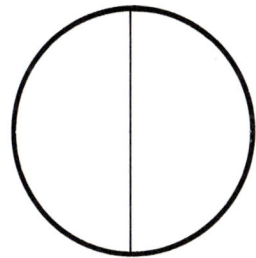

42. $\frac{3}{4}$
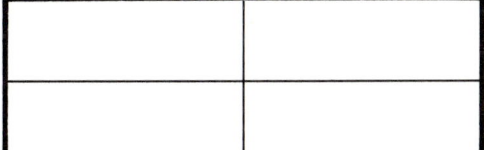

Do these problems.

43. 300 cm = ■ m

44. ■ cm = 4.28 m

45. 300 cents = $ ■

46. 136 cents = $ ■

47. Plums cost 5¢ each. How much do 6 plums cost?

48. At 5¢ each, how much do 10 plums cost?

49. Kareem paid 36¢ for 4 apples. How much does 1 apple cost?

50. Jared bought some milk that cost 46¢. He gave the storekeeper a $5 bill. How much change should he get?

51. How much do the glove and bat cost together?

52. Allison lives 2.5 kilometers from school. She rode her bicycle there and back. How far did she ride?

Mrs. Hayes is 1.70 meters tall.
Barry is 1.16 meters tall.

53. Who is taller?

54. How much taller?

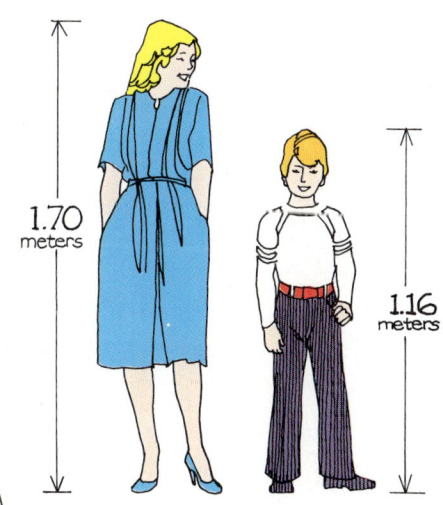

LESSON 106

Try to find a pattern.

1. $1 + 3 = \blacksquare$

2. $1 + 3 + 5 = \blacksquare$

3. $1 + 3 + 5 + 7 = \blacksquare$

4. $1 + 3 + 5 + 7 + 9 = \blacksquare$

5. $1 + 3 + 5 + 7 + 9 + 11 = \blacksquare$

6. $1 + 3 + 5 + 7 + 9 + 11 + 13 = \blacksquare$

7. $1 + 3 + 5 + 7 + 9 + 11 + 13 + 15 = \blacksquare$

8. $1 + 3 + 5 + 7 + 9 + 11 + 13 + 15 + 17 = \blacksquare$

9. $2 \times 2 = \blacksquare$

10. $3 \times 3 = \blacksquare$

11. $4 \times 4 = \blacksquare$

12. $5 \times 5 = \blacksquare$

13. $6 \times 6 = \blacksquare$

14. $7 \times 7 = \blacksquare$

15. $8 \times 8 = \blacksquare$

16. $9 \times 9 = \blacksquare$

How many cubes?

LESSON 107

1.

2.

3.

4.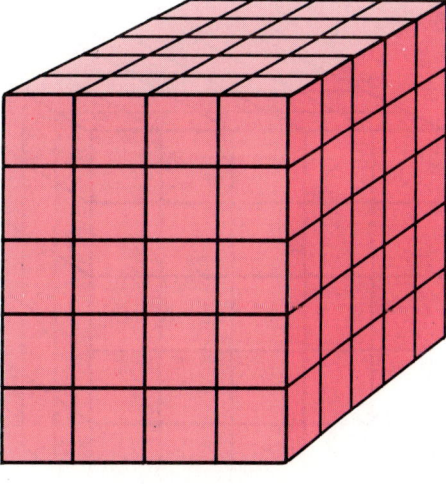

225

How many cubes?

1.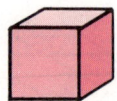

2.

3.

4.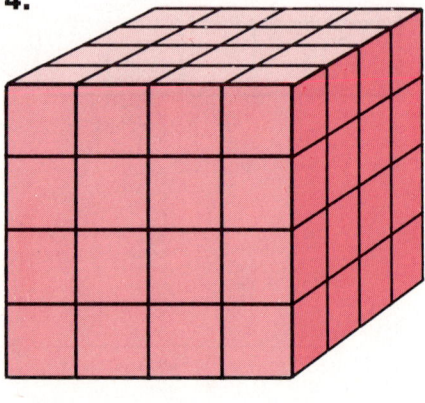

5.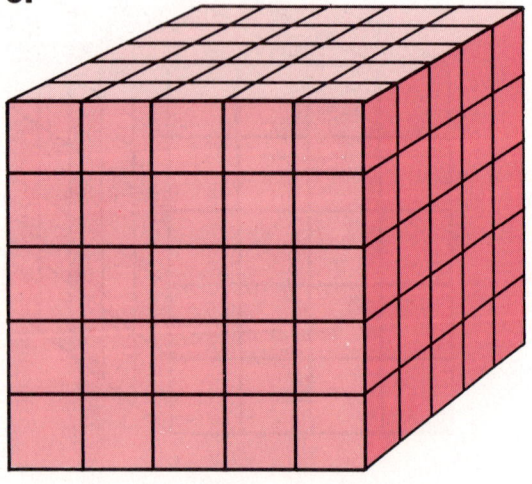

Pouring Fractions

The cubic centimeter is a unit of volume. This cube has a volume of 1 cubic centimeter.

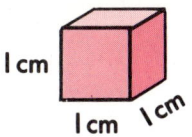

Find out how many of these cubes are in the box. Then give the volume of the box.

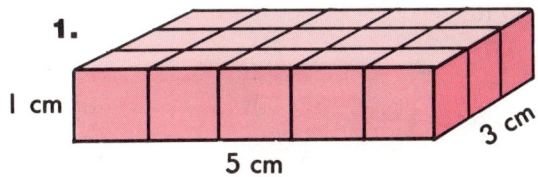

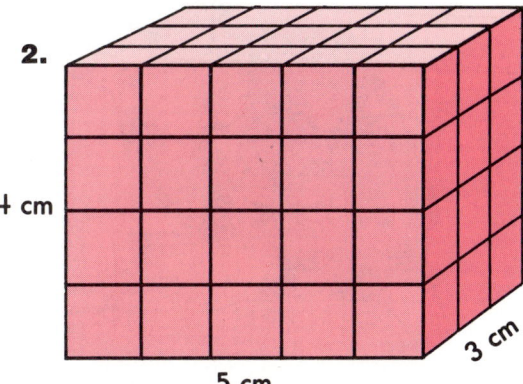

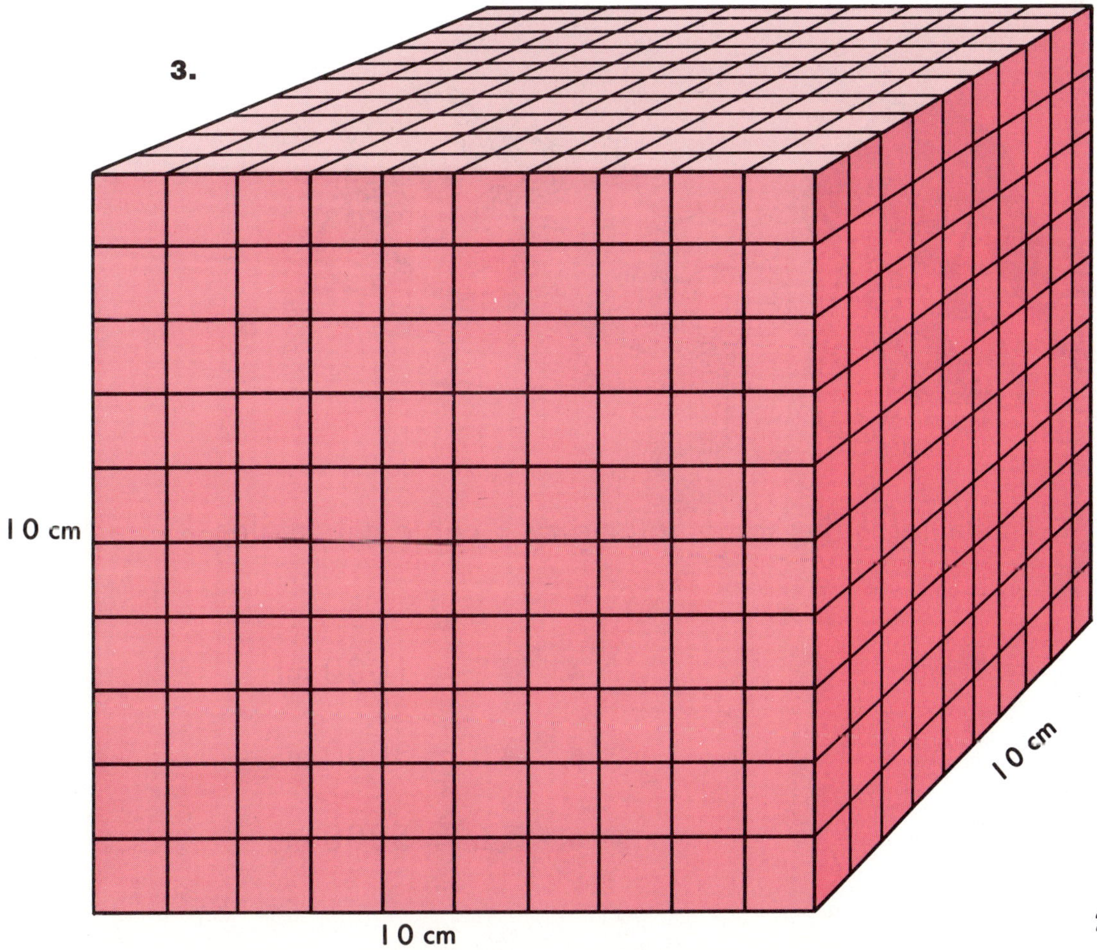

The liter and milliliter are units of volume.

There are 1000 milliliters in 1 liter.
1000 mL = 1 L

1 milliliter is the same volume as 1 cubic centimeter.

1. 1 L = ■ mL

2. 2 L = ■ mL

3. 7 L = ■ mL

4. ■ L = 1000 mL

5. ■ L = 3000 mL

6. ■ L = 5000 mL

Write the name of the unit that makes sense. Write *milliliters* or *liters*.

1. About 250 ▪ of milk

2. About 10 ▪ of water

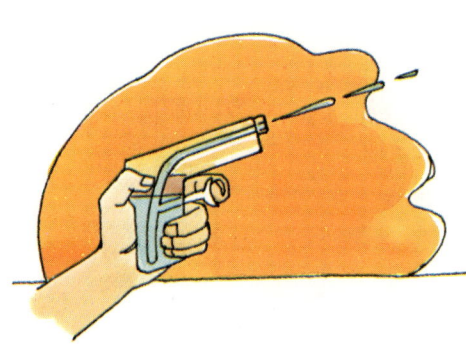

3. About 100 ▪ of water

4. About 1 ▪ of soup

Estimating and Measuring Volume

I think that holds about 750 milliliters.

The cup, pint, quart, and gallon are units of volume.

There are 2 cups in 1 pint.

There are 2 pints in 1 quart.

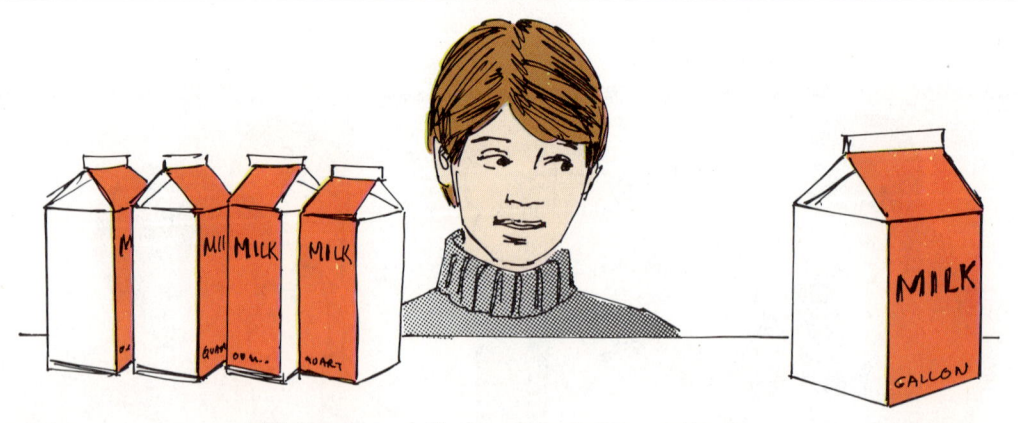

There are 4 quarts in 1 gallon.

Do these problems.

1. 1 quart = ■ cups
2. 2 quarts = ■ cups
3. 1 gallon = ■ cups
4. 1 gallon = ■ pints

5. $\frac{1}{2}$ gallon = ■ pints
6. $\frac{1}{2}$ gallon = ■ quarts
7. $\frac{1}{4}$ gallon = ■ quarts
8. 8 pints = ■ quarts

Which unit makes more sense?

9. About 1 (gallon, cup)

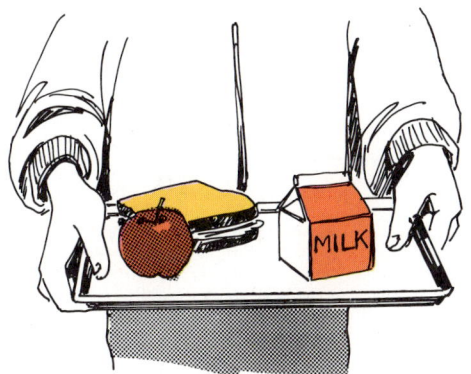

10. About $\frac{1}{2}$ (gallon, pint)

Estimating and Measuring Volume

I think that holds about 3 gallons.

Do these problems. Watch the signs.

1. $5 \times 8 = \blacksquare$
2. $56 \div 7 = \blacksquare$
3. $6 \times 7 = \blacksquare$
4. $3 \times 9 = \blacksquare$
5. $3 \times 4 = \blacksquare$
6. $40 \div 5 = \blacksquare$
7. $4 \times 7 = \blacksquare$
8. $8 \times 100 = \blacksquare$

9. $8 \overline{)48}$
10. $6 \overline{)54}$
11. $2 \overline{)12}$
12. $2 \overline{)13}$

13. $\begin{array}{r} 8 \\ \times 3 \\ \hline \end{array}$
14. $\begin{array}{r} 5 \\ \times 2 \\ \hline \end{array}$
15. $\begin{array}{r} 8 \\ \times 4 \\ \hline \end{array}$
16. $\begin{array}{r} 7 \\ \times 5 \\ \hline \end{array}$
17. $\begin{array}{r} 9 \\ \times 7 \\ \hline \end{array}$

18. $\begin{array}{r} 543 \\ -261 \\ \hline \end{array}$
19. $\begin{array}{r} 3.12 \\ -1.59 \\ \hline \end{array}$
20. $\begin{array}{r} 207 \\ -138 \\ \hline \end{array}$
21. $\begin{array}{r} 426 \\ 512 \\ +394 \\ \hline \end{array}$

LESSON 110

Write the Arabic numeral for each of these Roman numerals.

1. III
2. V
3. X
4. XX
5. C
6. L

7. XV
8. XVI
9. IX
10. XIX
11. LX
12. LXII

13. XXVII
14. XXIX
15. LXIX
16. CC
17. CCL
18. CCLVII

Roman Numeral Game

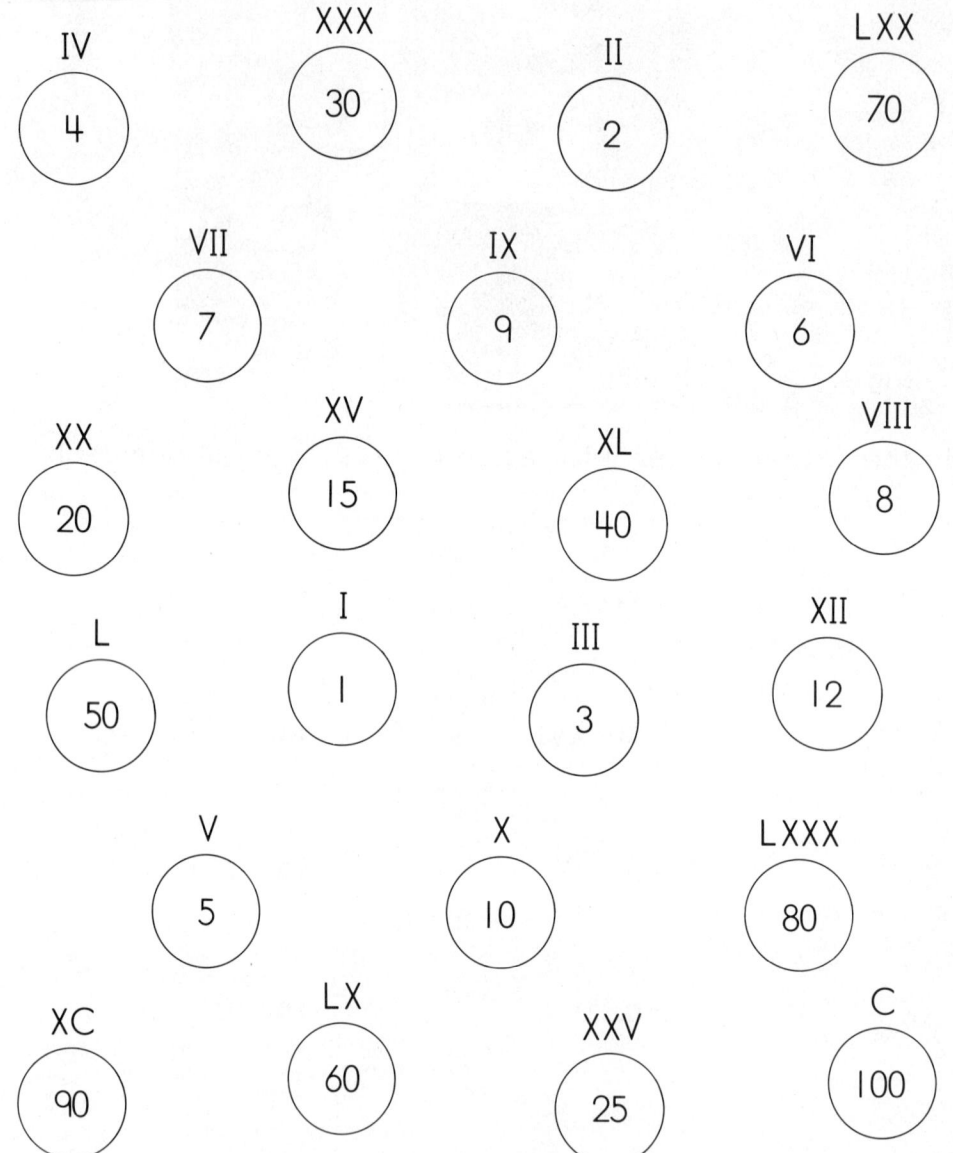

Guess the Marker

Do these problems. Watch the signs.

1. $2 + 5 =$ ■
2. $7 - 4 =$ ■
3. $7 + 4 =$ ■
4. $15 - 8 =$ ■
5. $15 - 7 =$ ■

6. $10 + 6 =$ ■
7. $9 + 6 =$ ■
8. $15 - 6 =$ ■
9. $17 - 8 =$ ■
10. $17 - 9 =$ ■

Multiply.

1.   6   2.   7   3.   8   4.   5   5.   4
     ×5   ×4   ×6   ×5   ×3

6.   9   7.   9   8.   6   9.   8   10.   3
     ×2   ×9   ×7   ×7   ×2

Divide.

11. $5\overline{)25}$ 12. $6\overline{)30}$ 13. $7\overline{)28}$ 14. $9\overline{)81}$

15. $10\overline{)30}$ 16. $4\overline{)28}$ 17. $6\overline{)36}$ 18. $2\overline{)12}$

19. $5\overline{)10}$ 20. $4\overline{)32}$ 21. $3\overline{)27}$ 22. $8\overline{)32}$

Do these problems. Watch the signs.

LESSON 112

1. 652
   +208

2. 7571
   -3651

3. 857
   +632

4. 300
   -175

5. 927
   +631

6. 7265
   +8319

7. 200
   -199

8. 50,000
   -49,999

9. 400
   -390

10. 340
   + 10

11. 600
   -300

12. 470
   -460

13. 25
    25
    25
   +25

14. 50
    50
    50
   +50

Guess the Marker

237

Norman and Joan are rolling a 0-5 and a 5-10 cube. Joan is keeping a tally of the number of rolls. Norman is using a graph to keep track of how many times each sum is rolled.
This is Norman's graph after 5 rolls.

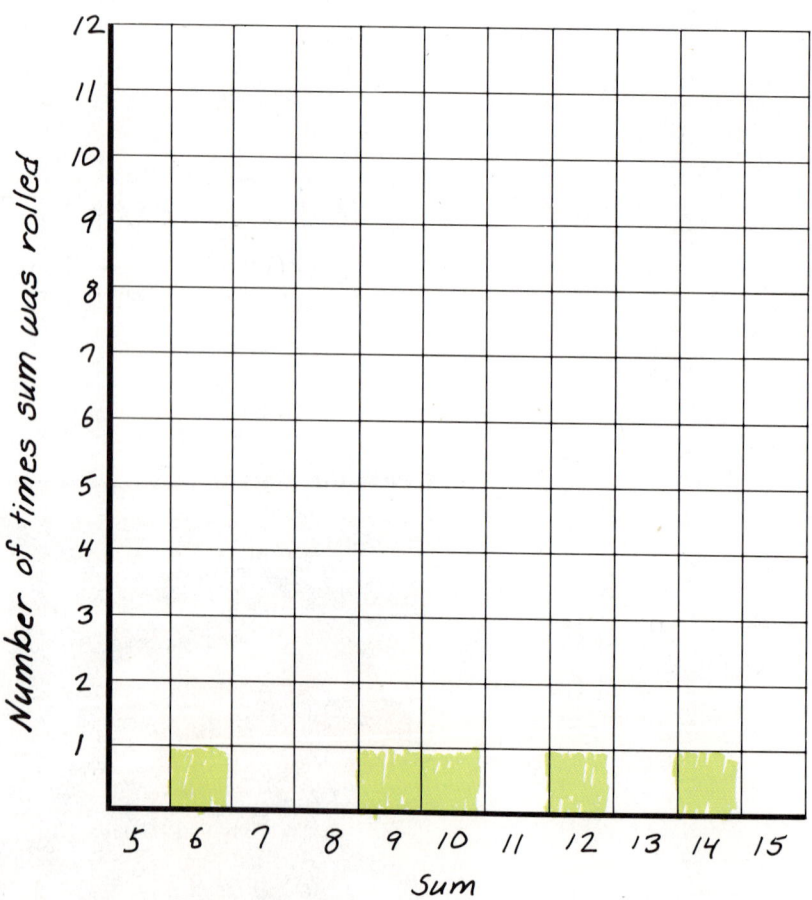

Which sum will reach the top of the graph first?

Total number of markers: ▪

There are 40 markers in the can. Bruce's class is trying to figure out how many red markers and how many white markers are in the can. Mrs. Hoffman is taking samples from the can. After each sample of 10 markers, Bruce can change his prediction. This is Bruce's record after the first sample of 10.

First sample

Color	Number
Red	3
White	7

First prediction

Color	Number
Red	10
White	30

Second sample

Color	Number
Red	
White	

Second prediction

Color	Number
Red	
White	

Third sample

Color	Number
Red	
White	

Third prediction

Color	Number
Red	
White	

Actual number of markers

Color	Number
Red	
White	

Make charts like Bruce's so that you can keep a record when you try to guess what is in the can.

1. How much will 4 bags of peanuts cost?

2. How much will 7 bananas cost?

3. How much will 6 apples cost?

4. How much will 2 bags of peanuts, 3 bananas, and 4 apples cost?

5. How much will 3 bananas and 1 bag of cherries cost?

6. How much will 2 bananas, 8 apples, and 1 bag of peanuts cost?

Clara's class made this scale drawing.
Make a scale drawing of your classroom.

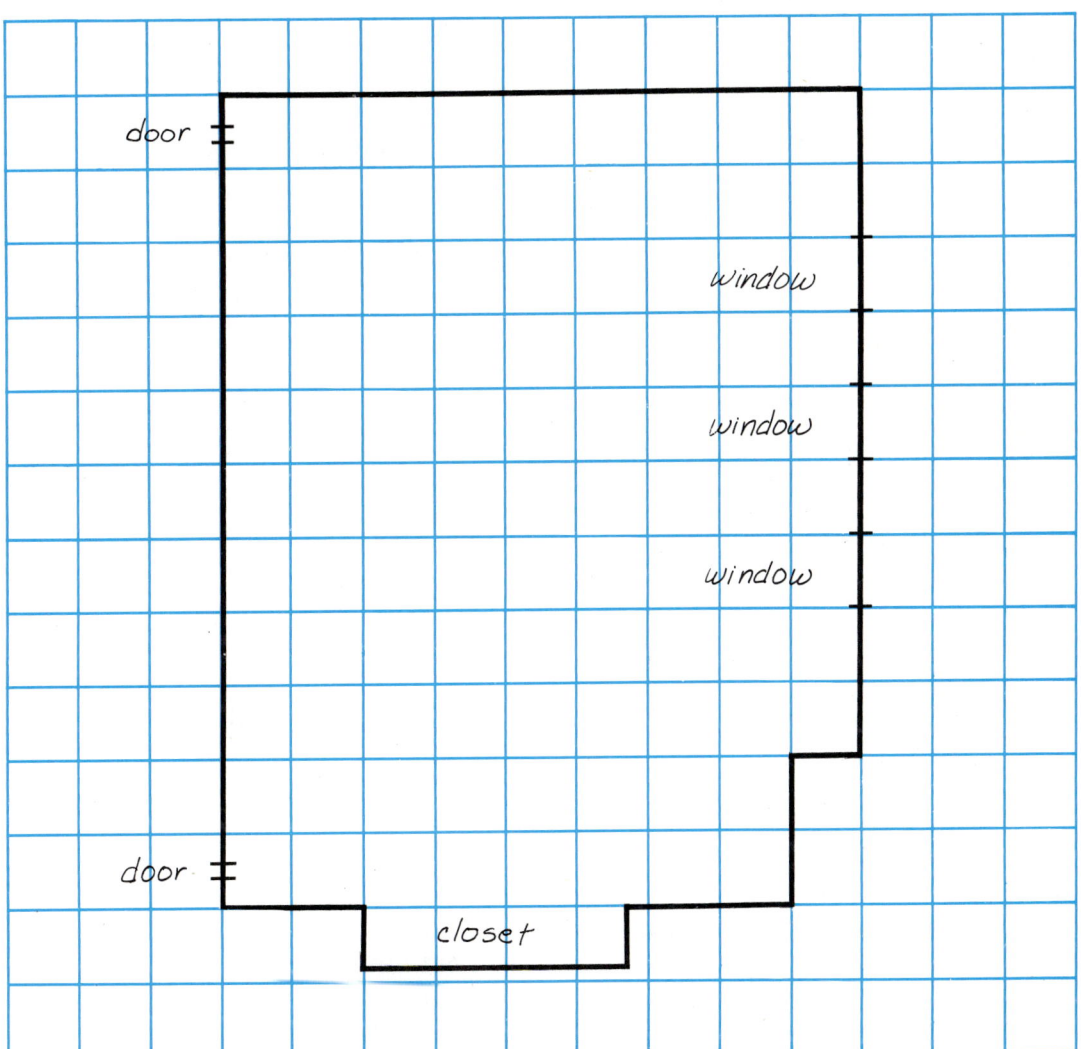

1. About how wide is Clara's classroom?
2. About how long is Clara's classroom?
3. About how wide is the closet in Clara's classroom?

Do these problems. Watch the signs.

1. 8 × 0 = ⬛
2. 4 × 3 = ⬛
3. 7 × 8 = ⬛
4. 16 ÷ 4 = ⬛
5. 5 ÷ 5 = ⬛
6. 9 × 1 = ⬛
7. 7 × 6 = ⬛
8. 28 ÷ 4 = ⬛

9. 15 ÷ 3 = ⬛
10. 8 × 9 = ⬛
11. 10 × 4 = ⬛
12. 90 ÷ 10 = ⬛
13. 24 ÷ 8 = ⬛
14. 8 × 6 = ⬛
15. 63 ÷ 9 = ⬛
16. 6 × 9 = ⬛

Discuss the Thinking Story®

LESSON 115

Sam's group made this scale drawing of the top of a table.
Make a scale drawing of 2 things in your classroom.

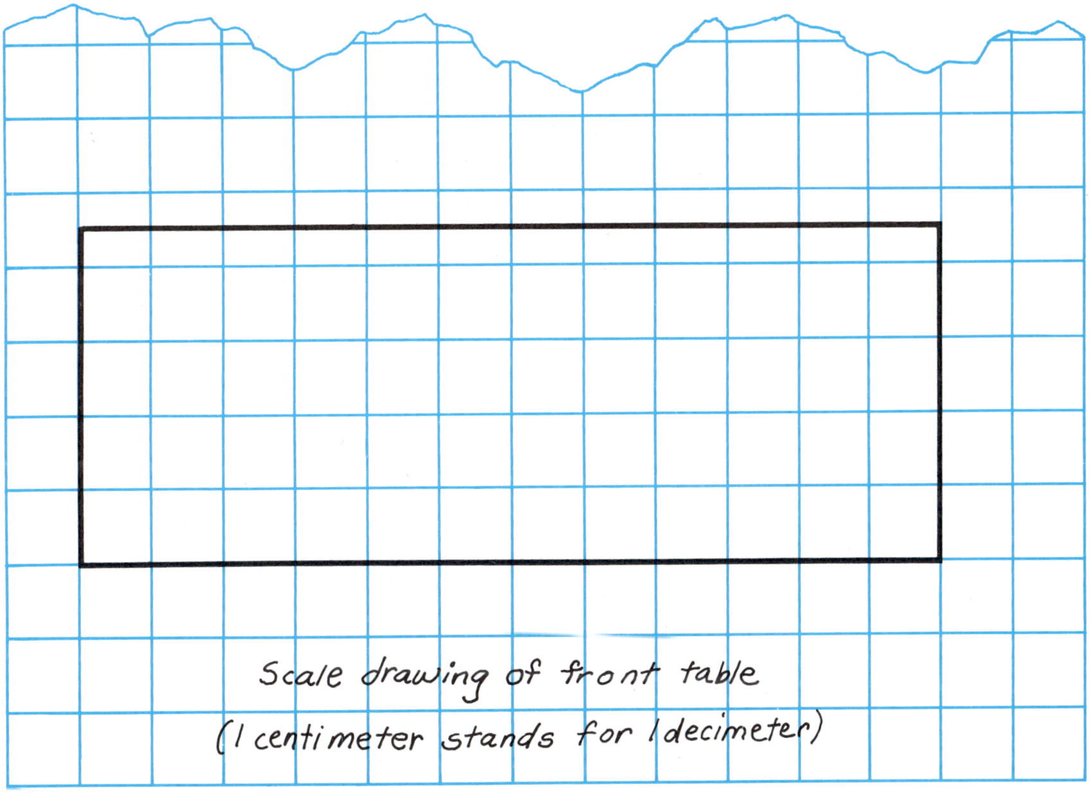

Scale drawing of front table
(1 centimeter stands for 1 decimeter)

1. How long is the table that Sam's group drew?
2. How wide is it?

243

Do these problems. Watch the signs.

1. $6 \times 4 = \blacksquare$
2. $35 \div 7 = \blacksquare$
3. $4 \times 5 = \blacksquare$
4. $14 \div 2 = \blacksquare$
5. $8 \times 8 = \blacksquare$

6. $18 \div 9 = \blacksquare$
7. $42 \div 6 = \blacksquare$
8. $9 \times 6 = \blacksquare$
9. $8 \times 6 = \blacksquare$
10. $10 \div 1 = \blacksquare$

11. $\begin{array}{r} 7.5 \\ -2.5 \\ \hline \end{array}$
12. $\begin{array}{r} 10.8 \\ +4.4 \\ \hline \end{array}$
13. $\begin{array}{r} 6.5 \\ -3.25 \\ \hline \end{array}$
14. $\begin{array}{r} 8.45 \\ +3.6 \\ \hline \end{array}$

Multiply.

15. $7 \times 10 = \blacksquare$
16. $7 \times 100 = \blacksquare$
17. $10 \times 10 = \blacksquare$
18. $100 \times 10 = \blacksquare$

19. $5 \times 10 = \blacksquare$
20. $10 \times 25 = \blacksquare$
21. $100 \times 13 = \blacksquare$
22. $40 \times 10 = \blacksquare$

1. Point to where these 2 lines will meet.

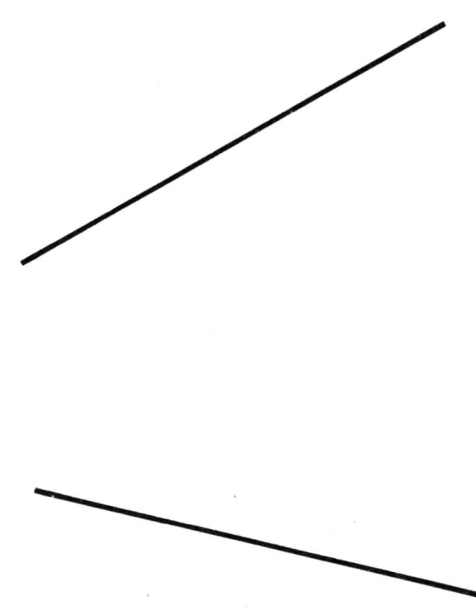

2. Point to where these 2 lines will meet.

1. Where will these 2 lines meet?

2. Where will these 2 lines meet?

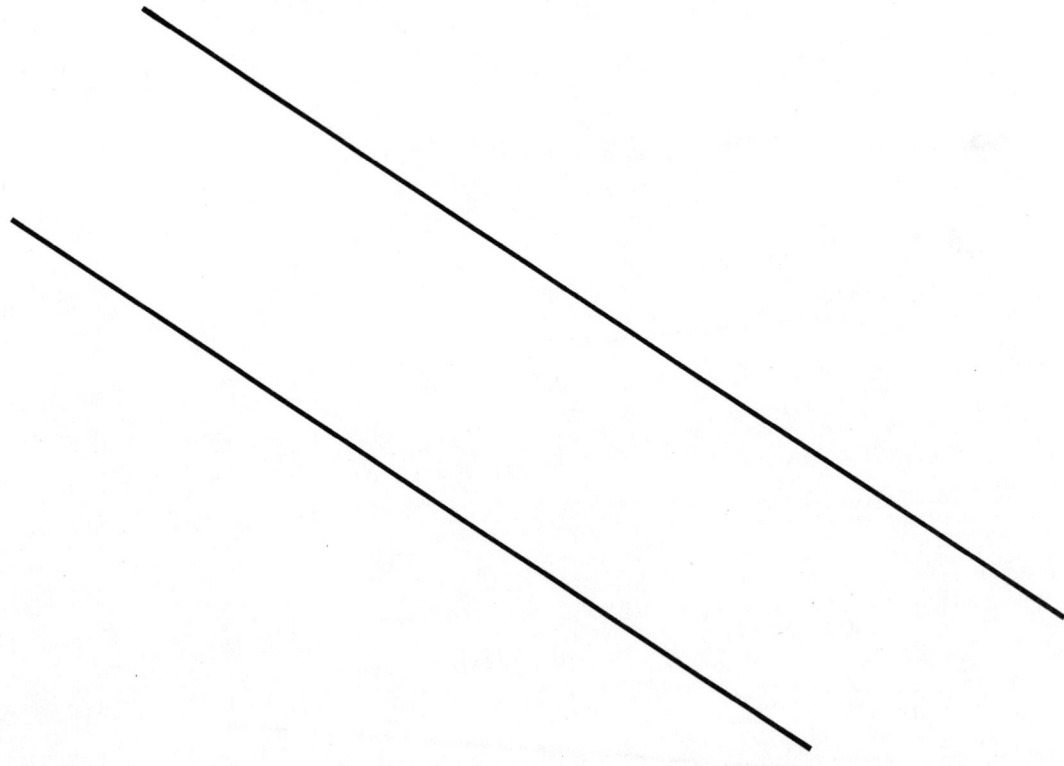

246

Do these problems. Watch the signs.

1. $6 \times 3 =$ ▪
2. $48 \div 8 =$ ▪
3. $9 \times 8 =$ ▪
4. $24 \div 6 =$ ▪
5. $8 \times 7 =$ ▪
6. $36 \div 6 =$ ▪
7. $3 \times 5 =$ ▪
8. $42 \div 7 =$ ▪
9. $9 \times 4 =$ ▪

10. $50 \div 10 =$ ▪
11. $5 \times 5 =$ ▪
12. $16 - 9 =$ ▪
13. $10 + 7 =$ ▪
14. $9 \times 9 =$ ▪
15. $17 - 9 =$ ▪
16. $9 - 8 =$ ▪
17. $4 + 8 =$ ▪
18. $56 \div 7 =$ ▪

Angles of a Triangle

LESSON 117

Write the name of each figure.

1.

2.

3.

4.

5.

6.

7.

Road Sign Shapes

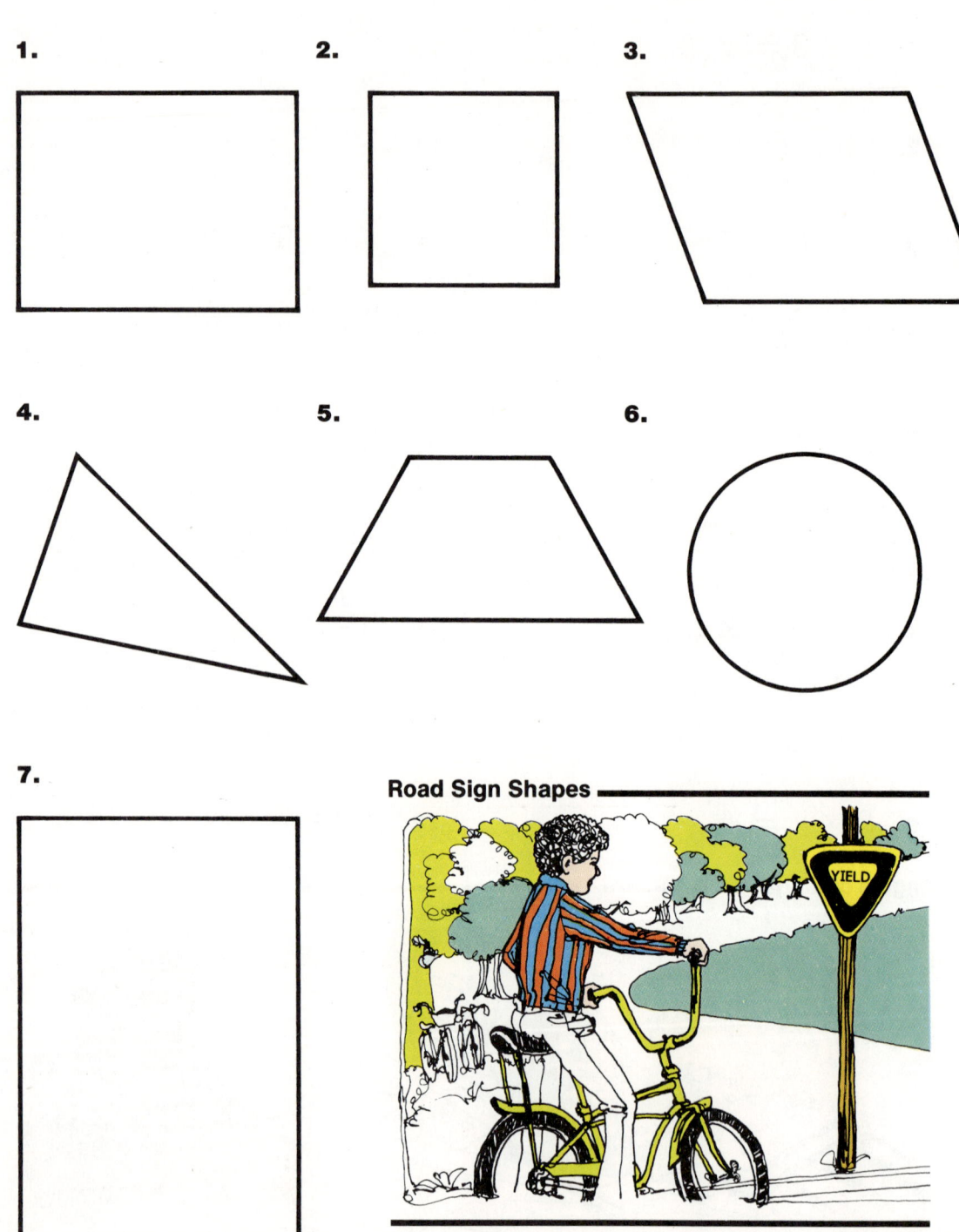

How many special figures can you find?

Squares ■

Rectangles ■

Parallelograms ■

Trapezoids ■

Circles ■

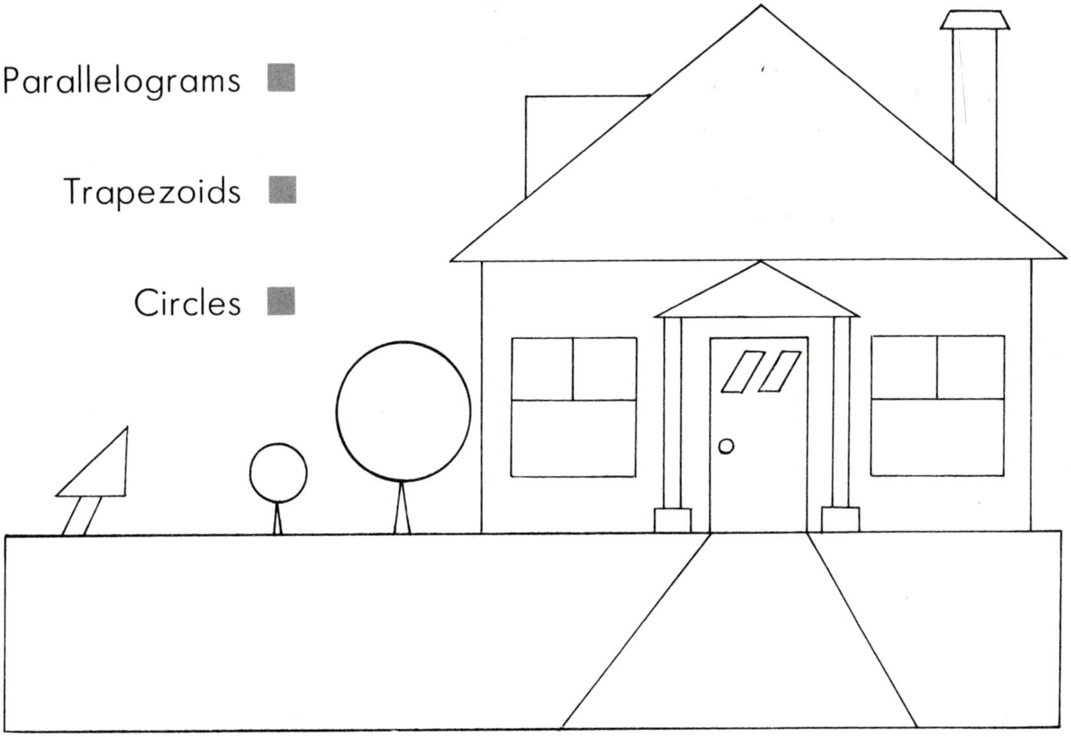

Angles of a Quadrilateral

249

LESSON 118

Carmen made a dartboard. She played a game with Julia. Find the score for each dart. Measure the distance from each dart to the center.

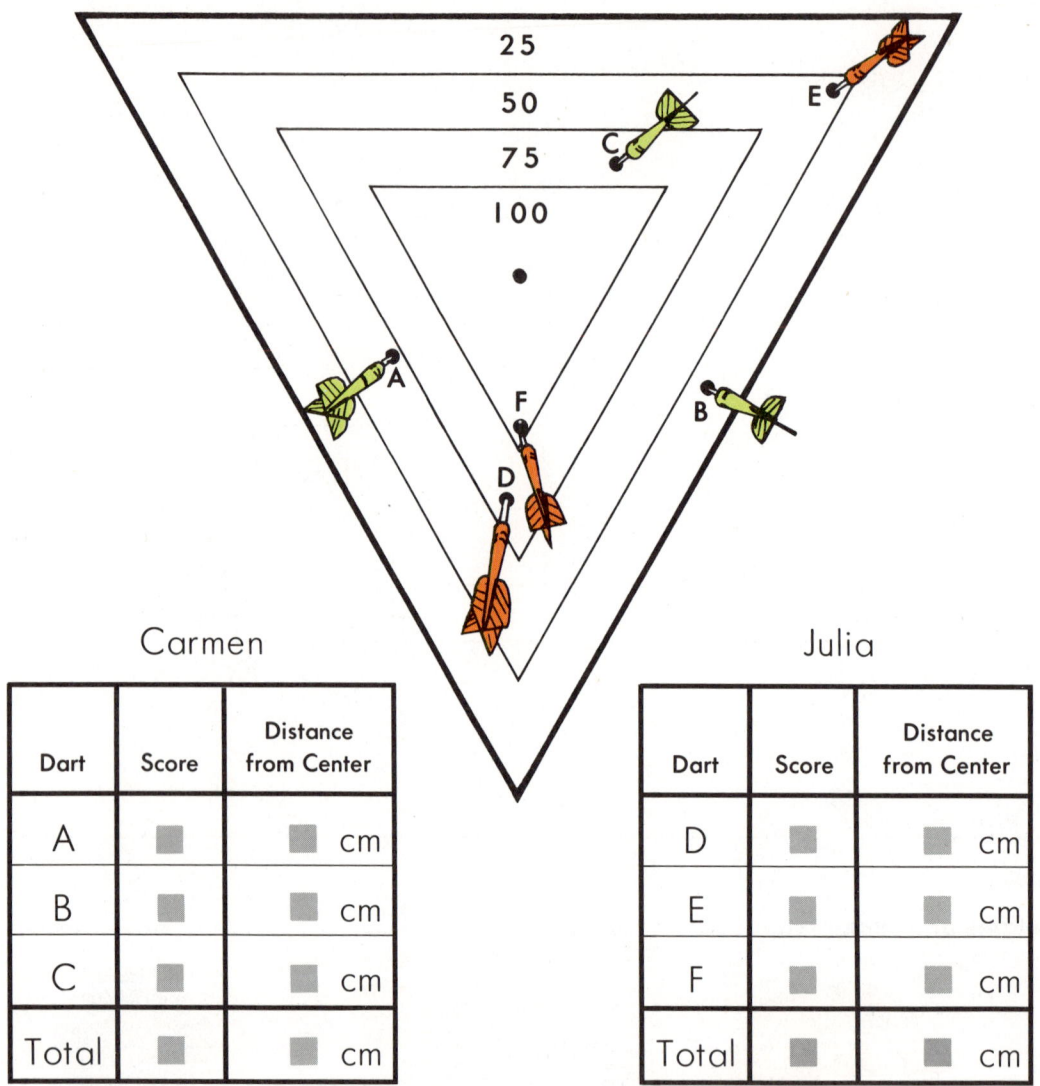

1. Who had a higher score?

2. Which player do you think had more skill?

3. How would you design a dartboard?

Do these problems. Watch the signs.

1. 6 × 5 = ■
2. 27 ÷ 3 = ■
3. 9 × 6 = ■
4. 8 × 7 = ■
5. 64 ÷ 8 = ■
6. 16 ÷ 4 = ■
7. 7 × 9 = ■
8. 10 × 6 = ■

9. 5 × 5 = ■
10. 14 ÷ 2 = ■
11. 9 × 8 = ■
12. 24 ÷ 6 = ■
13. 3 × 8 = ■
14. 6 × 7 = ■
15. 20 ÷ 5 = ■
16. 7 × 7 = ■

Making Target Games

LESSON 119

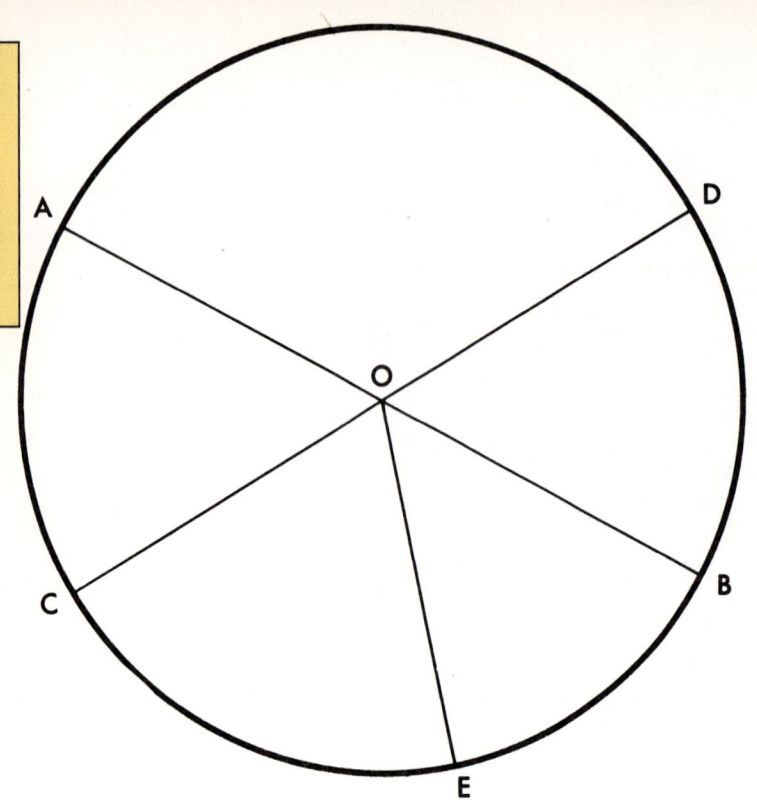

1. Diameter AB is ▇ centimeters long.

2. Diameter CD is ▇ centimeters long.

3. Radius OE is ▇ centimeters long.

4. Radius OB is ▇ centimeters long.

Making and Measuring Circles

Measurements of My Circle

Length of Diameters	Length of Radii

Multiply.

1. 6
   × 8

2. 7
   × 7

3. 4
   × 3

4. 2
   × 9

5. 10
   × 8

6. 5
   × 7

7. 6
   × 3

8. 7
   × 9

9. 4
   × 7

10. 8
    × 5

11. 7
    × 1

12. 3
    × 8

13. 9
    × 9

14. 4
    × 5

15. 7
    × 6

Add.

16. 37
    49
    63
    +218

17. 92
    137
    300
    +180

18. 3695
    2780
    +1500

19. 106
    127
    +159

What is the area?

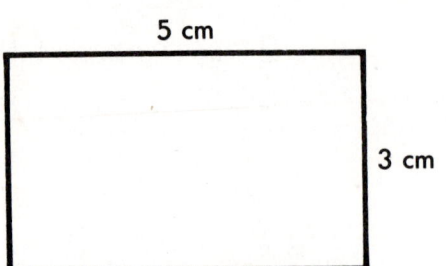
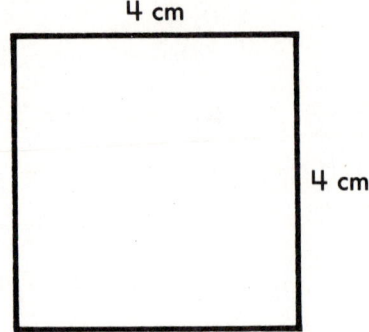

1. ▪ square centimeters   **2.** ▪ square centimeters

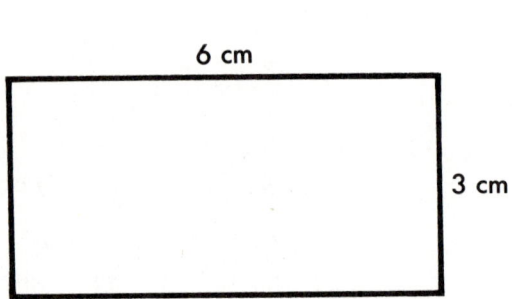
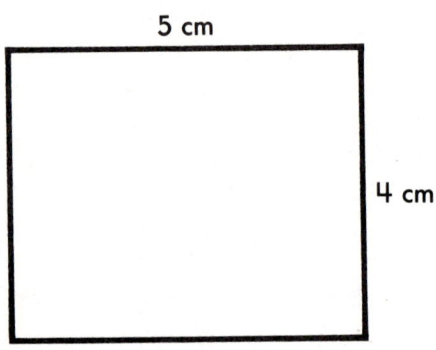

3. ▪ square centimeters   **4.** ▪ square centimeters

5. Area of the whole rectangle = ▪ square centimeters

6. Area of the blue triangle = ▪ square centimeters

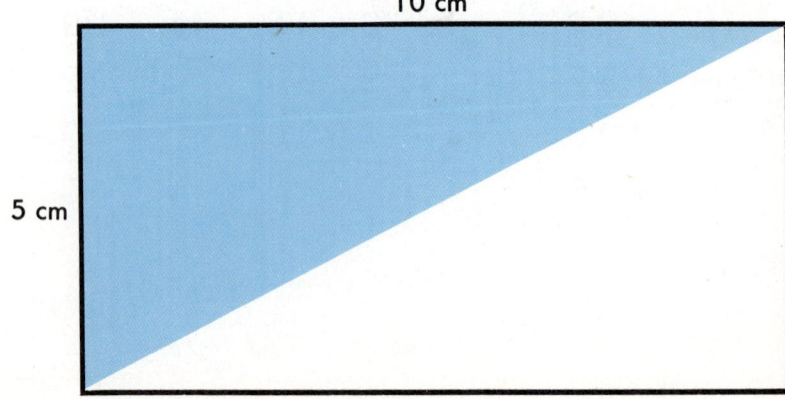

Multiply.

1. $\begin{array}{r}6\\ \times\,5\\ \hline\end{array}$ 2. $\begin{array}{r}8\\ \times\,3\\ \hline\end{array}$ 3. $\begin{array}{r}9\\ \times\,7\\ \hline\end{array}$ 4. $\begin{array}{r}7\\ \times\,8\\ \hline\end{array}$ 5. $\begin{array}{r}4\\ \times\,5\\ \hline\end{array}$

6. $1 \times 1 =$ ◼
7. $2 \times 2 =$ ◼
8. $3 \times 3 =$ ◼
9. $4 \times 4 =$ ◼
10. $5 \times 5 =$ ◼

11. $6 \times 6 =$ ◼
12. $7 \times 7 =$ ◼
13. $8 \times 8 =$ ◼
14. $9 \times 9 =$ ◼
15. $10 \times 10 =$ ◼

Discuss the Thinking Story®

Robin was going shopping. She made a chart of what she needed to buy.

1. Write the missing amounts.

Item	Number Needed	Unit Price	Amount of Money Needed
Bags of Peanuts	3	10¢	■
Apples	6	8¢	■
Oranges	2	9¢	■
Pretzels	4	5¢	■

2. How much money will Robin need altogether?

3. If Robin gives the shopkeeper $2, how much change will she get?

4. Suppose Robin wants to buy twice as many of each item. How much money will she need?

Mrs. Brown wants to buy a carpet for her living room. The floor is a rectangle that is 7 meters long and 5 meters wide. The carpet costs $10 a square meter.

1. How many square meters of carpet will Mrs. Brown need?

2. How much will that cost?

Ellen City is in the shape of an L. Copy or trace the map. Then draw a line to divide Ellen City into two rectangles.

3. What is the area of one of the rectangles?

4. What is the area of the other rectangle?

5. What is the total area of Ellen City?

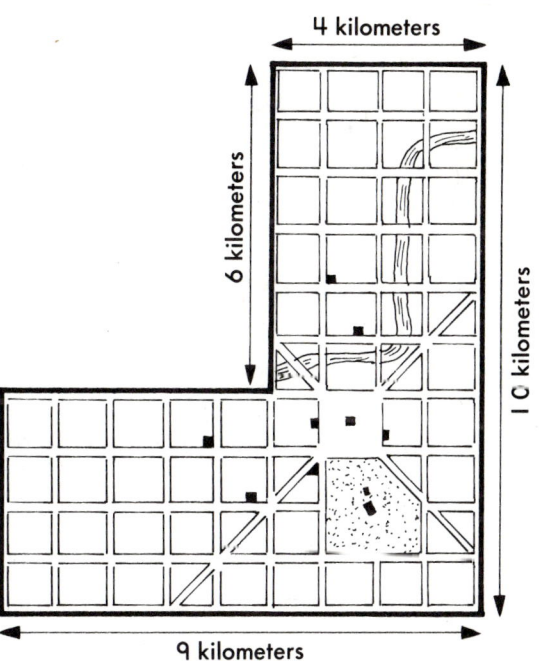

257

$27 \times 4 = $ _____?

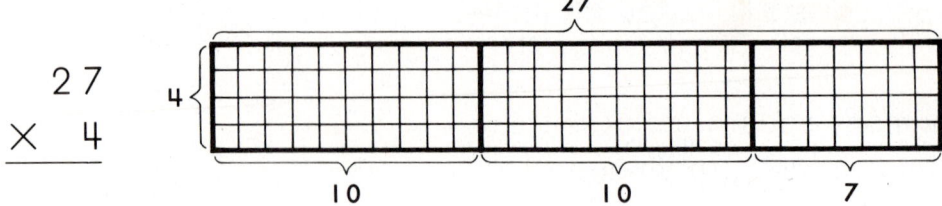

$$\begin{array}{r} 27 \\ \times\ 4 \end{array}$$

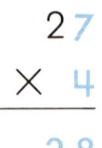

$$\begin{array}{r} 27 \\ \times\ 4 \\ \hline 28 \end{array}$$

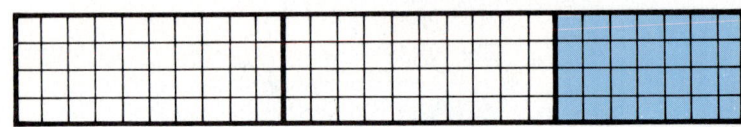

$7 \times 4 = 28$

$$\begin{array}{r} 27 \\ \times\ 4 \\ \hline 28 \\ 80 \end{array}$$

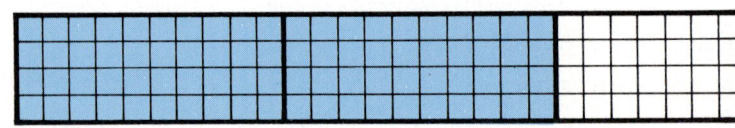

4×2 tens $= 80$

$$\begin{array}{r} 27 \\ \times\ 4 \\ \hline 28 \\ 80 \\ \hline 108 \end{array}$$

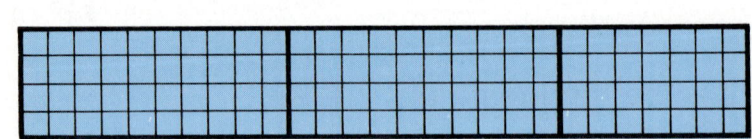

$28 + 80 = 108$

LESSON 122

258

You may draw pictures to help. Multiply. Discuss whether answers are reasonable.

1. 35
  × 4

2. 28
  × 7

3. 48
  × 1

4. 15
  × 6

5. 83
  × 9

6. 90
  × 8

7. 72
  × 5

8. 45
  × 2

9. 67
  × 3

10. 41
   × 5

11. 45
   × 8

12. 80
   × 7

LESSON 123

Do these problems. Watch the signs.

1. 5 × 5 = ◼
2. 6 × 7 = ◼
3. 8 × 5 = ◼
4. 8 × 7 = ◼
5. 5 × 3 = ◼

6. 25 ÷ 5 = ◼
7. 42 ÷ 6 = ◼
8. 40 ÷ 8 = ◼
9. 56 ÷ 7 = ◼
10. 15 ÷ 5 = ◼

11. 6
    +7
    ___

12. 8
    −2
    ___

13. 9
    +9
    ___

14. 8
    +6
    ___

15. 14
    − 7
    ___

Roll a Problem Game

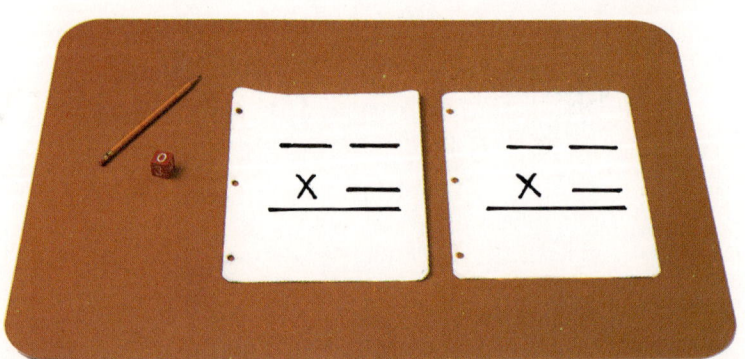

260

Multiply.

1. 83   2. 47   3. 26   4. 76   5. 11
   × 5   × 5   × 1   × 5   × 4

6. 38   7. 29   8. 26   9. 30   10. 30
   × 5   × 7   × 0   × 8   × 9

11. 58   12. 62   13. 55   14. 91   15. 90
   × 9   × 6   × 3   × 4   × 4

LESSON 124

1. Melissa saves $3 each month. Will she save enough in 1 year to buy the radio?

2. How many horseshoes are needed to shoe 13 horses?

3. Mr. Segal can finish a 1-kilometer race in 3 minutes. How long do you think it would take him to finish a 10-kilometer race?

Discuss the Thinking Story

Students from Los Amigos School are going on a field trip. 350 people are going. Each bus can seat 45 people.

1. How many people can 7 buses seat?

2. How many buses should the school use?

3. It costs $52 to rent 1 bus for a day. How much will it cost to rent 8 buses?

4. If the school rents 8 buses, how many extra seats will there be?

5. Suppose that each person going on the trip pays $1. Will that be enough to pay for 8 buses?

LESSON 125

134 × 8 = ____?____

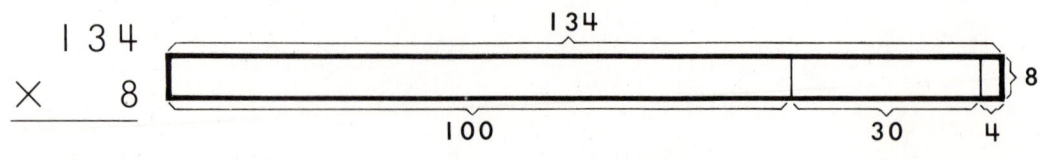

$$\begin{array}{r} 134 \\ \times\ \ \ 8 \\ \hline \end{array}$$

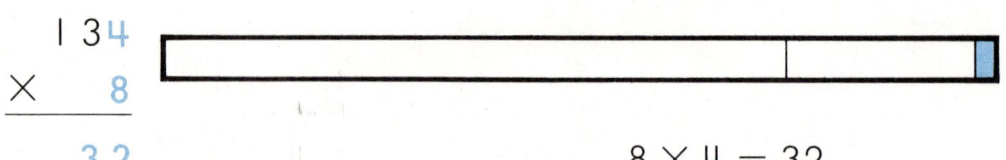

$$\begin{array}{r} 134 \\ \times\ \ \ 8 \\ \hline 32 \end{array}$$
    8 × 4 = 32

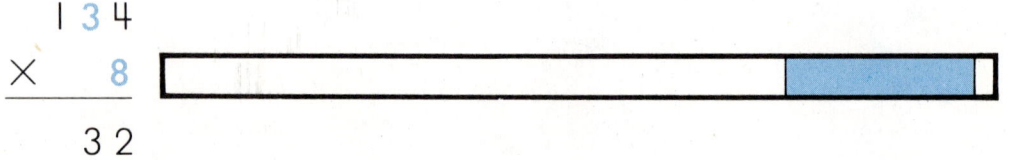

$$\begin{array}{r} 134 \\ \times\ \ \ 8 \\ \hline 32 \\ 240 \end{array}$$
    8 × 3 tens = 240

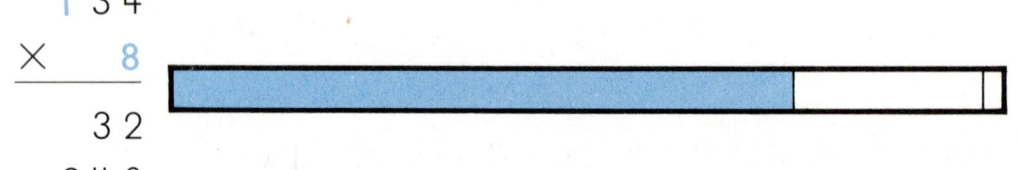

$$\begin{array}{r} 134 \\ \times\ \ \ 8 \\ \hline 32 \\ 240 \\ 800 \end{array}$$
    8 × 1 hundred = 800

$$\begin{array}{r} 134 \\ \times\ \ \ 8 \\ \hline 32 \\ 240 \\ 800 \\ \hline 1072 \end{array}$$
    32 + 240 + 800 = 1072

Multiply. Use shortcuts where possible. Compare and discuss your methods. Which are easiest?

1. 247 × 3

2. 108 × 7

3. 596 × 8

4. 111 × 6

5. 432 × 4

6. 909 × 9

7. 356 × 6

8. 732 × 0

9. 480 × 5

10. 379 × 2

11. 876 × 1

12. 380 × 6

LESSON 126

Multiply.

1. 555 × 7

2. 204 × 6

3. 373 × 7

4. 250 × 4

5. 694 × 9

6. 447 × 8

7. 109 × 2

8. 311 × 9

9. 378 × 3

10. 984 × 1

11. 800 × 7

12. 900 × 6

Do these problems. Watch the signs.

1. $\begin{array}{r}475\\+362\\\hline\end{array}$ 2. $\begin{array}{r}312\\+769\\\hline\end{array}$ 3. $\begin{array}{r}52.35\\-27.26\\\hline\end{array}$ 4. $\begin{array}{r}61.2\\-8.5\\\hline\end{array}$

Divide.

5. $6\overline{)48}$ 6. $7\overline{)42}$ 7. $8\overline{)48}$ 8. $9\overline{)18}$

9. $3\overline{)27}$ 10. $2\overline{)20}$ 11. $2\overline{)18}$ 12. $4\overline{)16}$

13. $7\overline{)63}$

14. $8\overline{)40}$

Roll Four Multiplication Game

1. Muffin eats about 250 grams of dog food each day. About how many grams does he eat in 7 days?

2. Miss Haber earns about $125 each week. About how much money does she earn in 4 weeks?

3. If a quarter of a kilogram of cheese costs 93¢, how many cents will 1 kilogram cost?

4. Write that amount in dollars and cents.

Cube-100 Game

Walter wanted to know about how many hours he spent doing certain things each year. He made some estimates and wrote them in a chart.

1. Write the missing amounts.

Activity	Hours Each Day	Number of Days Each Year	Hours Each Year
Sleeping	8	365	■
Eating	2	365	■
Reading at home	2	250	■
Staying in school	5	180	■
Watching television	1	175	■

2. Does Walter spend more time eating or reading each year?

3. Does Walter spend more time sleeping than he spends doing all the other activities put together?

4. About how many hours do you spend reading each year?

269

Multiply.

1. 37
   × 5
   ___

2. 43
   × 8
   ___

3. 60
   × 6
   ___

4. 364
   ×   9
   ____

5. 109
   ×   9
   ____

6. 841
   ×   3
   ____

7. 560
   ×   2
   ____

8. 367
   ×   4
   ____

9. 35
   × 8
   ___

10. 205
    ×   7
    ____

Discuss the Thinking Story

Tina wanted to buy a radio. So she tried to figure out how much money she could save in 1 year. She made a chart to help her. Copy and fill in the chart. (There are 365 days in 1 year.)

Save This Much Each Day	Amount Saved in 1 Year	
	Cents	Dollars and Cents
1¢		
2¢		
3¢		
4¢		
5¢		
6¢		
7¢		
8¢		
9¢		
10¢		

LESSON 129

34 × 26 = ____?____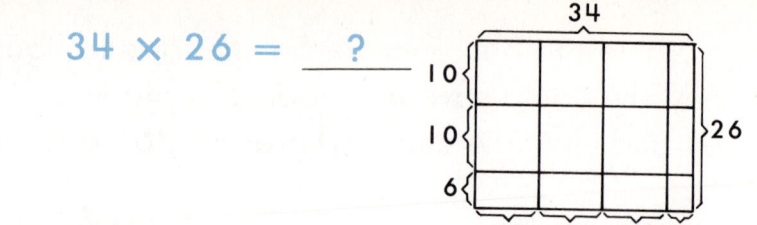

```
   3 4
 × 2 6
```

```
   3 4
 × 2 6
 ─────
   2 4        6 × 4 = 24
```
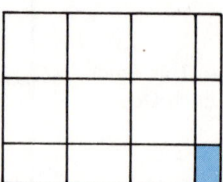

```
   3 4
 × 2 6
 ─────
   2 4
 1 8 0        6 × 3 tens = 180
```
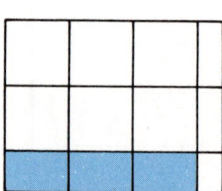

```
   3 4
 × 2 6
 ─────
   2 4
 1 8 0
   8 0        2 tens × 4 = 80
```
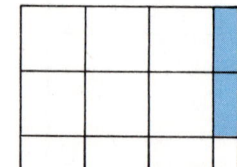

```
   3 4
 × 2 6
 ─────
   2 4
 1 8 0
   8 0
 6 0 0        2 tens × 3 tens = 600
 ─────
 8 8 4
```
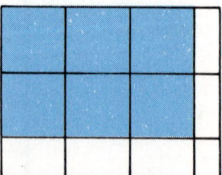

Multiply. You may draw pictures. Discuss your answers.

1. 25
   ×25

2. 74
   ×38

3. 56
   ×22

4. 49
   ×22

5. 91
   ×34

6. 81
   ×18

7. 75
   ×75

8. 35
   ×44

9. 24
   ×57

10. 64
    ×28

11. 45
    ×14

12. 79
    ×21

Multiply.

1. $3 \times 6 =$ ▪
2. $7 \times 4 =$ ▪
3. $8 \times 1 =$ ▪
4. $6 \times 0 =$ ▪
5. $3 \times 9 =$ ▪
6. $6 \times 7 =$ ▪

7. $8 \times 7 =$ ▪
8. $7 \times 8 =$ ▪
9. $10 \times 10 =$ ▪
10. $9 \times 7 =$ ▪
11. $9 \times 8 =$ ▪
12. $9 \times 9 =$ ▪

13. 40
    ×40

14. 41
    ×39

15. 35
    ×35

16. 30
    ×30

Multiply.

1. 31
   ×31

2. 32
   ×30

3. 88
   ×12

4. 88
   ×10

Do these problems. Watch the signs.

5. 3542
   −2542

6. 7810
   +3689

7. 6005
   −2147

8. 2121
   +2879

9. 2394
   −1475

10. 1000
   +1000

11. 9999
   +9999

12. 3260
   −1979

13. Greenville and Fulton are both straight ahead. How far apart are the 2 towns?

GREENVILLE 15 KILOMETERS
FULTON 25 KILOMETERS

1. There are 24 cans of soup in each carton. How many cans are there in 12 cartons?

2. There are 12 eggs in each carton. How many eggs are there in 12 cartons?

3. Each carton of eggs costs 89¢. How much do 12 cartons cost?

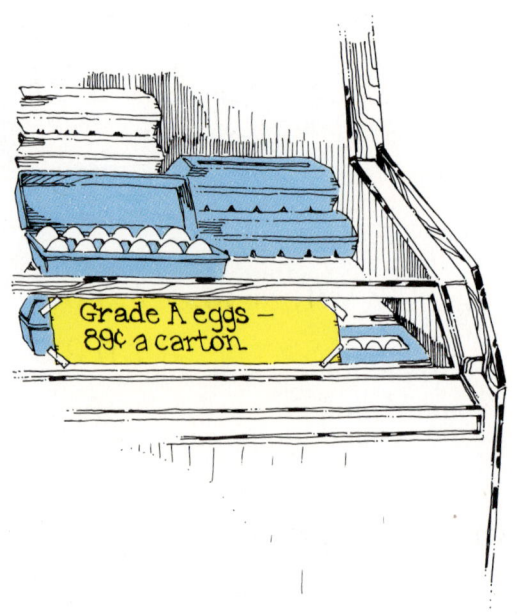

4. Write that amount in dollars and cents.

5. There are 60 minutes in 1 hour. How many minutes are there in 24 hours?

1. Beth had 15 quarters.
   How many cents is that worth?

2. Write that amount in dollars and cents.

3. There are 24 classes in the Hill School.
   There are about 25 children in each class.
   About how many children are in the school?

4. How many months old are you?

5. Each box is 11 centimeters thick. Can Mr. Walker fit a stack of 14 boxes under the table?

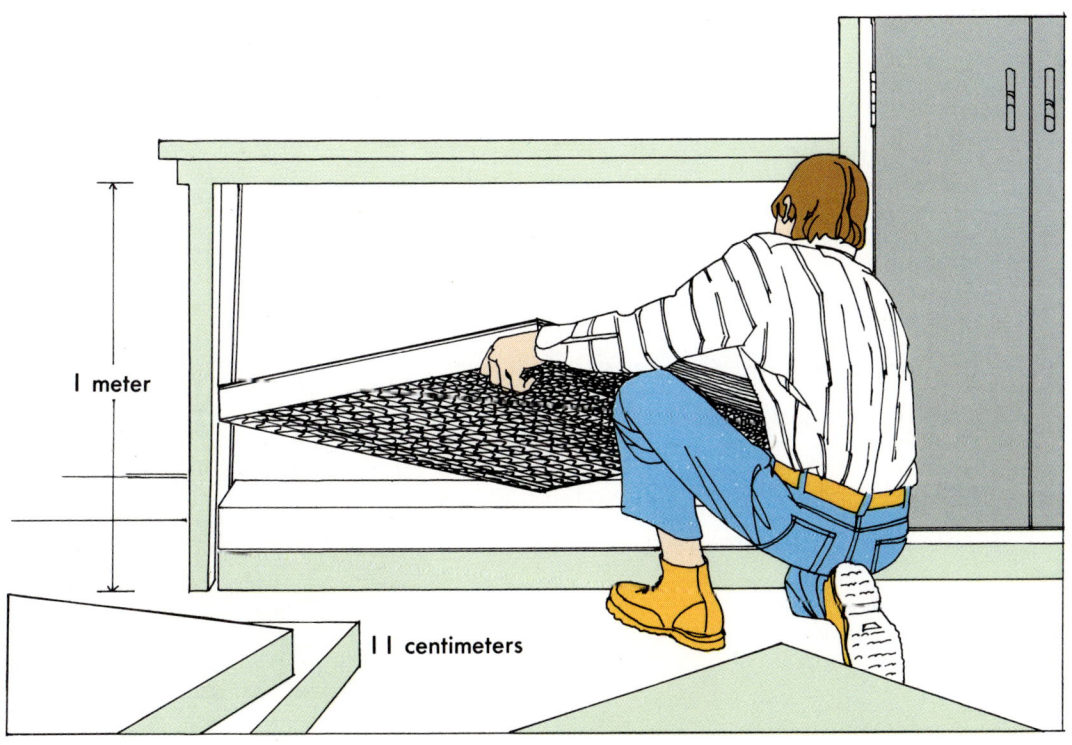

277

Esther earned $12 each month for a whole year.

1. How much did she earn that year?

2. Esther put her earnings in the bank each month.
At the end of the year she had $147.50.
How much interest did she get from the bank?

There are 24 hours in 1 day.

3. April has 30 days.
How many hours are there in April?

4. May has 31 days.
How many hours are there in May?

5. Rani's classroom is 13 meters long.
How many decimeters is that?

6. Pablo's table is 22 decimeters long.
How many centimeters is that?

LESSON 132

1. One book costs 347 cents. How many cents do 8 books cost?

2. One book costs $3.47. How much do 8 books cost?

3. Each table is 127 centimeters long. How many centimeters long are 6 tables placed end to end?

4. Each table is 1.27 meters long. How many meters long are 6 tables placed end to end?

5. One ticket to the movie costs $3.25. How much do 4 tickets cost?

Multiply.

1. 2.43   2. 3.02   3. 4.25   4. 1.75
×   5   ×   7   ×   4   ×   5

5. 6.33   6. 4.5   7. 3.7   8. 7.5
×   3   ×   6   ×   9   ×   4

9. 3.00   10. 2.5   11. 1.25   12. 3.2
×   8   ×   4   ×   8   ×   7

Tell the Truth Multiplication Game

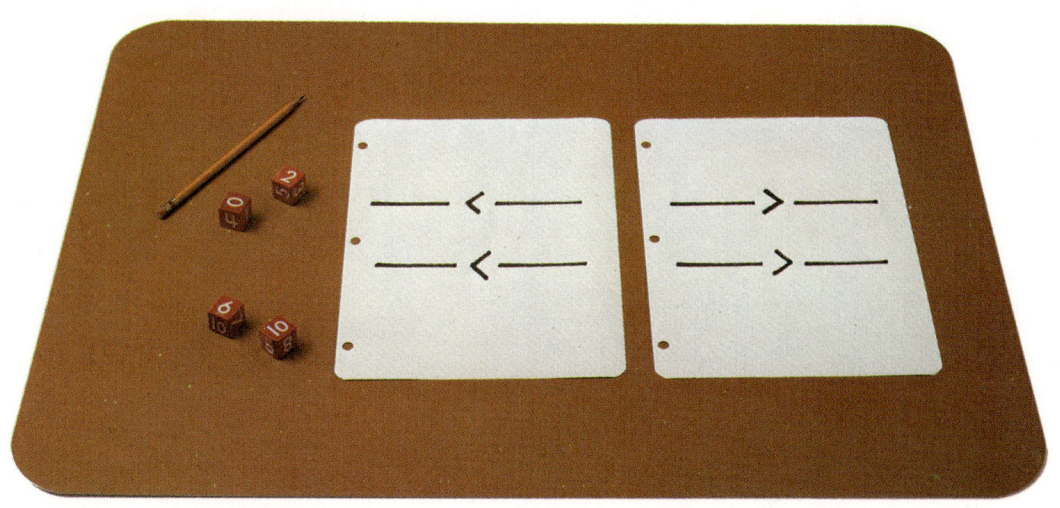

Draw the right sign. Draw <, >, or =.

1. 243 ● 342
2. 25 × 25 ● 24 × 25
3. 38 × 27 ● 27 × 38
4. 7 × 345 ● 7 × 3.45
5. 30 × 40 ● 12 × 100
6. 25 × 35 ● 6 × 100
7. 7 × 3.45 ● 7 × 4
8. 20 × 30 ● 6 × 100

Mrs. Ferroni wants to buy the same present for each of her 7 grandchildren. About how many dollars will she need if she buys each grandchild

1. a model airplane?

2. a T-shirt?

3. a football?

4. a storybook?

5. a poster?

6. a paint set?

In each problem, 2 of the answers are clearly wrong and 1 is correct. Choose the correct answer.

LESSON 134

1. 57 + 92 =
   a. 86
   b. 37
   c. 149

2. 1001 − 900 =
   a. 253
   b. 300
   c. 101

3. 320 + 430 =
   a. 841
   b. 750
   c. 940

4. 8135 + 1200 =
   a. 9335
   b. 8450
   c. 4375

5. 63 − 28 =
   a. 35
   b. 152
   c. 63

6. 6437 − 2375 =
   a. 9999
   b. 2075
   c. 4062

7. 21.1 + 36.2 =
   a. 573
   b. 57.3
   c. 18.7

8. 55.2 + 37.4 =
   a. 9.26
   b. 926
   c. 92.6

9. 9 − 4.5 =
   a. 13.5
   b. 8.55
   c. 4.5

10. 3.15 + 6.78 =
    a. 9.93
    b. 99.3
    c. 993

In each problem, 2 of the answers are clearly wrong and 1 is correct. Choose the correct answer.

1. 20 × 45 =	a.	90	**2.** 34 × 3 =	a.	1020
	b.	900		b.	75
	c.	9000		c.	102
3. 63 × 2 =	a.	126	**4.** 59 × 3 =	a.	197
	b.	315		b.	177
	c.	33		c.	77
5. 19 × 19 =	a.	361	**6.** 36 × 90 =	a.	2751
	b.	523		b.	1025
	c.	190		c.	3240
7. 325 × 3 =	a.	555	**8.** 80 × 7 =	a.	560
	b.	78		b.	750
	c.	975		c.	870
9. 31 × 29 =	a.	60	**10.** 6 × 20 =	a.	120
	b.	899		b.	12
	c.	6009		c.	720

1. Diana has a $10 bill. Does she have enough to buy 4 baseballs?

2. There are 42 rows of seats in the auditorium. There are 31 seats in each row. Are there enough seats for 1000 people?

3. Mr. Fenwick paid $100 for a box of 50 T-shirts. Will he make money if he sells the shirts for $1.89 each?

Discuss the Thinking Story

Count up. Fill in the missing numbers.

1. | 97 | 98 | | | | 102 | |

2. | 997 | 998 | | | 1001 | |

3. | 9999 | 10,000 | | | 10,003 |

4. | 10,998 | | | | 11,002 |

5. | 100,998 | | | 101,001 |

6. | 900,997 | | 900,999 | |

7. | 909,998 | | | 910,001 |

8. | 999,998 | | | 1,000,001 |

Copy and fill in the chart.

Distance in Meters	Distance in Centimeters
1	■
10	■
100	■
1000	■

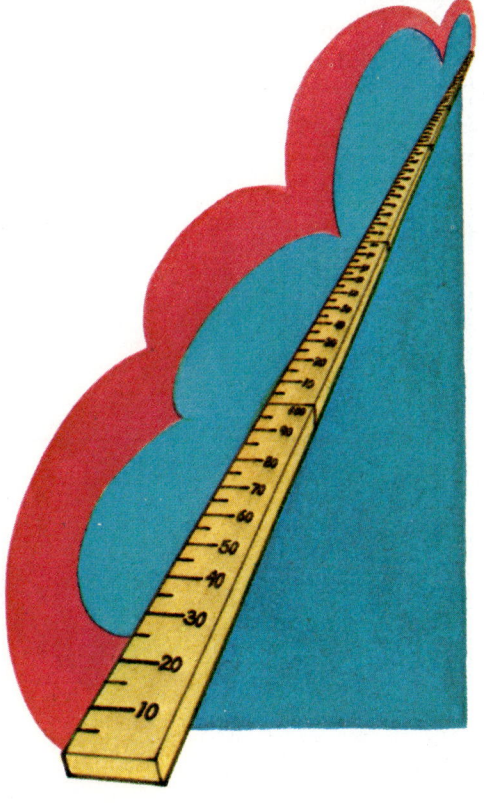

There are 100,000 centimeters in 1 kilometer.
How many centimeters are there in 10 kilometers?

Think!
About how long is 1 centimeter?

About how long is 10 kilometers?

Can you think of a place that is 10 kilometers from your school?

How much is 1,000,000?

Copy and fill in the chart.

Amount in Dollars	Amount in Cents
1	100
10	■
100	■
1000	■
10,000	■

Think!
What can you buy for 1 cent?
What can you buy for 1,000,000 cents?

Copy and fill in the chart.

Number of 1-Cent Coins	Weight		
1	About	3	grams
10	About	■	grams
100	About	■	grams
1000	About	■	grams
10,000	About	■	grams

Think!
About how many cents do you think you can carry?

Add.

1. 6 + 8
2. 7 + 2
3. 8 + 6
4. 2 + 9
5. 7 + 7

6. 36 + 72
7. 85 + 97
8. 346 + 763
9. 602 + 147

10. 7218 + 6318
11. 3190 + 2530
12. 65,151 + 37,629

13. 8,745,648 + 6,639,425
14. 12,795,000 + 36,312,128

LESSON 136

Subtract.

1. 14 − 7
2. 8 − 2
3. 16 − 8
4. 17 − 9
5. 13 − 7

6. 94 − 36
7. 75 − 28
8. 420 − 105
9. 657 − 348

10. 8675 − 4382
11. 9400 − 3250
12. 97,520 − 86,672

13. 3,642,758 − 2,642,635
14. 14,756,821 − 13,647,945

LESSON 138

Multiply.

1. 6   2. 7   3. 8   4. 9   5. 4
   ×5   ×4   ×7   ×3   ×7

6. 10   7. 4   8. 8   9. 5   10. 3
   ×10   ×9   ×6   ×5   ×6

Divide.

11. 6)48   12. 3)24   13. 6)24   14. 2)12

15. 48 ÷ 8 = ■   19. 36 ÷ 6 = ■

16. 56 ÷ 7 = ■   20. 27 ÷ 3 = ■

17. 64 ÷ 8 = ■   21. 14 ÷ 2 = ■

18. 25 ÷ 5 = ■   22. 8 ÷ 1 = ■

Multiply.

1. 35
   × 7

2. 375
   ×   6

3. 34
   ×25

4. 60
   ×40

Do these problems. Watch the signs.

5. 7241
   +3689

6. 2931
   +6129

7. 8703
   −2694

8.   7,652,871,999
   +10,743,426,000

9. Stan hit a ball that landed about 10 meters from the centerfield fence. About how far did he hit the ball?

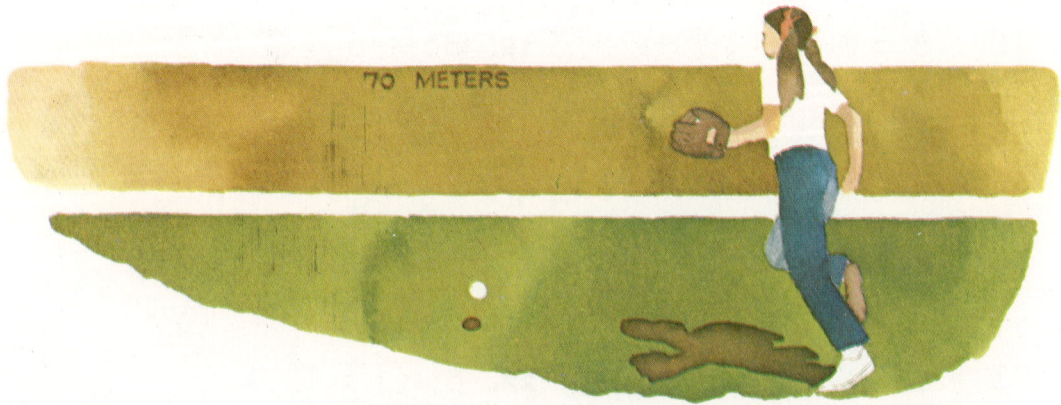

Do these problems. Watch the signs.

1. 5 + 8 = ▩
2. 7 + 9 = ▩
3. 12 − 7 = ▩
4. 18 − 9 = ▩

5. 7 + 8 = ▩
6. 6 − 0 = ▩
7. 11 − 4 = ▩
8. 7 + 6 = ▩

Count up. Fill in the missing numbers.

9. | 89 | 90 | 91 | ▩ | ▩ | ▩ | 95 | ▩ | ▩ |

10. | 998 | 999 | ▩ | ▩ | 1002 | ▩ |

11. | 1,099,999 | ▩ | ▩ | 1,100,002 |

12. | 1,999,999 | ▩ | 2,000,001 | ▩ |

Do these problems. Watch the signs.

13. 45   14. 62   15. 703   16. 346
    +36   −28   −249   +679

17. 8,704,956   18. 12,048,759
    +4,283,504   − 9,237,825

What fraction is colored?

19.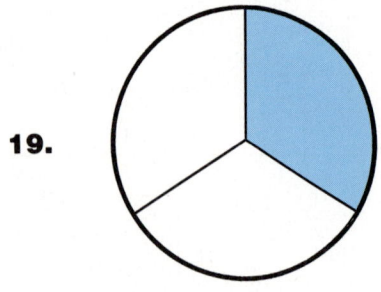

20.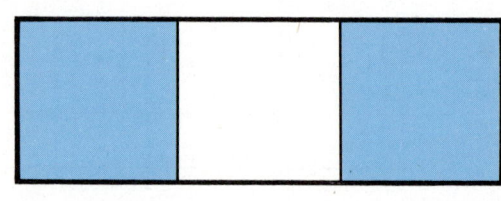

21.

22.

Multiply.

23. 6 × 7 = ■   **26.** 8 × 6 = ■

24. 7 × 8 = ■   **27.** 3 × 3 = ■

25. 3 × 6 = ■   **28.** 6 × 3 = ■

Divide.

29. 56 ÷ 7 = ■   **32.** 30 ÷ 3 = ■

30. 24 ÷ 4 = ■   **33.** 24 ÷ 6 = ■

31. 30 ÷ 5 = ■   **34.** 35 ÷ 7 = ■

Draw the right sign. Draw <, >, or =.

35. 43 ● 37   **38.** 1.08 ● 1.4

36. 98 ● 106   **39.** 32.6 ● 12.9

37. 6.2 ● 3.9   **40.** 7.3 ● 7.30

Do these problems. Watch the signs.

41. 3.42
   +1.98
   ———

42. 8.6
   −4.8
   ———

43. 16.85
   + 8.4
   ———

44. 7.7
   −3.55
   ———

45. 67
   × 5
   ———

46. 241
   × 6
   ———

47. 507
   × 9
   ———

48. 43
   ×58
   ———

49. 45
   ×45
   ———

50. 4.67
   × 3
   ———

51. What is the area of this rectangle?

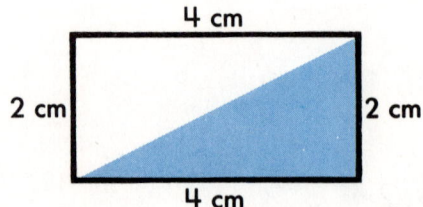

52. What is the area of the blue triangle?

53. Each pen costs 20¢.
How much do 4 pens cost?

Tami is 135 centimeters tall.
Kay is 128 centimeters tall.

54. Who is taller?

55. How much taller?

56. There are 20 rows of seats in the room. There are 30 seats in each row. How many seats are in the room?

Use this code to answer the questions.

A	B	C	D	E	F	G	H	I	J	K	L	M
21	14	1	25	9	17	26	10	23	18	3	11	19

N	O	P	Q	R	S	T	U	V	W	X	Y	Z
4	7	16	15	8	24	6	22	13	2	12	20	5

1. What shell could trap a man?

13×2 $47 - 24$ 3×7 $2 + 2$ $42 \div 7$

1×1 $6 + 5$ 7×3 $11 + 8$

2. What animal lives the longest?

3×2 $3 + 4$ $10 - 2$ —

$54 \div 9$ $49 \div 7$ $18 + 5$ 8×3 $8 + 1$

3. What is the world's most poisonous snake?

$12 + 12$ $19 - 10$ 3×7

$18 + 6$ $16 - 12$ $17 + 4$ 3×1 $45 \div 5$

CALCULATOR ACTIVITY 1

A. Do these problems with your calculator and without your calculator. Do you get the same answer each way?

1. 7 + 8 = ■
2. 70 + 80 = ■
3. 700 + 800 = ■
4. 7000 + 8000 = ■
5. 0 + 5 + 5 = ■

6. 14 − 9 = ■
7. 140 − 90 = ■
8. 1400 − 900 = ■
9. 14,000 − 9,000 = ■
10. 8 + 10 + 10 = ■

11. 0 + 5 + 5 + 5 + 5 + 5 = ■

12. 8 + 10 + 10 + 10 + 10 + 10 = ■

B. Use the number line to help do these problems. Also do them with the calculator. Are the answers the same?

1. 12 − 3 − 3 − 3 = ■
2. 10 − 3 − 3 − 3 − 3 = ■
3. 7 − 2 − 2 − 2 = ■
4. 7 − 2 − 2 − 2 − 2 = ■
5. 1 − 6 = ■

6. −3 + 2 = ■
7. −3 + 2 + 2 = ■
8. 0 + 5 = ■
9. 0 − 5 = ■
10. −7 + 10 = ■

RACE FROM 15 TO −15 AND BACK GAME

Players: 2
Materials: One 0–5 cube and 1 5–10 cube
Object: To get from 15 to −15 and back first

Rules
1. Players take turns rolling the 0–5 cube or the 5–10 cube and add or subtract the number rolled. A player *must* roll the 0–5 cube 2 times before finishing.
2. Players start at 15, go to or past −15, and then back to 15.
3. First player back to 15 who has rolled the 0–5 cube 2 times or more wins.

Sample Game
(A * marks the times the 0–5 cube was rolled. Scores are in parentheses.)

Wendy rolled:	Wendy scored:	Peter rolled:	Peter scored:
5	15 − 5 = (10)	8	15 − 8 = (7)
7	10 − 7 = (3)	8	7 − 8 = (−1)
10	3 − 10 = (−7)	8	−1 − 8 = (−9)
8	−7 − 8 = (−15)	0*	−9 − 0 = (−9)
8	−15 + 8 = (−7)	4*	−9 − 4 = (−13)
6	−7 + 6 = (−1)	3*	−13 − 3 = (−16)
4*	−1 + 4 = (3)	8	−16 + 8 = (−8)
4*	3 + 4 = (7)	9	−8 + 9 = (1)
10	7 + 10 = (17)	9	1 + 9 = (10)

Wendy won this game.

CALCULATOR ACTIVITY 2

A. Complete each pattern.

1. 0, 5, 10, 15, __, __, __, __, __, 45
                   20, 25, 30, 35, 40

2. 26, 28, 30, __, __, __, __, __, __, 44
                   32, 34, 36, 38, 40, 42

3. 42, 45, 48, __, __, __, __, __, __, 69
                   51, 54, 57, 60, 63, 66

4. 1, 6, 11, 16, __, __, __, __, __, __, 51
                   21, 26, 31, 36, 41, 46

5. 2, 7, 12, __, __, __, __, __, __, __, 52
                   17, 22, 27, 32, 37, 42, 47

B. Write the total number of steps you need to take to reach the goal. If you will not reach the goal, write N.

	Goal	First Two Steps	Total Steps
1.	52	2, 7, 12	10
2.	55	2, 7, 12	N
3.	94	4, 9, 14	18
4.	98	4, 9, 14	N
5.	98	2, 5, 8	32
6.	48	2, 5, 8	N
7.	101	2, 4, 6	N
8.	102	2, 4, 6	50

301

CALCULATOR ACTIVITY 3

A. Make 3 copies of the grid below. Then do each of the following exercises on a separate grid.

1. Color the boxes you reach when counting by twos and circle the number in the boxes you reach when counting by fives. Place an X in the boxes you reach when counting by tens.

2. Circle the number in the boxes you reach when counting by nines and place an X in the boxes you reach when counting by elevens.

3. Circle the number in the boxes you reach when counting by eights and color the boxes you reach when counting by twelves.

0	1	2	3	4	5	6	7	8	9
10	11	12	13	14	15	16	17	18	19
20	21	22	23	24	25	26	27	28	29
30	31	32	33	34	35	36	37	38	39
40	41	42	43	44	45	46	47	48	49
50	51	52	53	54	55	56	57	58	59
60	61	62	63	64	65	66	67	68	69
70	71	72	73	74	75	76	77	78	79
80	81	82	83	84	85	86	87	88	89
90	91	92	93	94	95	96	97	98	99

B. Look at the grid. How is it different from the grid on page 302?

C. Make 3 copies of the grid below. Then do each of the following exercises on a separate grid.

1. Color the boxes you reach when counting by twos and circle the number in the boxes you reach when counting by fives.

2. Circle the number in the boxes you reach when counting by nines and place an X in the boxes you reach when counting by sevens.

3. Circle the number in the boxes you reach when counting by fours and color the boxes you reach when counting by tens. Place an X in the boxes you reach when counting by eights.

0	1	2	3	4	5	6	7
8	9	10	11	12	13	14	15
16	17	18	19	20	21	22	23
24	25	26	27	28	29	30	31
32	33	34	35	36	37	38	39
40	41	42	43	44	45	46	47
48	49	50	51	52	53	54	55
56	57	58	59	60	61	62	63

CALCULATOR ACTIVITY 4

A. Do these problems. If you use a calculator, you must push the keys for all the numbers and signs shown.

1. 1 + 1 = ▇
2. 10 + 10 = ▇
3. 100 + 100 = ▇
4. 11 − 7 = ▇
5. 110 − 70 = ▇
6. 1100 − 700 = ▇
7. 100 − 1 = ▇
8. 1000 − 1 = ▇
9. 100 − 20 = ▇
10. 8 + 5 = ▇
11. 80 + 50 = ▇
12. 800 + 500 = ▇
13. 7 + 9 =
14. 807 + 509 = ▇
15. 500 + 500 = ▇
16. 700 + 300 = ▇

B. Write C if you would use a calculator to do the problem. Write N if you would not. Then do each problem.

1. ○ 1000 − 1 = ▇
2. ○ 7856 + 1947 = ▇
3. ○ 4763 − 1763 = ▇
4. ○ 6047 − 2539 = ▇
5. ○ 25 + 75 = ▇
6. ○ 250 + 750 = ▇
7. ○ 251 + 749 = ▇
8. ○ 1992 − 1983 = ▇
9. ○ 4703 − 2865 = ▇
10. ○ 5000 − 3000 = ▇
11. ○ 10 + 10 = ▇
12. ○ 4567 − 3456 = ▇

CALCULATOR ACTIVITY 5

A. Do these problems.

1. 3 + 8 = ◼
2. 3 − 8 = ◼
3. 13 − 8 = ◼
4. −3 + 8 = ◼
5. 300 + 800 = ◼
6. 300 − 800 = ◼
7. 130 − 80 = ◼
8. −30 + 80 = ◼

B. Write the total number of steps you need to take to reach the goal. If you will not reach the goal, write N.

	Goal	First Two Steps	Total Steps
1.	107	2, 7, 12	◼
2.	107	3, 7, 11	◼
3.	109	2, 7, 12	◼
4.	123	0, 3, 6	◼
5.	124	0, 3, 6	◼

C. Complete each pattern.

1. 21, 23, 25, ◼, ◼, ◼, ◼, ◼, 37
2. 13, 16, 19, ◼, ◼, ◼, ◼, ◼, ◼, ◼, 43

305

CALCULATOR ACTIVITY 6

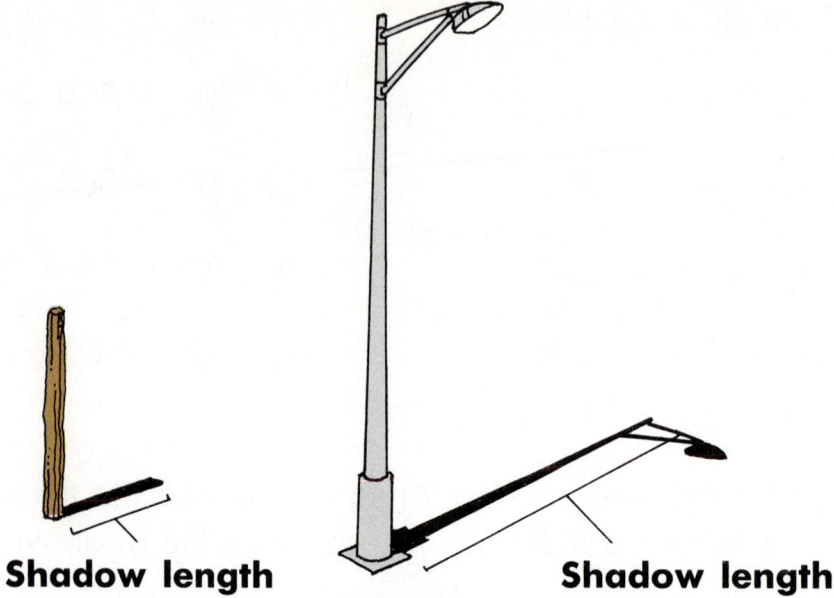

Shadow length   **Shadow length**

Choose two outside objects that stand up straight. For example, you might choose a lamppost and a fence post. Measure the heights of both objects and the lengths of their shadows at several different times today. Repeat these measurements at the same time of day once a week. Do this for several weeks. Record your findings in charts like the one below.

Name of object _____

Date	Time	Height	Shadow length

Answer each question.

1. How many months are in a year?

2. If you were born exactly 8 years ago, how many months old are you?

3. If it is now March and your eighth birthday was in January, how many months old are you?

4. If it is now March and your eighth birthday will be in July, how many months old are you?

5. If it is now February and your twelfth birthday is in February, how many months old are you?

6. If it is now April and your ninth birthday was last September, how many months old are you?

7. How old are you in months?

8. Have a friend tell you his or her birthdate. How many months old is your friend?

9. Who was born first, you or your friend?

10. How many months earlier was this person born?

CALCULATOR ACTIVITY 7

A. Measure the height and base of each triangle. Then use your calculator to divide the height by the base.

1.
2.
3.

(with triangles labeled h and b)

(h) height = ■ cm   (h) height = ■ cm   (h) height = ■ cm

(b) base = ■ cm   (b) base = ■ cm   (b) base = ■ cm

$\frac{h}{b}$ (h ÷ b) = ■ $\frac{h}{b}$ (h ÷ b) = ■ $\frac{h}{b}$ (h ÷ b) = ■

B. Find the answers to these questions.

1. Look at the shadow length data you collected in Calculator Activity 6. Did the height of each object change during the day? If so, how?

2. During the day, did the length of each object's shadow change? If so, how?

3. Look at your charts from Calculator Activity 6. Add another column to each chart and title it h ÷ s $\left(\frac{h}{s}\right)$. For each object, calculate the height divided by the shadow length for each day that measurements were recorded. Write your answers in the charts.

308

134 129 126 137 134 142 127 128 130 134

131 130 128 132 139 129 125 137 136 128

136 132 126 126 130 135 132 130 132 129

A. The numbers above give the ages in months for the members of a third-grade class.

 1. List the numbers in order from smallest to largest.

 2. What method did you use to sort the numbers?

 3. What is the smallest number in your list?

 4. What is the largest number?

 5. Which numbers appear most often?

83 85 91 62 85 74 95 68 92 94

85 97 73 78 80 86 88 91 93 87

81 79 76 83 82 96 84 82 85 86

B. The numbers above give the test scores of a third-grade class.

 1. What is the lowest score?

 2. What is the highest score?

 3. What is the most common score?

C. In the chart below, the number 91 is written as 9 tens and 1 one. The number 83 is written as 8 tens and 3 ones. The number 85 is written as 8 tens and 5 ones.

Tens	Ones
9	1
8	3, 5
7	
6	

1. Copy the chart above. Use the scores from Part B to complete it.

2. Is it now easier to find the lowest, highest, and most common score?

3. Could you now easily put the scores in order from lowest to highest?

D. Find out the heights in centimeters of all the members of your class.

1. Record the heights on a sheet of paper.

2. Arrange the heights in order from shortest to tallest.

3. What is the shortest height in your list?

4. What is the tallest height?

5. What is the most common height?

A. Do these problems.

1. How many sticks?

   1, 2, 3,   4, 5, 6,
               7, 8, 9,
               10, 11

   3 + 8 = ▪

2. How many pennies?

   1, 2, 3, 4,   9, 10, 11, ...
   5, 6, 7, 8,

   8 + 8 + 8 = ▪

   3 × 8 = ▪

3. How many balls?

   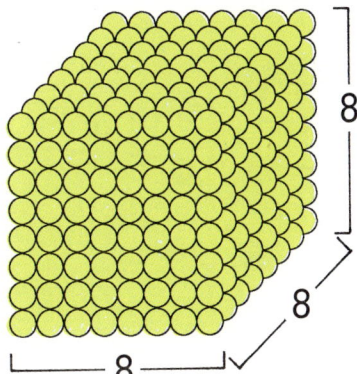

   1, 2, 3, ...
   8 + 8 + 8 + 8 + ...

   8 × 8 × 8 = ▪

   8^3 = ▪

4. You know that for all numbers, n and m, n + m = m + n. Here are some examples.

   a. 4 + 2 = ▪   2 + 4 = ▪

   b. 7 + 9 = ▪   9 + 7 = ▪

   c. 283 + 579 = ▪   579 + 283 = ▪

5. You know that for all numbers, n and m, $n \times m = m \times n$. Here are some examples.

   a. $4 \times 2 = \blacksquare$ $\quad\quad$ $2 \times 4 = \blacksquare$

   b. $7 \times 9 = \blacksquare$ $\quad\quad$ $9 \times 7 = \blacksquare$

   c. $283 \times 579 = \blacksquare$ $\quad\quad$ $579 \times 283 = \blacksquare$

6. Is it true that for all numbers, n and m, $n^m = m^n$? To find out, try these examples.

   a. $5^7 = \blacksquare$ $\quad\quad$ $7^5 = \blacksquare$

   b. $2^5 = \blacksquare$ $\quad\quad$ $5^2 = \blacksquare$

   c. $3^5 = \blacksquare$ $\quad\quad$ $5^3 = \blacksquare$

   d. $2^3 = \blacksquare$ $\quad\quad$ $3^2 = \blacksquare$

   e. $2^4 = \blacksquare$ $\quad\quad$ $4^2 = \blacksquare$

   f. $1^{10} = \blacksquare$ $\quad\quad$ $10^1 = \blacksquare$

   g. $3^6 = \blacksquare$ $\quad\quad$ $6^3 = \blacksquare$

B. Super Challenge

   1. For what values of n and m is $n^m = m^n$?

   2. For what values of n and m is $n^m > m^n$?

A. Write the total number of steps you need to take to reach the goal. If you will not reach the goal, write N.

Goal	First Two Steps	Total Steps
1. 168	0, 5, 10	
2. 168	3, 8, 13	
3. 168	0, 3, 6	
4. 168	2, 5, 8	

B. Copy the grid below. Circle the numbers you reach when counting by twos. Draw a square around those you reach when counting by threes. Place an X over the numbers you reach when counting by fives and sevens.

0	1	2	3	4	5
6	7	8	9	10	11
12	13	14	15	16	17
18	19	20	21	22	23
24	25	26	27	28	29
30	31	32	33	34	35

C. Do these problems.

1. $7 + 5 = $ ▪
2. $7 - 5 = $ ▪
3. $5 - 7 = $ ▪
4. $-7 + 5 = $ ▪
5. $-7 - 5 = $ ▪
6. $-5 - 7 = $ ▪

7. $-5 + 7 = $ ▪
8. $5 + 7 = $ ▪
9. $5^7 = $ ▪
10. $7^5 = $ ▪
11. $2^{10} = $ ▪
12. $10^2 = $ ▪

D. Write these 20 numbers in order from smallest to largest. Count to make sure you have 20 numbers in your list.

75 86 72 91 68 97 85 88 78 90

102 83 79 84 90 86 82 74 93 85

E. Measure the diagonal (d) and the side (s) of the square. Then divide the diagonal by the side.

$d = $ ▪ cm

$s = $ ▪ cm

$\dfrac{d}{s} = $ ▪

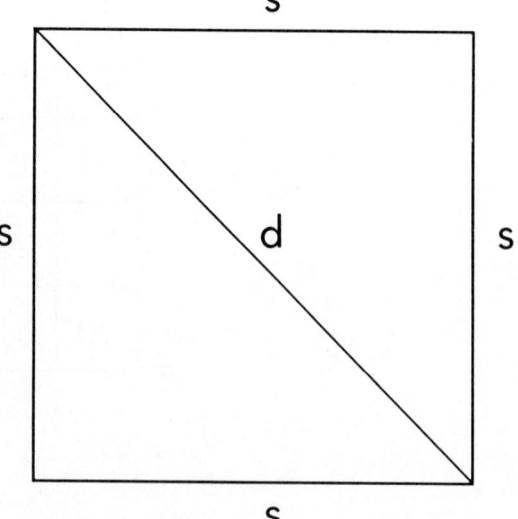

GAME RULES

GAME RULES

ADD THE PRODUCTS GAME

Players: 2, 3, or 4
Materials: Two 0-5 cubes
Object: To score a total of 50 or more

Rules
1. Take turns rolling both cubes.
2. On each turn, find the product of the 2 numbers you roll.
3. Add the product to your last score.

If your score was:	And you rolled:	Your new score would be:
12	3 2	18
36	4 0	36
25	5 1	30

4. The first player whose score totals 50 or more is the winner.

Other Ways to Play This Game
1. Use one 0-5 cube and one 5-10 cube. Try to score a total of 150 or more.
2. Use two 5-10 cubes. Try to score a total of 450 or more.

Can you think of other ways to play this game?

Note: Rules for mat games are on the mats.

COUNTING AND WRITING NUMBERS GAME

Players: 2
Materials: Pencil, paper
Object: To say and write the ending number

Rules
1. The first player chooses both a starting and an ending number more than 1000 and less than 10,000. He or she counts 1, 2, or 3 from the starting number, saying and writing the numbers. For example, if the starting number is 1351, the first player's first turn might be any of these:

    1352
    1352, 1353
    1352, 1353, 1354

2. The second player starts where the first player leaves off, saying and writing the next 1, 2, or 3 numbers. For example, if the first player stops at 1353, the second player could say and write any of these:

    1354
    1354, 1355
    1354, 1355, 1356

3. Take turns counting, saying, and writing 1, 2, or 3 numbers.
4. The player who says and writes the ending number wins the round.

Other Ways to Play This Game
1. Pick how many numbers are to be counted. For example, play a Get from 50 to 90 by Ones or Threes Game.
2. Subtract instead of adding. For example, play a Get from 100 to 75 by Twos or Threes Game.

Can you think of other ways to play this game?

CUBE-100 GAME

Players: 2 or more
Materials: Two 0-5 cubes, two 5-10 cubes
Object: To score as close to 100 as possible without going over

Rules
1. Roll the cubes one at a time, adding the numbers as you roll.
2. After any roll, instead of adding that number you may multiply it by the sum of the previous numbers. But then your turn is over.
3. The player with the score closest to, but not over, 100 wins the round.

Sample Game

Wendy rolled **6**, then **3**.
6 + 3 = 9

Then she rolled **9**.
9 × 9 = 81

She stopped after 3 rolls.

Todd rolled **5**, then **5**.
5 + 5 = 10

Then he rolled **6**.
10 + 6 = 16

He rolled **6** again.
16 × 6 = 96

Wendy's score was 81.

Todd's score was 96.

Todd won the round.

Can you think of any other ways to play this game?

DOLLARS AND CENTS GAME

Players: 2

Materials: Two 0-5 cubes, two 5-10 cubes, a score form like the one on page 179

Object: To make the larger total amount of money

Rules

1. Take turns rolling all 4 cubes and making two 2-digit numbers from the numbers rolled.
2. Add the two 2-digit numbers and write the total to the left of the first or the next available equal sign on your score form. For example, if your sum is 156, you would write:

    _156_ ¢ = $ _____ and _____ ¢

3. Fill in the blanks to the right of the equal sign. You must write less than 100 in the right-hand cents blank.

    _156_ ¢ = $ _1_ and _56_ ¢

4. When all 5 lines on the score form are filled in, add the number of dollars and the number of cents and write these totals.
5. Change the totals to a number of dollars and cents (with the number of cents less than 100). For example, 623¢ would be changed to $6 and 23¢. Write the new total on the score form.
6. The player with the larger total amount of money is the winner.

Can you think of other ways to play this game?

DOLLARS AND DIMES GAME

Players: 2

Materials: Two 0–5 cubes, two 5–10 cubes, a score form like the one on page 171

Object: To make the larger total amount of money

Rules

1. Take turns rolling all 4 cubes and adding the numbers rolled. For example, if you roll **10, 8, 5,** and **0,** your sum is 23.
2. Write this sum (the number of dimes) in the blank to the left of the first or the next available equal sign on the score form. For example, if your sum is 23, you would write:

    __23__ ⊄ = $ _____ and _____ ⊄

3. Fill in the blanks to the right of the equal sign. You must write in a number less than 10 in the right-hand dimes blank.

    __23__ ⊄ = $ __2__ and __3__ ⊄

4. After filling in all 5 lines on the score form, add to get the totals of the 2 right-hand columns.
5. Change the totals to the number of dollars and dimes (with the number of dimes less than 10). Write the new total in the bottom blank.
6. The player with the larger total amount of money is the winner.

Can you think of other ways to play this game?

ROLL FOUR MULTIPLICATION GAME

Players: 2
Materials: Two 0-5 cubes, two 5-10 cubes
Object: To get the greater product

Rules
1. Take turns rolling all 4 cubes. If a **10** is rolled, roll that cube again.
2. Combine the numbers you roll to make a 3-digit by 1-digit multiplication problem. You must use the smallest number rolled as the multiplier.

If you rolled: These are some problems you could make:

		875	857	758	587
8 7 3 5		× 3	× 3	× 3	× 3

3. Calculate the product. The player with the greater product wins.

Sample Game

Terri rolled **4, 2, 7,** and **8**.
She made this problem:

$$\begin{array}{r} 874 \\ \times\ \ 2 \\ \hline \end{array}$$

Earl rolled **3, 0, 6,** and **5**.
He made this problem:

$$\begin{array}{r} 653 \\ \times\ \ 0 \\ \hline \end{array}$$

Terri's product was 1748 and Earl's product was 0. Terri won the round.

FOUR ROLLS OF FOUR CUBES GAME

Players: 2, 3, or 4
Materials: Two 0-5 cubes, two 5-10 cubes
Object: To make the largest total score

Rules

1. Take turns rolling all 4 cubes and making two 2-digit numbers to add. Do this 4 times in each turn. (If you roll a **10,** roll again.)
2. Each time you roll, all the players add the 2 numbers you make. The player after you writes each sum for you, but all 4 sums count in your score.
3. After you have rolled 4 times, the next player rolls 4 times, and so on until all players have rolled.
4. Each player adds his or her 4 sums to get a total score.
5. The player with the largest total score wins the round.

Sample Game

Beth rolled:	Beth made:	For a sum of:	
7 9 2 5	95 and 72	167	
6 5 0 3	63 and 50	113	Andy wrote these
5 8 1 5	85 and 51	136	down for Beth.
9 8 2 0	92 and 80	172	

Andy rolled:	Andy made:	For a sum of:	
6 8 0 0	60 and 80	140	
7 7 5 1	75 and 71	146	Beth wrote these
9 5 0 5	90 and 55	145	down for Andy.
6 5 4 5	65 and 54	119	

Beth's total was 588. Andy's was 550. Beth won this round.

GUESS THE CUBE GAME

Players: 4 or 5
Materials: Two 0–5 cubes, two 5–10 cubes
Object: To guess the other player's number

Rules
1. Divide into two groups. Two students are players, and the rest are multipliers.
2. Each player chooses a cube and shows a number on it to the multipliers. The players do not show each other their numbers.
3. The multipliers tell the product of the 2 numbers.
4. Each player tries to guess the other player's number.

INEQUALITY GAME

Players: 2
Materials: Two 0–5 cubes, two 5–10 cubes
Object: To fill in an inequality statement correctly

Rules
1. The first player makes one of these game forms on a sheet of paper:

2. He or she rolls all 4 cubes, makes two 2-digit numbers, and writes their sum on either side of the inequality sign. (If the player rolls a 10, he or she rolls that cube again.)
3. The second player rolls all 4 cubes, makes two 2-digit numbers, and writes their sum in the remaining space.
4. If the inequality statement is true, the second player wins. If the inequality statement is false, the first player wins.
5. Players take turns being first.

MAKE 1000 GAME

Players: 2
Materials: Two 0–5 cubes, two 5–10 cubes
Object: To make the higher sum not over 1000

Rules

1. Take turns being the first player. The first player chooses and writes down the starting number, which must be greater than 250 and less than 750.

2. The second player rolls all 4 cubes and uses 1 or more of the cubes to make a 1-, 2-, or 3-digit number. (If you roll a **10**, roll again.)

3. The second player adds the number made to the starting number. If the sum is over 1000, the second player automatically loses the round.

4. The player with the higher sum not over 1000 wins the round.

Sample Game

Charles chose 472 as the starting number.
Norma rolled **7, 6, 2,** and **4** and made the number 476.

$$\begin{array}{r} \text{Norma added:} \quad 472 \\ +\,476 \\ \hline 948 \end{array}$$

Then Norma and Charles switched roles. Norma chose 285 as the starting number. Charles rolled **8, 7, 2,** and **1** and made the number 712.

$$\begin{array}{r} \text{Charles added:} \quad 285 \\ +\,712 \\ \hline 997 \end{array}$$

Charles won this round.

Can you think of other ways to play this game?

MISSING DIVISOR GAME

Players: 2
Materials: About 7 counters, a 0-5 cube, a 5-10 cube, the 7 problems from page 123
Object: To cover more problems

Rules

1. Take turns rolling either cube.
2. If the number you roll is the missing divisor in a problem not yet covered, place a counter on the space for that problem and write the entire problem on your paper.
3. The game ends when all 7 problems are covered.
4. The player who has covered more problems is the winner.

MULTACKTOE GAME

Players: 2
Materials: 2 Multacktoe cards (like those on page 82), two 0-5 cubes, about 6 counters or play coins for each player
Object: To cover 3 boxes in a line

Rules

1. Each player chooses 1 of the 2 Multacktoe cards.
2. The players take turns rolling the two 0-5 cubes.
3. Both players calculate the product of the 2 numbers rolled. If the product is on a player's card, he or she puts a counter in that box.
4. The first player to cover 3 boxes in a line (horizontally, diagonally, or vertically) is the winner of the round.

ROLL A 15 GAME

Players: 2
Materials: Two 0-5 cubes, two 5-10 cubes
Object: To get the sum closer to 15

Rules
1. Take turns rolling the cubes one at a time.
2. Add the numbers as you roll. The sum of all the numbers you roll should be as close to 15 as possible.
3. You may stop after 2, 3, or 4 rolls.

If you rolled:	The sum would be:
7 and 1 and 4 and 7	19
8 and 5	13
4 and 4 and 8	16
9 and 3 and 3	15
5 and 10	15

4. The player with the sum closer to 15 wins the round. (The best score is 15; the next best score is 14 or 16; and so on.)

Other Ways to Play This Game
1. Roll all the cubes at once. Decide in advance which cubes you will roll.
2. Play with more than 2 players.

Can you think of other ways to play this game?

ROLL A NUMBER GAME

Players: Whole group or 2, 3, or 4
Materials: A 0-5 cube
Object: To make the greatest 3-digit number

Rules

1. Draw blanks for a 3-digit number on your paper, like this:
   ___ ___ ___
2. The first player rolls the cube 3 times.
3. Each time the cube is rolled, write that number in 1 of the 3 blanks you made. After all 3 rolls, you will have made a 3-digit number.
4. The player who makes the greatest 3-digit number is the winner of the round.

Sample Game

Number Rolled	Amy's Number	Jack's Number	Ellen's Number
First roll: 3	3 __ __	__ __ 3	__ 3 __
Second roll: 1	3 __ 1	__ 1 3	__ 3 1
Third roll: 5	3 5 1	5 1 3	5 3 1

Ellen won this round.

Other Ways to Play This Game
1. Instead of a cube, use slips of paper numbered from 0 to 9 and draw them from a container (a coffee can, for example).
2. Make a 4-digit number.
3. The greatest odd (or even) number wins.
4. Use a 5-10 cube. If you roll a **10,** roll again.

Can you think of other ways to play this game?

ROLL A PROBLEM GAME

Players: 2 or more
Materials: A 0–5 cube
Object: To get the largest sum (or smallest difference)

Rules
1. Use blanks to outline an addition (or subtraction) problem on your paper like this:

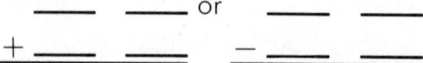

2. The first player rolls the cube 4 times.
3. Each time the cube is rolled, write that number in one of the blanks in your outline.
4. When all the blanks have been filled in, find the sum (or difference) of the 2 numbers.
5. The player with the largest sum (or smallest difference) wins the round.

Other Ways to Play This Game
1. Instead of a cube, use strips of paper numbered from 0 to 9 and draw them from a container (a coffee can, for example).
2. Add (or subtract) 3- or 4-digit numbers.
3. Add columns of 2-, 3-, or 4-digit numbers.
4. Use a 5–10 cube. If you roll a **10,** roll again.
5. Use decimals. Draw blanks to outline an addition (or subtraction) problem on your paper. For example:

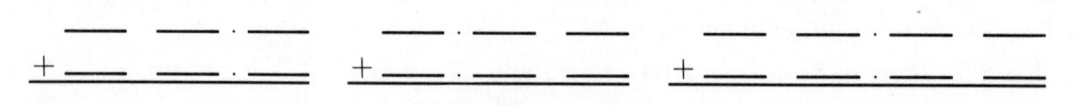

6. Outline a multiplication problem. The player with the largest product wins.

ROMAN NUMERAL GAME

Players: 2
Materials: Two 0-5 cubes, two 5-10 cubes, 22 play dimes or markers, the game board from page 234
Object: To capture more markers

Rules
1. Cover the circles on the game board with play dimes or markers.
2. Roll all 4 cubes on each turn. Use any combination of the 4 operations (addition, subtraction, multiplication, and division) on the numbers rolled to make a new number.
3. Pick up the dime or the marker at the Roman numeral for this number. If you pick up the correct marker, you can keep it. If incorrect, replace the marker.
4. You lose your turn if you make a number that is not on the board or a number whose marker has already been taken.
5. The player who has taken more markers is the winner.

Another Way to Play This Game
Cover the Roman numerals instead of the circles on the game board. (You will see 30, for example, but not XXX.)
   Write the Roman numeral for the number made. Pick up the marker above that number. If you've written the correct Roman numeral, keep the marker.

Can you think of other ways to play this game?

ROLL AND SUBTRACT GAME

Players: 2 or 3
Materials: Two 0-5 cubes, two 5-10 cubes
Object: To make the smallest difference

Rules
1. Take turns rolling all 4 cubes. If you roll a **10,** roll again.
2. Use any combination of the numbers rolled to make two 2-digit numbers. Find the difference of these numbers.
3. The player with the smallest difference is the winner.

ROLL 20 TO 5 GAME

Players: 2
Materials: Two 0-5 cubes, two 5-10 cubes
Object: To score closer to 5

Rules
1. Take turns rolling the cubes, one at a time. Subtract the first number rolled from 20. From that result, subtract the next number rolled, and so on.
2. Make a difference as close to 5 as possible. (The best score is 5; the next best is 4 or 6; the next after that is 3 or 7; and so on.)
3. You may stop after 2, 3, or 4 rolls.
4. The player who scores closer to 5 is the winner.

Other Ways to Play This Game
1. Decide how many and which of the cubes to roll. Roll the cubes all at once and subtract the total rolled from 20. If you roll more than 20, you automatically lose.
2. Play with more than 2 players.

GLOSSARY

Glossary

addend A number that is added to another number to make a sum. For example:

```
  35 — addend
+ 48 — addend
  83 — sum
```

$7 + 8 = 15$ — sum
| |
addend addend

arrow operation A way to write down an action of a function machine. In 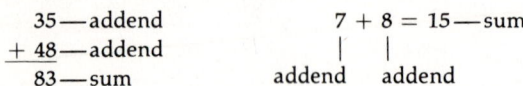 56, 7 goes in and is multiplied by 8 to give 56. The *function rule* in this case is $\times 8$.

circle A perfectly round figure. All the points on a circle are the same distance from a point called the center. In this figure, for example, points A, B, and C are the same distance from point O, the center of the circle:

decimal point A dot used to separate the units digit from the tenths digit.

denominator The part of a fraction written below the line. The part written above the line is called the *numerator*. The denominator tells how many equal parts something is divided into. The numerator tells how many of those parts there are. In the fraction $\frac{3}{4}$ the denominator (4) says that something is divided into four equal parts. The numerator (3) says there are three of those parts.

diameter A line, going through the center of a circle, that starts at one point on the circle and ends at the opposite point on the circle. AB is a diameter of this circle:

difference The amount that one number is greater or less than another. For example:

```
  43 — minuend
- 16 — subtrahend
  27 — difference
```

$10 - 7 = 3$ — difference
                 └── subtrahend
                 └──── minuend

digit Any of the numbers 0, 1, 2, 3, 4, 5, 6, 7, 8, and 9. The two digits in 15 are 1 and 5.

dividend A number that is divided by the divisor. For example:

```
              43 — quotient
divisor — 8)347 — dividend
              32
              27
              24
               3
```

$6 \div 3 = 2$ — quotient
       └── divisor
└──── dividend

equality A statement that says that two numbers are equal.

even number Any multiple of 2. 0, 2, 4, 6, 8, and so on are even numbers.

factor See *multiplicand*.

fraction $\frac{1}{2}$, $\frac{3}{4}$, and $\frac{7}{8}$ are examples of fractions. (See *denominator* and *numerator*.)

function machine A machine (sometimes imaginary) that does the same thing to every number that is put into it. (See *arrow operation*.)

function rule See *arrow operation*.

heptagon A polygon with seven sides.

hexagon A polygon with six sides.

hundredth If a whole is divided into 100 equal parts, each part is one-hundredth of the whole.

inequality A statement that tells which of two numbers is greater. For example: $4 > 3$ is read "4 is greater than 3." $3 + 6 < 10$ is read "3 plus 6 is less than 10."

inverse operation An operation that "undoes" the results of another operation. Multiplication and division are inverse operations; addition and subtraction are inverse operations.

—(×3)→ is the inverse of —(÷3)→
—(-6)→ is the inverse of —(+6)→

minuend A number from which another number is subtracted. (See *difference*.)

multiple A number that is some whole number of times another number. 12 is a multiple of 3 because $3 \times 4 = 12$.

multiplicand A number that is multiplied by another number, the multiplier. For example:

    5 — multiplicand   3 × 5 = 15 — product
  × 3 — multiplier   — multiplicand
   15 — product   — multiplier

The multiplier and multiplicand are also called the factors of the product.

multiplier See *multiplicand.*

numerator The part of a fraction written above the line. (See *denominator.*)

odd number A whole number that is not a multiple of 2. All whole numbers that are not even are odd. 1, 3, 5, 7, 9, 11, and so on are odd numbers.

parallel lines Lines in a plane that do not ever meet. Lines *AB* and *CD* are parallel:

Lines *EF* and *GH* are not parallel:

pentagon A polygon with five sides.

perimeter The distance around a figure. The perimeter of this rectangle is 6 centimeters:

place value The value of a digit in a number. The value of 7 in 27 is 7 units; in 74 its value is 70, or 7 tens; in 726 its value is 700, or 7 hundreds.

polygon One of a certain type of figure. These figures are polygons:

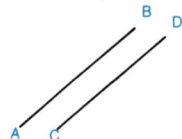

These are not:

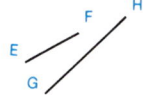

Here are the names of some common polygons and the number of sides:

Number of Sides	Name
3	triangle
4	quadrilateral
5	pentagon — a regular pentagon has five equal sides:
6	hexagon — a regular hexagon has six equal sides:
7	heptagon — a regular heptagon has seven equal sides:

product The result of multiplying two numbers together. (See *multiplicand.*)

quadrilateral A polygon with four sides.

quotient The result (other than the remainder) of dividing one number by another. (See *dividend.*)

radius A line that goes from the center of a circle to a point on the circle. *OA* is a radius of the circle shown here. The radius of this circle is 1 centimeter.

rectangle A quadrilateral in which all four angles are right angles.

regroup To rename a number to make adding and subtracting easier.

Example of regrouping in subtraction:

   1 15   (To subtract in the units column, 2 tens
   2̶ 5̶   and 5 is regrouped to 1 ten and 15.)
 − 1 7
     8

333

Example of regrouping in addition:

```
   1      (After adding the tens column, 13 tens is
  2 9 6    regrouped to 1 hundred and 3 tens.)
+ 4 4 2
  7 3 8
```

relation signs The three basic relation signs are > (greater than), < (less than), and = (equal to). (See *inequality*.)

remainder A number less than the divisor that remains after the dividend has been divided by the divisor as many times as possible. For example, when you divide 25 by 4, the quotient is 6 with a remainder of 1:

```
      6 R1
   4)25
     24
      1
```

square A quadrilateral with four equal sides and four equal angles.

subtrahend A number that is subtracted from another number. (See *difference*.)

sum The result of adding two or more numbers. (See *addend*.)

tenth If a whole is divided into 10 equal parts, each part is one-tenth of the whole.

triangle A polygon that has three sides.

whole number The numbers that we use to show how many (0, 1, 2, 3, and so on). 3 is a whole number, but $3\frac{1}{2}$ and 4.5 are not whole numbers.

zero The number that tells how many things there are when there aren't any. Zero times any number is zero; zero plus any number is that number: $0 \times 3 = 0, 0 + 3 = 3$.